Marks of Weakness

Marks of Weakness

GERALDINE JONES

QUARTET BOOKS
London   New York

An Anthony Blond Book

First published in Great Britain by Quartet Books Limited 1988
A member of the Namara Group
27/29 Goodge Street
London W1P 1FD

Copyright © 1988 by Geraldine Greineder

British Library Cataloguing in Publication Data

Jones, Geraldine
  Marks of weakness.
  I. Title
  823'.914[F]

ISBN 0-7043-2680-9

Typeset by Reprotype Limited, Peterborough, Cambs.
Printed and bound in Great Britain by the
Camelot Press Plc, Southampton

For my mother

Acknowledgement

Four lines from the song 'I Hate Men', composed and written by Cole Porter, copyright © 1948 by Buxton-Hill-Music Corporation, are reproduced by kind permission of Chappell Music Ltd.

One

Frau Keller was a big woman of fifty-five whose robust stoutness gave the lie to modern notions that fat people are unhealthy. Every Tuesday she came to clean Catherine Hemmersbach's house and applied herself to the task with a zeal and energetic thoroughness which filled Catherine with admiration. Indeed, although Catherine was in general far from shy or lacking self-confidence, there was more than a little awe in her attitude to the charwoman. It sprang only in part from her awareness that Frau Keller's definition of what passed as a clean house was considerably more stringent than her own. What most impressed Catherine was the older woman's indifference to chit-chat and her firm, though courteous, refusal to allow their relationship to go beyond the barest business formalities.

At first, Catherine had looked for a specific cause for this reserve: her conscience was doubly burdened, for she not only imagined that Frau Keller might very well be envious of her own affluence, she also feared residual hostility to the English, originating in some indignity Frau Keller had suffered as a young woman in the British Zone of Occupation. Gradually, however, she convinced herself that such speculations were idle and, accepting that Frau Keller was one of those unusual human beings who are completely self-contained, she gave up any attempt at conversation and left her to work undisturbed. In trying to stay out for as much of the morning as possible, her own Tuesday expeditions acquired a pattern of moderate self-indulgence and she increasingly looked forward to them.

Catherine just now felt particularly in need of agreeable diversion. Whereas a year before she had been in a comfortable state of almost total contentment, she had for the last few months been unsettled. She had quite lost the invigorating sense of freedom that had come to her when she gave up her job, without in any degree wanting to return to work. Her house, her cooking and her books all continued to give her pleasure but the pleasure was dulled by a restlessness, by a new fear that her activities were futile. She found this mood of self-doubt extremely disturbing, the more so as she had long prided herself on being ruled by reason alone and, rationally judged, her way of life was as satisfactory as ever. Not for her the anguished self-absorption of so many educated women: although others might see her as the slave of a conventional marriage, as one who had subjugated all her own interests to the advancement of her husband's career, she saw herself as having the best of all possible worlds. She had not greatly enjoyed teaching and she had no ambition to do anything else. Her compensation for managing the household and making her husband's needs her first priority was a surplus of leisure which, she flattered herself, she knew how to use intelligently.

With Frau Keller busy swilling the terrace, Catherine took her time choosing which suit to wear for her weekly excursion to Bonn. Since they had been able to afford good clothes for her, she had found her own appearance pleasing: slightly severe, well-cut suits and silk blouses suited her and she looked very much like many German women of her age and class. She sounded like them, too, although having derived her spoken German principally from her husband, she had never acquired the specifically feminine affectations of bourgeois speech. She decided at last on navy blue, a colour which, twenty years after leaving school, still reminded her of her uniform. 'I was the perfect schoolgirl,' she thought and then, aware of a certain poignancy in the reflection, gave herself a little shake. She feared she might be losing her grip on the way she ran her life: believing firmly that, ever since her marriage, she had consciously chosen what she wanted to do, she had a horror of discovering now, at thirty-eight, that she had made the wrong decisions. 'It's all Günter's fault,' she muttered petulantly, recalling recent changes in his behaviour.

It had all begun with his taking up jogging – an activity which Catherine considered as ridiculous as it was uncomfortable – and she had contemptuously brushed aside his suggestion that they go together. She had never taken any voluntary exercise in her life and, if he were determined to follow such a foolish fashion, he would have to go alone. At first, Günter protested that, as she was alone throughout his long working day during the week, she should not also spend much of Saturday and Sunday alone. She replied, acidly, that panting through woods in a tracksuit was too high a price to pay merely to escape solitude. Secretly, she assumed that his enthusiasm would in any case be short-lived; and certainly he did not seem to enjoy any of the much-publicized benefits of greater physical fitness since, far from turning into one of those lean and dynamic men *d'un certain âge* who adorn the pages of *The Sunday Times*, he became morose and preoccupied. At the same time, he had begun to nag Catherine, challenging her to go out more, to look for a job again, voicing fears that she was in danger of stagnating, of turning into a boring *Hausfrau*. The previous evening's conversation had culminated in an unusual show of temper from her. Goaded by his charge that a woman of her talents had no right to be content just keeping house, she had exploded: 'As you very well know, I do not *just* keep house and I would even go as far as to say that my intellectual interests are a good deal wider than yours. Certainly *my* reading is not limited to thrillers and illustrated news magazines.' Whereupon, to underline her point, she had picked up a book on the degree to which Coleridge had plagiarized Schlegel, a book which, in truth, she found far from compulsive reading. But for the rest of the evening she refused to lift her eyes from it and ostentatiously put her fingers in her ears when Günter switched on the television.

Catherine went downstairs and showed Frau Keller the lavish arrangements she had made for her mid-morning break. She was proud to have pierced the German's food chauvinism with her own raised pies and terrines and believed Frau Keller would be disappointed if she were offered only the more usual cooked meats. 'I'm going to the hairdresser's,' she explained, superfluously, for Frau Keller made it clear that it was none of her business where Frau Hemmersbach went. 'I shall probably not be home before one-thirty, so I'll pay you now. You can let yourself out.' The money changed hands, considerably above the going rate for charwomen but inflated by Catherine to assuage a muddled sense of guilt that she should be able to afford to pay someone else to clean her windows and scrub her floors. She got into her car, one of the smaller Volkswagen models, and drove off. The Autobahn was only four kilometres away and she was in the centre of Bonn, parked in the underground garage beneath the Marktplatz, in less than half an hour.

They had bought the land on which their house stood, in a small market town to the south west of Bonn, when it seemed probable that Günter would be moved to his firm's new factory in the Rhineland. They had acquired it cheaply, before the civil servants of the federal capital had fully accepted that, if they were ever to own their own homes, they must look for property beyond the limits of the old university town and its neighbouring spa, Bad Godesberg. The plot was generous and, in the few years since the house had been completed, the conifers had grown tall and now quite shut them off from the gaze of passers-by. Catherine loved her house and had never fully overcome her surprise that it really belonged to her. She had grown up in a cramped little semi-detached in a Liverpool suburb, where fitted Axminster was considered the height of luxury and a family's respectability was judged by the neatness of its privet hedges. As their move had coincided with her giving up her job, she had been more closely involved with the actual building than Günter and she had derived great satisfaction from her successful dealings with the architect and contractors. When the house at last stood ready for them to move in, she looked upon it very much as her personal achievement.

The hairdresser was not far from the car park, a couple of hundred yards through the pedestrian precinct past the elegant little shops selling dresses, furs and leather goods. Herr Kloessgen – no easy familiarity here of calling a stranger by his Christian name just because he cut your hair – had been doing Catherine's hair for several years and she took a mild pleasure from the fact that he had never supposed her to be anything but German. It was not that she actively wanted to be wholly German: much of her remained stubbornly English. But living most of her adult life abroad had led to a dilution, too, of her Englishness; she was less at ease with the British than she used to be and it was agreeable to escape, if only during anodyne conversations with the hairdresser, from the ambiguity that surrounded her identity in more intimate connections.

'I fear the grey hairs at your temples are becoming more noticeable, Frau Hemmersbach. Why don't you allow me to colour them? Your hair is such a lovely shade of dark-brown that it would not be at all difficult to match. No one would ever know.'

Now Catherine hated the idea of having her hair dyed but when she said so, her words seemed to lack force and Herr Kloessgen only increased his efforts to persuade her. In the end, she fell back on saying her husband would not approve, an argument which she detested herself for using since she considered Günter's views on such a matter irrelevant. Herr Kloessgen, however, was silenced and when after a pause he spoke again it was to tell her of his plans to take his wife and small daughter to Tunisia during

5

the October half-term break. The weather was certain to be good, he said, and they had chosen a first-class hotel, but could they be sure that Arabian hygiene would be adequate? Catherine said something soothing but in her mind she marvelled at the paradox of the Germans being among the world's leading foreign tourists when their obsession with cleanliness and their susceptibility to intestinal infection should have kept them firmly at home.

Her hair done, she browsed for half an hour in a bookshop and then, at a shop that sold only perfume and expensive cosmetics, took advice on which cream to buy to prevent her neck ageing more noticeably than her face. Privately she suspected that she might as well rub lard into her wrinkles but she enjoyed listening to the competent, white-coated saleswoman too much to disappoint her by not purchasing one of her overpriced little pots. Finally, she stopped at her favourite stall in the vegetable market and bought carrots, parsley, plums and salad. On her way home, she pulled in at one of the vast supermarkets that spring up on the outskirts of well-to-do residential areas. It was extremely clean and very well arranged but too impersonal for Catherine to like shopping there more than once every couple of weeks: it was the place to buy dry groceries and soap powder but she would never be received by the cashier with the respectful attention lavished on her by the butcher and wine merchant. She had read how some refugees from the east, on arriving at last in the Federal Republic, were disgusted by the opulence of huge food halls but Catherine, as she pushed her trolley round, rejected their puritanism: she approved of a world where pensioners could find miniature bottles of sparkling wine next to the packet soups – and could afford to buy them too.

When she got home, she ate an apple and immediately started preparations for supper; unusually, she had been invited to have tea with a neighbour, and she would soon have to go out again. She made carrot soup and pastry for a plum tart, washed the lettuce and rubbed garlic and pepper into a couple of fillet steaks before brushing them with olive oil. Then she powdered her nose, fetched a little bunch of flowers from the garden and set off up the road to Frau von Frohndorf. Catherine's relations with her neighbours were distantly cordial. Although hardly any were working wives, their days seemed to be too full of housekeeping and superintending their children's homework to leave time for the casual dropping in for a mug of Nescafé that goes on among housebound Englishwomen. Occasionally, invitations such as this one would be issued – to greet a newcomer or say goodbye – and then the table would be laid with a lace cloth and fine china and there would be an impressive choice of expertly baked home-made cakes. Frau von Frohndorf had only been in her house, the last finished in the street, for a couple of months and the tea party was by way of thanking her neighbours for the welcoming gestures they had made to her. Her husband was in the army and had been a military attaché in London before his present secondment to the Ministry of Defence. Frau von Frohndorf was extremely anglophile and had been overjoyed to learn that Catherine was English. There had even been an attempt at English conversation practice, but Catherine had disappointed her pupil by failing to praise her fluent, though limited, command of the language and then had bored her by dwelling at length on niceties of style which were beyond her comprehension. So now they conversed only in German.

Frau von Frohndorf, having briefly rhapsodized over Catherine's dahlias, led the way to the sitting-room, where four other ladies were already seated. 'Then I will make tea,' the hostess announced, 'or would anyone prefer coffee?' Catherine said that she would, to the particular astonishment of everyone present: 'And you an Englishwoman!' they exclaimed. It was odd how tea had caught on in Germany: it was very much the chic thing to drink, just as coffee had, in Catherine's youth, been much more fashionable in England than tea. But coffee, she thought, as she tasted the Kirschtorte, went so much better with rich cream cakes than insipid tea did. The conversation passed from complaints at the builders' shortcomings to the problems arising from the children having to change school. Catherine, being childless, was silent at first but, when the talk became more general and touched on the iniquities of the comprehensive system which the Social Democrats were trying to introduce, she told of her own experiences years before teaching at a comprehensive in Liverpool.

'And have you taught here as well?' they asked.

'Oh, yes, for nearly ten years altogether, when we were living near Frankfurt.'

'Then why don't you work now?'

'I don't really want to. I'm very lazy and I enjoy my leisure.'

'But you have no children. What do you do all day?'

'Oh, I potter about – I read a lot, write letters, and cooking takes up a lot of my time.' This sort of interrogation was not new to Catherine but she could not today muster her usual degree of conviction when she asserted that hers was the enviable way of life and that it was the people who only began to take themselves seriously when they got a job who were to be pitied. So she was glad when the subject changed and Frau von Frohndorf began boasting of her social conquests in London.

'Have you ever been to Ascot?' she asked, turning to Catherine.

'Certainly not. My origins are very plebeian.' This was an intentionally mischievous choice of epithet: *plebejisch,* in German, is one of those difficult foreign loan-words best avoided in ordinary conversation, since so few people are sure of their meaning. But Catherine was irritated by the woman's snobbery.

Frau von Frohndorf smiled uneasily and went on to explain how the embassy received tickets every year for the royal enclosure, and how their own visit had been one of the highlights of their three-year tour. She fondly remembered some of their English friends, mentioning them only by their first names and adding, directly to Catherine: 'You English are so much friendlier and warmer than we are; in London *everyone* was *"per du"*.'

'That's not actually correct,' said Catherine, determined to quarrel, 'the familiar form died out in England a couple of hundred years ago. What we really do is use the polite form to everyone – including children and dogs. It's rather less friendly, if anything.'

'Oh, well, I found it friendly.' And Frau von Frohndorf nimbly moved the conversation to Bayreuth which, naturally, she always visited in the season. Catherine cared nothing for Wagner and her thoughts drifted away. She wondered why she was so bad-tempered. She had looked forward to coming and enjoying the modest distraction of housewives' chatter; now she was here she was being either argumentative or sullen.

Frau von Frohndorf was offering her guests liqueurs. She also had sherry: the sojourn in London had at least been useful in forming a taste for that drink and Catherine gratefully took what seemed like a very un-London-sized glass. The atmosphere became less strained, the talk less dominated by their host's boasting. Catherine's glass was refilled and she talked agreeably about holidays in the Black Forest, talk which managed to remain agreeable even when it touched, inevitably, on acid rain. Whatever the tragedy of dying forests, it did not touch these ladies with intolerable force, and they all felt better for having demonstrated to each other, in spirited little speeches, how much they cared for the environment. They were surprised when it was discovered – on Herr von Frohndorf's returning from his office – that it was nearly six o'clock. The party broke up and, although Catherine hardly expected Günter for another hour or more, she hurried home to see to his dinner.

His car, however, was already standing in the drive and Catherine found him in the kitchen eating a banana. She apologized effusively for being out. 'For God's sake, Catherine,' he said, 'you don't have to be in when I get home.'

'Of course I know that, but it was only a silly tea party and I really would rather have been here to greet you. Supper won't be long – will you have a drink?'

'No.' Günter took the morning paper, which had arrived after he had left for work and started to read it. Catherine lit the flame under her soup and heated a small frying-pan for the steaks. While it was getting hot, she cut up some butter into tiny cubes. She browned the meat quickly and then added a glass of white wine to the pan. After it had bubbled for a few minutes she removed the steaks to the oven and tipped the butter into the pan juices. She shook vigorously and added some tarragon, then poured the sauce over the steaks. She stirred parsley and *crème fraîche* into her soup and served it. 'We must eat,' she said, leading the way to the dining-room, 'the steak doesn't like to be kept warm.'

Günter took a piece of bread, barely tasted the soup and put his spoon down. 'There's too much cream in it.'

'Then why didn't you stop me putting it in? You could easily have had yours without.'

'Oh, you're always so damned dogmatic about your cooking.' Catherine, anxious to avoid argument, said nothing but ate her own soup with a pleasure only slightly marred by her husband's ill temper.

'Will you open the wine that's there?' she asked, as she went to fetch the meat.

'I don't want any. Can you bring some mineral water?'

'Certainly, but as I do want wine, I'd still like you to open the bottle.' Catherine sounded cross, in spite of herself. She dressed the salad and brought it and the meat to the table.

'Herr Kloessgen wanted to dye my hair today,' she began, with a somewhat forced brightness. 'He wouldn't take no for an answer until I said you *forbade* me to colour my hair. It's really rather touching that he still believes in a world of tyrannical husbands and submissive wives.'

'He's an idiot.'

'Not as much of one as our neighbour, Frau von Frohndorf. She was probably not very sensible to begin with, but her years in London have given her German affectations a quite awful veneer of English snobbery. She did nothing but show off about the splash she had made in London society.'

'I don't know why you bother with such people.'

'It would have been churlish to refuse her invitation when she knows I spend every afternoon at home and, anyway, there aren't that many people of my calibre around. I have to make do with what's available.' Günter was in no mood for irony and only grunted. Catherine noticed that he had not touched his steak but decided not to comment on it until she had finished her own meal.

He broke the silence. 'Why can't you cook something cheap and simple for a change?'

'Because I don't see why we should eat cheap food when we can afford better – anyway, this was a very simple meal; you saw yourself how quickly I got it ready.'

'What you spend on a couple of days' meat would keep a family in India alive for weeks.'

'And what I spend on meat helps keep the butcher's family alive here: at any rate, he's jolly glad to have my custom. Your thriving economy needs buyers as well as producers.' Catherine drank some more wine before adding, 'There should have been a plum tart, but I wrongly assumed that you had come home so early because you were hungry, and would not want to wait for it to bake. Perhaps you'd like some cheese?'

'I'm not at all hungry. I sometimes think our marriage has been nothing but one long, elaborate dinner party.'

'I don't believe in underestimating the pleasures of good food.'

'But for God's sake, Catherine, that shouldn't be all you have to offer.'

'No, well, in all humility, I don't really believe that is. Nevertheless, I want some cheese.'

She went out to get it and he shouted after her, 'I wish you could forget about eating for a minute and listen to me.'

She came back with some Camembert and a few

grapes. 'And can't I manage to listen and eat a bit of cheese at the same time? Surely my mind hasn't atrophied to the point where I can only do one simple thing at a time.'

'I want a divorce.'

She did not immediately think him serious. 'Good heavens! You can't want a divorce just because I gave you a fillet steak when you were longing for lentils!'

'No, I want a divorce because I don't want to live with you any more. Because I'm in love with someone else.' He stood up and turned away from her in a melodramatic manner.

She felt her heart beat faster and that slightly sick feeling come into her stomach such as she experienced when a car, travelling too fast, only just missed colliding with her on a narrow road. But there was no change in the tone of her voice as she asked: 'And do I know the lucky woman?'

'It's Anna Boehnke – she came here with Wolfgang.'

'Oh, her. Yes, I remember her well.'

They talked until nearly midnight: that is, Günter did most of the talking. She learned that what she had taken to be her personal strengths – her equanimity and good sense – had increasingly made her intolerable to live with. Nothing could touch her, nothing could excite or upset her: she hadn't even seemed to mind much about her infertility.

'What's the point of getting worked up about things you can't change?' she asked.

'And what's the point of being alive if nothing can ever really move you?' he retorted.

Then he told her that Anna was pregnant and that he was thrilled. She saw that now he would have to leave her: without the baby she might have tried to hang on until Anna grew tired of him or, God help him, he began to miss her own restraint and good cooking.

As soon as he realized that she was not going to fight him he began, superfluously, to list his grievances against her more fully. Clearly, her even temper had been hardest to bear. There was no passion between them, neither the passion of love nor the passion of anger.

'It was a comfortable relationship,' she murmured.

'Such comfort,' he snarled, 'is contemptible, more suited to pigs in a sty than to human beings.'

He told her how he had suffered from her cynicism: she mocked his work and failed to take him quite seriously. Günter worked for an American multi-national which produced toilet articles. Catherine, unaware that she was wounding his sensibilities, had raised many a laugh telling people that he worked 'in nappies'. Of course she knew that the expanding continental market in disposable diapers provided not only their bread and butter but also the jam on it; nevertheless she had not supposed – and still could not quite believe – that her husband needed her respectful approval for the part he was playing in ensuring there would never be a return to the bad old days of terry towelling and gauze. But the longer he spoke, the more oppressed she became by the extent of the gulf between them.

At last, frustrated by her refusal to counter his accusations, Günter decided that they should go to bed. There followed the sort of farce which is never far beneath the surface of domestic tragedy. It was much too late for him to drive to Anna's and, in any case, she should not be disturbed: expectant mothers need their sleep. But now that Catherine knew of his infidelity he was loath to share her bed again.

'It hasn't troubled you before and I don't see why *your* sense of propriety should be suddenly more acute, just because *I* know. But if it will make you happier I'll get a bed ready for you in the spare room.'

'I hate to put you to any trouble,' he answered, as though he were an unexpected guest, forced by a snowstorm to spend the night. 'I'd make the bed myself, only I don't know where the sheets are.'

Catherine smiled grimly as she reflected that he would probably not be permitted to enjoy such convenient ignorance with his new wife. Then, when eventually she was alone, she cried unrestrainedly. She felt most bitter at Günter's condemnation of her placidity since, far from its being a congenital characteristic, she had worked hard to acquire it after the exhausting battles of the first year of their marriage had taught her that, as her husband would not change his ways to please her, she must, if they were to remain married, change hers. She wondered if she had been pusillanimous – certainly Günter, with his new abrasiveness, would say so now, but at the time she believed she had done the only reasonable thing. Their quarrels had indeed made her think of leaving him, but an awareness of his vulnerability and even of something which could best be described, unfashionably, as her duty, led her instead to make the best of what she had. Unexpectedly, virtue had been rewarded by years of happiness: Günter responded to the new tolerance and indulgence with which she treated him by becoming in turn gentler and more loving. Often, he had infuriated their married friends by boasting that he and Catherine never had rows. At some point, she now realized, her happiness had become mere complacency: having learned to manage her marriage satisfactorily, she had become blind to its limitations. Yet the habit of complacency is hard to break and still she comforted herself that, even if she had sensed Günter's growing discontent, she could not easily have changed herself all over again. Probably, in any case, his infatuation with Anna had preceded his becoming critical of her: it was easier to desert her if he could convince himself that she had failed him.

Her tears gave way to irritation that she was being cast into the role of victim. She would, in the forthcoming weeks, have to prepare herself to be generally pitied: she was the classically good wife usurped by the younger woman. Not much given to underestimating herself, she found it hard to accept that, unless youth were to be the only criterion, any impartial judge would consider Anna's attractions greatly superior to her own. She had come to their house about a year before as the girlfriend of one of Günter's second cousins, a young man who was studying at the University of Bonn and whom, out of family piety, they regularly invited for a meal. She looked like many of her generation, in washed-out jeans and a cotton smock from the Third World shop, her pinched face dominated by a ludicrously large pair of circular spectacles. Catherine had gone to great trouble preparing vegetarian food for her, but had still failed, according to her own lights, to make the girl feel properly at ease. While Wolfgang, getting agreeably drunk on their wine, taunted them for having sold out to the bourgeois gods, Anna sat slightly apart, leafing through old newspapers, her glass untouched. Catherine took Wolfgang's rejection of their Persian rugs and antique furniture as a good-humoured pose which he would cast off the moment he exchanged his penurious student allowance for a proper salary, but Anna's disapproval struck her as painfully genuine; was she perhaps a potential recruit for one of those dreary terrorist groups whose alleged activities filled the papers but whose actual existence impinged so little on the everyday life of Germany's worldly citizens?

It had, therefore, come as a great surprise to her when Anna, on being jilted by Wolfgang – he was about to take his final examinations and was well on his way to securing a job with General Foods – turned to them for sympathy. She had arrived just before lunch one Sunday and, distractedly waiving her principles, had partaken of their roast lamb *en croûte* and drunk nearly a bottle of claret. She told them that Wolfgang was an arsehole and life a load of shit. They took her for an afternoon walk in the woods where, along with a couple of hundred other people, they breathed relatively fresh air and worked up an appetite for their afternoon coffee and cake. When they got home again she ate three pieces of Linzer Torte and showed no inclination to leave. Günter withdrew for a nap and she helped Catherine fill the dishwasher before settling down with a gin and tonic. Much later, after salmon mousse and Chablis, Günter drove her home. Perhaps he did seem to be away a long time but the thought that he might have been seduced – even mildly tempted – by a tipsy, muddle-headed girl barely half his age, simply had not entered Catherine's head.

Eventually, she dropped off to sleep at about three o'clock, but not before her instinctive vanity had led her to prepare cotton-wool pads soaked in witch-hazel for her swollen eyelids. She was not above taking a modest revenge upon Günter by keeping the outward signs of her distress to a minimum. The alarm went, as usual, at six o'clock. She got up, her head aching from last night's crying and lack of sleep, took a shower and dressed quickly, escaping downstairs before Günter needed the bathroom. She made the breakfast and wondered if he would eat any; he really must be very hungry after last night's abstinence. When he came down he said, 'Oh, how kind of you to have made coffee, but you really shouldn't have got up so early.'

'Günter, will you for heaven's sake stop treating me like a good-natured landlady. I have been making your breakfast for sixteen years and I don't see why *I* should change, just because *you* have decided to indulge your aberration with this tiresome girl.'

She had not spoken so angrily before and it seemed to do him good. He sliced the top off his egg before answering. 'I'm afraid it isn't an aberration. I only wish it were.'

'Humbug! You have as much control over the affair as you wish to exercise – or you would have had if you hadn't let her get pregnant.'

'I don't think you know what it's like to be really in love.'

'That depends on your definition. I certainly would never have dreamt of leaving *you* on a mere selfish whim – perhaps some people would call that love.'

'But isn't it wrong to stay together once the relationship has died?'

'And is it not possible that you are confusing the vitality of your affair with Anna with the death of your marriage to me?'

Günter pondered this question as he spread a piece of

wholewheat bread with skimmed-milk Quark: breakfast was the one meal at which Catherine indulged his wish to adopt the latest health-food fad. 'If you are so sure that there's nothing wrong with our marriage, why aren't you more upset that I want to end it?'

'How do you know I'm not upset?'

'You're so very calm. You even look as though you slept all night.'

'If you assure me that a fit of hysterics is all that is needed to stop you leaving me, then I shall happily tear my hair and throw my coffee cup at your head. Otherwise, I'd rather keep my dignity.'

'But you know I've got to go to Anna now.'

'Exactly. And your determination to go does, I think, take away any right you might have had to tell me how to behave.'

Günter finished his breakfast in silence and then stood up to leave. 'I don't think I'll be back this evening.'

'Very well. You remember that I'm going to Liverpool at the end of the week for Sarah's engagement party?'

'Oh, yes. How long will you be away?'

'I had planned a flying visit but now I think I might as well drive over and maybe stay a few weeks.'

'Well, I'll pop in to see you before you go. Goodbye.'

For the first time in sixteen years, Catherine did not go with Günter to the front door. As he left, her resolve to retain her dignity faltered and she started to cry. She cried for a long time.

Two

Catherine spent a wretched day, restlessly roaming the house which she and Günter had planned together and then lovingly filled with the beautiful objects her jealous brother had once called their 'Ersatz children'. Although Günter had never been her whole existence in Byron's sense – she had never loved him with a consuming passion – her marriage had none the less provided the context for her entire adult life. She was bitterly aware that it was she alone who had decided to live her life within such narrow limits; if she had kept some sort of job she would at least have been obliged to carry on and thus been saved from spending every single minute, as she was now, in contemplation of her own misery. But she had insisted that to look for work outside the house when neither financial considerations nor her own ambition required it would be to admit that the life she had chosen for herself was insufficient. If it had been right to marry Günter and to stay married to him, then surely she should be able to find satisfaction enough from her own resources. Even now she would not concede that, while supposing herself happily married, it would have been wiser to pursue a career merely as an insurance against purely hypothetical desertion.

She was used to the house being quiet during the day but in her present state its customary stillness seemed somehow ominous; it reinforced her feeling of total desolation. She had been wrong not to seek friends of her own. True, she was a tenacious letter-writer and kept in touch with a dozen old acquaintances whom she rarely saw, but she had allowed her regular social contacts to depend too much on the people Günter wanted to see and there was a high degree of formality about most of them. Certainly she had nobody at hand to whom she could turn for sympathy. It was fortuitous, therefore, that she had already been planning to go to Liverpool at the end of the week. She could not imagine being able to tolerate her own company for long. Surrounded by familiar faces and diverted by the varied concerns of her closest relatives, she would be able to look more calmly on her own situation and decide what to do next. However, the more she thought of disclosing, especially to her mother, the details of what had happened, the more she was forced to reflect that her relations with her family had, over the years, become sadly complicated.

Catherine was the youngest of three children: her brother, Peter, and her sister, Jennifer, had been in their early teens when she was born. Her father, Tom Quinn, was the third of eleven children born to second-generation Irish immigrants in a street off Scotland Road. His father was a builder's labourer and his mother, perennially short of money, had frequently depended on credit from the corner shop to feed her large family. The corner shop was owned by a couple called Stewart, whose Protestantism showed itself most noticeably in their prejudice against Catholics. Since, however, the majority of their customers was Catholic, they were, for the period, discreet in their bigotry – until, that is, their daughter, Joyce, told them she intended to marry young Tom Quinn. For the Stewarts such a marriage was a tragedy in every respect, for on top of Tom's religion was the fact that he did not have a proper job. A bright child, he had easily won a scholarship to the Jesuit grammar school but he had had to leave when he was sixteen to make way for a younger brother whose schooling, since he wanted to become a priest, took priority over his own.

Of course the Stewarts did their best to talk their daughter out of such a marriage but she would not be persuaded, in spite of the threat, ruthlessly carried out, that they would never speak to her again. Until the war, the young couple led a hand-to-mouth existence but then their fortunes changed dramatically: Joyce's parents were killed in the blitz and she learned that, the long years of neglect notwithstanding, they had left her all their money. It was enough for her to buy a small house in Childwall, a suburb worlds away from Scotland Road and the rented rooms in which she had spent the previous ten years. At the end of the war Tom, with his pre-war School Certificate better qualified than many, was accepted for the emergency teacher-training programme and the family's respectability was complete.

Had Joyce Quinn possessed any choice in the matter, she would probably have chosen not to have Catherine, but once the child was actually there, she became totally besotted with it, giving full rein to the maternal instincts which had, in the case of Peter and Jennifer, been thwarted by the more pressing struggle for subsistence. Materially, there was no comparison between the surroundings in which Catherine grew up and those which, as small children, her brother and sister had known. But the difference went much further: Catherine was, from the day she was born, the centre of attention and indulged, not only by her mother, but by her tender-hearted father and the sweet-natured Jennifer. Peter was more inclined to be jealous, especially when his little sister's mental powers threatened to outshine his own, but she idolized her big brother and idolatry appeased him.

Catherine never knew the disagreements and tensions which, in adolescence, spoil so many children's relations with their parents: even had she been less conformist than she was, she would have been assured of wholehearted support at home. When at Oxford she found herself leading a disappointingly cloistered existence in her women's college, altogether unable to mix easily with the opposite sex, her family consoled her and, though they could be of no practical help, it was very comforting to return to Liverpool and meet with general approval, not just from adoring parents but also from the wider circle of friends belonging to Peter and Jennifer, who had both stayed on Merseyside after their marriages. When Catherine came home at the end of her last term, her spirits seemed so very low that Mrs Quinn decided that she must arrange some substantial diversion for her.

Sheila Buckley, an old friend of the Quinns, had been among the first party of teachers to take part in the post-war Liverpool–Cologne exchange. Unlike most of the group she had kept in touch with the family that had hosted her and now the younger daughter, recently married and living in Munich, was urging her to come for a holiday. Sheila planned to turn her visit into an extended tour of Germany and take in her friends in Cologne as well. She was toying with the idea of going by car but she was not a very confident driver and her knowledge of German was slight. So Joyce Quinn suggested that Catherine go with her, to assist both with the language and the driving. Catherine had taken her driving-test soon after her seventeenth birthday and passed with the aplomb that had attended all her other examinations. The proposal met with everyone's approval and Sheila's German host readily offered to put Catherine up as well.

The trip got off to a good start; Catherine had always felt at ease among older people and she had long been a favourite with Sheila. In Cologne she found that her schoolgirl German was surprisingly convincing – a feeling for grammar and an ear for pronunciation combined to help her speak, at least at a mundane level, near perfectly. Since foreigners generally do not expect the English to speak any language but their own, Catherine's proficiency drew special praise, and as she was just now particularly susceptible, the compliments had the effect of making her even more sweetly charming. Moreover, the fact that her German, though near faultless as far as it went, was still at a relatively simple level led to her making a very different impression from the one she made in England, where her seriousness and obvious intelligence quickly stamped her a bluestocking. Her hosts in Cologne thought of her as a pleasant, presentable-looking girl and described her as such on the telephone to their Munich relations as the two Englishwomen made their way south.

On hearing then that Catherine was '*jung, hübsch und solid*' (young, pretty and respectable), Monika Hemmersbach resolved to do a little matchmaking on behalf of her brother-in-law, Günter, who at twenty-eight had never had a serious girlfriend. He had just completed his thesis on 'comparative developments in the bankruptcy laws of industrialized countries' and was about to take a job with the American soapmakers for whom he was still working seventeen years later. In some ways he was rather like Catherine, though his solid academic achievements had probably cost him more effort than she had ever needed to make. But whereas his shyness was an integral part of his character, Catherine's – which had, in fact, become apparent only at Oxford – was rather a mere surface diffidence resulting from a sense of her own inadequacy in young, mixed company. Now, in Germany, happy that everyone she met found her superficial pleasantries amusing, she was at last able to overcome the agonizing self-consciousness that had dogged her at university. Doubtless Günter was ripe for matching and his sister-in-law's efforts to pair him off did not need to go beyond asking him to drop in for a glass of wine one evening. He came and while Monika, anxious to prove that her English was still fluent, caught up on Sheila's news, Günter, who had no linguistic pretensions, sat with his brother and Catherine, happily chatting in German. She was the first English girl he had met and, although she bore little resemblance to the mini-skirted dolly birds that typified Swinging London for the readers of Germany's illustrated papers, she nevertheless possessed for him a faintly exotic attraction, just by coming from the town of the Beatles and the land of Mary Quant. He quickly ascertained that she was not stupid, which was much in her favour, but at the same time the language barrier gave what she said a deference and hesitation which agreeably flattered his ego.

During the ten days that Catherine stayed in Munich, their courtship proceeded with an intensity that dazzled her. He took her round the churches and art galleries and introduced her to the beer halls and Weißwurst. When one evening on returning to the house before the others had got home from their separate excursion, he looked at her very solemnly and addressed her as '*du*', using for the first time the familiar form of the second-person pronoun, she found herself inexpressibly moved; indeed, she was more excited by this purely linguistic access of tenderness than by the embrace which followed it. Just before the end of her holiday they went for a walk in the Botanical Gardens and he asked her what was to happen next. Before she had a chance to reply, he answered himself: either they could say goodbye and go their separate ways or they could keep in touch and eventually get married. Personally, he favoured the latter alternative. Catherine, who had scarcely grown used to having a man pay her any sort of romantic attention, was quite unprepared for a proposal of marriage, but as she could think of no good reason why she should not become Günter's wife, she accepted him. He was satisfied with his success but anxious, for the present, that they keep the engagement to themselves; Monika was a dreadful chatterbox.

When Catherine returned to Liverpool, her mother was initially delighted that her daughter had so obviously enjoyed her holiday, though she was extremely disappointed when Catherine announced that she would be looking for supply teaching in Liverpool: Mrs Quinn had hoped her brilliant daughter, who had taken a first at Oxford, would show greater ambition. Catherine did not at once confide her marriage plans to her mother but Sheila's report that Günter had 'quite fallen for her', together with Catherine's departure for Munich during the October half-term holiday, aroused deep foreboding in Joyce. At Christmas Günter came to Liverpool and made an unhappy impression: he treated Catherine with an offhandedness which her mother found offensive, and seemed unwilling to make more than a perfunctory attempt to speak English. He pointedly addressed Catherine in German and disingenuously asked her to translate when Mrs Quinn told him she hoped he would use to the full the opportunity his visit afforded to improve his English. At Easter Catherine again went to Germany and was warmly welcomed by Günter's parents who by this time openly regarded her as their future daughter-in-law. On her return to Liverpool she told her own family that she would like to get married in the summer. Although more than half expecting it, her mother received the announcement with hysterical horror and for some weeks behaved as if Catherine had contracted a fatal disease. However, as she had indulged her daughter's every wish since infancy, it would have been surprising if she had maintained her hostility now; she really did want only Catherine's happiness and though she made no secret of the fact that Günter was not at all the son-in-law she would have wished for, she threw herself into the wedding preparations with an enthusiasm that would have done credit to a Victorian mamma.

The marriage took place at the end of July. Günter's parents, his brother and Monika travelled to Liverpool and received a cordial welcome from Mrs Quinn, who was anxious to fulfil her obligations as mother of the bride with becoming dignity. Nevertheless she did not omit to explain to Herr and Frau Hemmersbach, whose scant English meant they understood perhaps a quarter of what she said, that she did not consider Günter much of a catch and that her daughter was sacrificing opportunities of personal success such as few people could even dream of. She feared that Catherine's total inexperience with men was leading her into a precipitate marriage that she must live to regret. Frau Hemmersbach understood from this only that Günter was Catherine's first boyfriend and, being a very old-fashioned lady, she rejoiced in the information and heard nothing which might have soured relations between the two families.

After a brief touring holiday in the Eifel the young couple set up house in a small apartment just outside Frankfurt. For both of them the courtship was over but whereas its culmination in marriage left Günter free to devote his energies wholeheartedly to his budding career, Catherine was left with a great deal of time on her hands and very little notion of how she should spend it. There was no question of housekeeping occupying more than a couple of hours each day and Günter was away from shortly after seven in the morning until, at the earliest, six-thirty or seven in the evening. Moreover, when he eventually did come home, he seemed quite insensitive to Catherine's need for conversation and companionship: he wanted to eat his supper and drink his beer without exchanging more than the odd word about his office day, and he certainly had no inclination to indulge in the sort of prolonged discussion on books and people which had been the main solace of Catherine's undergraduate life. Increasingly, she reproached him for his neglect and, the loneliness of her day inclining her to melancholy, she frequently ended up in tears. Günter was baffled by her weeping: throughout their engagement she had been docile and sweet-tempered and she had never given him the smallest indication that she doubted she could be permanently happy with him. He felt cheated by the change in her and, instead of considering the reasons for it or offering her sympathy, he became not only even more silent but glumly disapproving as well.

Before the autumn was out Catherine took the excuse of a family celebration to go home, where it was not long before the warmth and real affection of her reception caused her to tell her mother and Jennifer that she was far from happy. They both behaved beautifully, listening sympathetically and not once even suggesting to Catherine that they had known this would happen all along. Although Mrs Quinn had long ago inferred that Günter was just the sort of man who would expect his wife to accept her inferior status uncomplainingly, she breathed no criticism of him to Catherine. Instead she skilfully emphasized that an early divorce would be the kindest thing for him too: they had both made a mistake but they should not be forced to spend a lifetime regretting it. Catherine went back to Frankfurt very nearly decided that she would tell him she was leaving him. Günter, however, disarmed her by seeming genuinely pleased to have her back and over the long weekend resulting from All Saints' Day falling on a Monday they visited the Hemmersbachs senior, where Catherine was, as the youngest and prettiest member of the family circle, made much of by uncles and aunts who rarely received such polite attention for their reminiscences from their own children as they did from her. Everyone in Munich seemed to be so bent on congratulating Günter on his good fortune in finding such a wife that Catherine sensed an inappropriateness, almost a grossness, in now asking for a divorce. Unfortunately, when she got back to their own flat, she was as miserable as ever and still Günter refused, apparently, to take her unhappiness seriously. She would cry and he would shrug his shoulders; she would continue to cry and he would go to bed. In reply to her accusations of cruelty, Günter told her she was hysterical; when she said that all she wanted was reassurance that he loved her, he said that he would not have married her without loving her but that she should not expect him to turn into the sort of sentimental fellow he had never pretended to be.

At Christmas they went again to Munich and again Catherine was revived by the admiration of the family there. When, in the spring, she next saw her mother she was still unable to break completely from Günter. In the end, she was helped out of the depression which afflicted her in her Frankfurt isolation by Günter's finding a job for her. His firm ran English-language courses for its managers and the teacher had had a heart attack which would keep him away for several months; although Catherine was, by German standards, extremely young, she was a native speaker with a degree and a year's teaching experience. In addition she was immediately available and prepared to accept the temporary nature of the appointment. The teaching she had to do was very carefully prescribed but the social effect of going out to work was exhilarating. As a married woman she assumed – perhaps naïvely – that men would not suppose her to be seeking their favours and, released from the shyness that had blighted her student days, she became newly attractive and vivacious. At home she was too busy telling Günter about the things she was doing to find time to reproach him for not telling her more about what *he* was doing. Naturally, he found her chatter more enjoyable than her scenes and he became less moody himself. When the course teacher was sufficiently recovered to return to work, Catherine found another job in adult education and there she remained until they moved to the Rhineland. By this time she had so grown in self-knowledge that she did not fear a long day at home on her own any more: on the contrary, she looked forward to having time to herself and a house in which to enjoy it that was very different from that first overcrowded little flat.

Perhaps she did sometimes vaguely regret having married the first man who asked her – for she now knew, as she had not known before, that Günter would not have been the only man to want to marry her – but she was by no means sure that she could have greatly increased her chance of happiness with anybody else. She did not have a passionate nature and her readiness to make the best of what she had was coupled with her private conviction that she knew what was best for Günter. It was a sense of superiority, not self-abasement, which motivated her to work the harder of the two at building a happy marriage and for a long time her efforts were rewarded with what seemed like total success.

The effect of this gradual transformation of Catherine's attitude to her husband and her life in Germany was, however, very damaging to her relations with her mother. Mrs Quinn, who rarely doubted the truth of her own instincts, had never expected Catherine to be happy with

Günter and those tearful visits home in the first year had confirmed her expectations. She never forgot what Catherine had told her then about Günter's coldness and indifference to her own unhappiness and she was not subsequently prepared to accept that the unhappiness might have been less profound than it appeared at the time. She felt that her daughter was showing great perversity in continuing to live with an ogre who, she knew, had never properly appreciated his wife's exceptional qualities. She considered herself doubly betrayed: having married a man of whom she disapproved, Catherine had then seemed to acknowledge her mistake, accepting all the sympathy that was lavished upon her, only to change her mind again and reject her mother's advice a second time. They never quarrelled, but a coolness grew up between them and Catherine's visits to Liverpool, though regular and frequent, became shorter and more formal.

And so it was that Catherine, bleakly reflecting on her situation now Günter was gone, began to see her trip to Liverpool as a possible aggravation of her distress. Her decision to take the car and stay longer than originally planned had been made on the spur of the moment to Günter; he was leaving her and she wanted to surround herself with those who loved her to make up for his desertion. She liked too the idea of putting physical distance between herself and him and Anna. The trouble was, the more she thought of it, the less real comfort she could envisage for herself once her family knew the nature of her misfortune. All day Wednesday she put off phoning her mother, either to tell her the major news or to inform her that she had altered her travel plans. The house seemed abnormally quiet and towards evening she put on a record, although she had little affinity for music, and it certainly had no power to console her – her breast, she was fond of saying, was not sufficiently savage. She picked at some bread and cheese, drank too much burgundy and went to bed early where, contrary to expectation, she immediately fell asleep.

Three

Catherine slept soundly until nearly nine o'clock the next morning. She took a shower and dressed carefully in a grey suit and pink blouse. She would go to Bad Godesberg, she decided, and breakfast in a café overlooking the Kurpark before exchanging her airticket for a berth on the Zeebrugge–Hull ferry; on no account would she waste another whole day moping about the house. While Catherine, pleased to find that she was able to busy herself with preparations for a drive to town, became slightly more cheerful, Günter was glumly asking his secretary if she would make him some coffee, as he had come out without any breakfast. When, the previous morning, he had telephoned Anna to tell her that he had finally told Catherine and would be coming home to her that evening, he had thought she sounded delighted. Yet when he actually arrived, her welcome was muted to the point of indifference.

'D'you want a drink?' she asked, sitting down again. 'There's only whisky.'

'Yes, all right. Can I get you one?'

'No.' They sat in awkward silence for a few moments and then she said, 'I hope you don't expect much to eat. It's big meals in the evening that make people fat.' He readily agreed with her but still he was taken aback by the extremely spartan nature of the supper to which they sat down: some thin slices of Swiss cheese, brown bread and a jar of pickled gherkins.

Anna, munching her third slice of bread, commented, 'Not quite what you're used to, I suppose?'

'It's not that. I just can't believe that I'm really here.'

When they had finished, she indicated that he should help carry the plates over to the sink and gave him a tea-towel with which to dry the dishes as she washed them. Afterwards they watched the television news and Anna gave vent to her contempt for the entire political establishment. Günter lacked political commitment to a degree incomprehensible to Anna, so he pretended generally to agree with her; and anyway he found the extravagance of her anger at the state of the world oddly appealing. They went to bed early and at last, in their love-making, found equal and uncomplicated pleasure. Günter fell asleep, for the first time at Anna's side, at least partially reassured that he had been right to come and live with her.

Next morning she remained stubbornly asleep when he got up. When he was dressed he went into the kitchen but could find neither milk nor ground coffee there. He went back to the bedroom and gently woke her.

'I wanted to make some breakfast,' he said, 'but I can't find the coffee.'

'There's a jar of Nescafé in the cupboard over the sink.'

'Is that all you have? Instant coffee doesn't agree with me.'

'Well I've nothing else.'

'What about tea?'

'Never drink it.' She turned over and resolutely shut her eyes.

'Perhaps you could think to buy some coffee when you go out then?'

She grunted slightly but as he was anxious to force some friendly words from her before he left, he said, in a conciliatory tone, 'Can I get you anything?'

'No, just leave me in peace. It's awfully early.'

'Should we go out to eat tonight? Surely we have something to celebrate.'

She did not answer but pulled the pillow tight around her ears.

He spent an unproductive day at work and left the office early. He was aware that he very much wanted to see Catherine, even though he had no clear idea of what he would say to her. Her sang-froid two nights ago had made it easier for him to break with her, particularly since his perception of the coldness in her character had done much to reinforce his preference for Anna. Catherine was right in believing that they had once been perfectly happy, but she was wrong in assuming that it was only Anna's arrival in his life that had spoiled their happiness: in fact, Günter had been increasingly unhappy for some months before Anna had invited him to bed with her.

His career, to which for so long he had devoted his main energy, had reached a plateau. A hope he had had a year before of being transferred to a better job in the States had been disappointed and he had found himself growing restless. Catherine, who had been unenthusiastic about leaving her house and familiar, settled life for what she regarded as New World brashness, underestimated the seriousness of her husband's discontent. She chaffed him for wanting to have his own little 'mid-life crisis', like the man in the *Spiegel* magazine cover-story and, when he failed to laugh off such a suggestion, accused him of having lost his sense of humour. If he had lost his job altogether, she would certainly have given him all the reassurance and moral support he sought; as it was, she considered it feeble-minded to remain disheartened for long over a rather minor setback. He soon felt frustrated not only at work but at home as well, galled by Catherine's blithe refusal to believe that he had any cause to be depressed. She continued to run the house, cook his meals and entertain their guests with effortless efficiency, but more and more her competence tended to irritate rather than console him. She tried to divert him from dwelling on his working life by ignoring it herself, chattering instead about the books she was reading and organizing theatre visits and weekend trips away for them both.

It therefore came as an exhilarating change for him when Anna, as he drove her home that Sunday night, encouraged him to talk about his general dissatisfaction with the turn his career had taken. Anna, modishly left-wing as she was, thought it the most natural thing in the world that anyone employed by a vast capitalist complex, especially an American one, should have doubts about the usefulness of his work, and Günter perhaps mistook the ideological nature of her condemnation of multi-nationals for sympathy with his personal predicament. What was of most significance for him, however, was that she was listening to his complaints without censure, whereas Catherine had implicitly rebuked him for not finding that all was for the best in the best of all possible worlds. The suggestion that they go to bed had come from Anna and was expressed with a startling directness which Günter found impossible to refuse. Ever since her infertility had been established beyond doubt Catherine had found his sexual advances irksome and, although she had never rejected them, she made it clear that they gave her little pleasure. That Anna, in contrast to his wife, should actually seek them came as a most agreeable surprise to his ego; her subsequent assertions that he had succeeded in delighting her beyond all reasonable expectations overwhelmed him.

In the ensuing months they had seen each other often but, in order not to arouse Catherine's suspicions, they had never been able to spend more than a few hours together – sometimes less – and these brief meetings were inevitably preoccupied with sexual relations. Anna, for all her liberated toughness, had been desolated by Wolfgang's rejection and she was, especially at the beginning, very susceptible to Günter's gentleness and clearly admiring wonder at the contrast she presented to Catherine. Her pregnancy had not been intended by either of them but their reactions to it were utterly different. Anna, whose earliest political activity had been involvement in the campaign to liberalize the abortion laws, assumed at first that a speedy termination would be the most acceptable solution for them both. Günter, on the other hand, was overcome by a wave of paternal sentiment that even Anna could not immediately resist. Although she had, privately, by no means ruled out the possibility of an abortion, she momentarily allowed herself to be carried along by her lover's enthusiasm. She was pleased, too, that her having a baby would bring matters to a head between Günter and Catherine, whom she had heartily disliked ever since Wolfgang, after their first visit to the Hemmersbachs, had told her how very much he admired his English cousin.

Perhaps she had not expected Günter to act so quickly; perhaps, in view of the respectful way he had always referred to Catherine, she had not, in her heart, expected him to act at all; certainly she had been caught off guard by the apparent finality of his moving into her flat. Her ungracious welcome reflected the muddle of her own feelings and sadly confused Günter, who had rashly begun to spin a dream of serene family happiness with a loving young wife. By five o'clock on Thursday, though anxious to escape from the office, he found himself dreading having to encounter again Anna's uncompromising refusal to exert herself in order to make him feel at home. He would rather first call on Catherine, if only in the hope that an interview with her would provide him with something to talk to Anna about.

Catherine returned from Bad Godesberg invigorated. She had changed her airticket, bought gifts for the family, and been talked by the fishmonger into buying more crawfish than she would probably be able to eat. She had prepared them on a couple of skewers with mushroom and bacon to grill later and was drinking sherry when Günter knocked at the door. She was happy to see him but determined not to show it.

'Have you lost your key?' she asked, walking straight back to the sitting-room. 'Will you have a drink?'

'Yes, thank you.' She poured him a sherry and sat down. 'I've been a bit worried about you,' he began.

'Really?' Her voice was sharp.

'Perhaps I was too harsh on Tuesday.'

'I was not hurt by the presentation but by the content of what you said.'

'But you were upset?'

'What difference does it make?'

'I hate to think of you being miserable.'

'Enough to tell Anna she can go to hell?'

'Catherine, I've explained how I feel about Anna.'

'Indeed you have. What I don't understand is what you want from me. Perhaps you'd like me to kill myself, then you'd be reassured that I really *had* cared, but no longer distressed by the thought of my actually being "miserable" somewhere.'

'God, how I hate your cynicism!' Catherine, infuriated by Günter's determination to put her in the wrong, would just then have liked to hit him, but that same overdeveloped fear of making herself look ridiculous which had, as a teenager, inhibited her from dancing the twist, held her back. Instead she asked how one set about getting a divorce. There had been much newspaper coverage of a new divorce law but, with what now seemed culpable complacency, she had not read beyond the headlines, assuming that such matters did not concern her. Günter seemed embarrassed by her question. 'Are you really so eager to be rid of me?'

'My dear Günter, surely I am already rid of you, whether I want to be or not. But I had supposed that you and Anna would be impatient to marry in order to legitimize the child.'

Günter smiled. 'How very conventional you are! I'm not sure Anna even really believes in marriage.'

Catherine felt vaguely cheered by these words. 'So of course you don't believe in marriage any more either?'

'Maybe it just doesn't seem all that important.'

'Nevertheless, the three of you will want to set up house together – presumably this house will have to be sold or,' Catherine frowned with distaste at the possibility, 'or, if you choose to live here, you'll have to buy me out.'

'Oh, perhaps, something like that. But there's really no

need to rush things. The baby's not due till the end of April. Anna's flat will do for the moment.'

'I thought she lived in some squalid student commune.'

'It wasn't squalid at all. But she moved out, anyway, to a place of her own a few months ago.'

'I'm disappointed. I didn't think that she would fall so quickly into the role of kept mistress.'

'I don't keep her. Her parents pay the rent. She still has three or four semesters before her exams, though I doubt she'll ever take a degree.'

'Because it would interfere too much with motherhood?'

'Well, yes, it might. But actually, even with the baby, I'm very anxious she should finish the course. It's just that she hardly does any work – she's much too involved in politics.'

'What sort of politics?'

'The new Green Party.'

Catherine nodded. Yes, of course, Anna would be a 'Green', one of the growing band of newly confident environmental agitators who could see greater affluence and comfort for more people than ever before only in negative terms, as leading directly to dying forests and polluted rivers. It was not that Catherine herself did not care at all about the dangers that threatened the environment, but rather that she feared the consequences of out-and-out 'green' policies: she was more alarmed at the prospect of having to give up her motor car and efficient central heating than she loved the forests or feared atomic power stations. And then a thought occurred to her which made her laugh.

'I do hope,' she said, 'that you are both aware of the ecological implications of throw-away nappies.'

Günter, quite discomfited, stood up. 'I really only came to pack some clothes,' he lied, 'I'll go and see to it.'

Catherine, still chuckling at her own joke, remained seated for a few minutes, and then followed Günter upstairs. She found him in the bedroom, distractedly opening drawers and stuffing the contents untidily into a large suitcase.

'Would you like me to help you?' she asked, responding automatically to his clumsiness.

'Why the hell should I?'

'Why shouldn't you? I've been packing your cases for a long time.'

'Well it was a mistake. I never wanted you to nanny me.'

'I see. So there goes another of my foolish delusions.' Catherine walked out of the room, very nearly in tears. She returned to the sitting-room, poured herself more sherry and fought very hard to prevent herself from weeping. Her self-control was considerable and when, a quarter of an hour later, Günter came down with his case packed, she appeared to be reading the newspaper. She looked at him so coldly that he could think of nothing to say.

'I'm driving to Belgium tomorrow morning,' she said. 'I should be in Liverpool by lunchtime on Saturday.'

'Right, well, drive carefully.' His voice trailed off lamely and he went towards the front door. She remained seated and before the sound of his car had died away she was howling without restraint. When at last she stopped crying she felt no relief from having given way. She had no appetite for supper and went to bed without taking the trouble to put any witch-hazel pads on her eyes.

Günter, meanwhile, drove away convinced that Catherine had mastered this crisis with the same ease as she made a béarnaise sauce. Far from being relieved, however, that he had not caused her intolerable distress, he was bitterly angry at what he took to be her immunity from normal human reactions. He reached Anna's flat bursting to pour out his scorn for the unnaturally controlled way Catherine was behaving. But Anna was not there. He found a scrawled note on the draining-board to say that she had gone to a local party meeting; he must have heard the news and would understand how excited she was. He should find himself something to eat as she would probably not be home until very late. Günter had not heard any news all day; indeed he had not even seen a newspaper because he had not bothered to stop at a kiosk and his own was delivered to the house. He looked round the kitchen and opened the fridge but disdained to eat either crispbread or yoghurt. He took the whisky bottle and a glass and went into the living-room to switch on the television. He was just in time for the eight o'clock news programme.

Günter had never seen life in party-political terms and he was at a loss as to what possible event could have occurred which would cause Anna such excitement that she preferred to go to a meeting to discuss it than out to dinner with him. Nor did the news bulletin enlighten him: the main item, dwelt on in stultifying detail by the commentators, was the withdrawal of the FDP, the junior partner, from coalition with the ruling Social Democrats. This, to Günter, seemed hardly earth-shattering: the papers had been full of the strains within the government for months; it had only been a matter of time before Schmidt was ousted as Chancellor and the FDP formed a new coalition with the conservative Christian Democrats. Günter, irritated by the repetitiveness of the television reporting, switched over to a cowboy film, an ancient black-and-white classic in which he would have found the dubbing of laconic outlaws and tough sheriffs by German actors with cut-glass accents hilarious, had his own spirits not been quite so low. Too lethargic to get up to switch the set off, he sat on, drinking and dozing, while the television twice more in the course of the evening told him how the coalition had broken up. When Anna at last got home he was fast asleep in front of a blank screen.

'Darling!' she shouted, shaking his shoulder. 'Wake up! I've so much to tell you. Isn't it all thrilling?' Günter, dull-witted from whisky and sleep, said nothing and she continued. 'There'll have to be new elections now and I know we're going to do well. People will be so sick of the old parties that they'll vote for us in droves.'

'Election? Already?'

'Well not next week. Nobody quite knows when exactly

but probably in the spring, at the very latest. And we're sure to do well. We'll be in the Bundestag!'

'We were going to go out to dinner.'

'We can do that another night. This is much more exciting.'

Günter, more drunk than he thought, stood up with difficulty. 'I really can't agree about that,' he said, his attempt to sound dignified undermined by the slight slurring of his words. 'I really can't agree,' he said again but, aware that it sounded no better the second time, decided he had better go straight to bed. He left the room and Anna, still light-headed by the evening's discussions and her own certainty that the next months would be exhilarating, did not pay too much attention to Günter. She ate a yoghurt and followed him to bed. Next morning when, feeling the full force of a hangover, Günter looked in the kitchen for fresh coffee but found none, he risked the damage that Nescafé would do to his stomach and left for work without even disturbing Anna.

Four

The plane that Catherine had planned to take to England would have got her to Liverpool on Friday evening. It was necessary, therefore, that she telephone her mother before she set out for Zeebrugge. As she ate her breakfast, she considered what she should say. Although she had been driving a car for over twenty years, she expected her mother to doubt her ability to drive all the way unaccompanied; she would probably panic if she heard that she was not only driving alone but doing so in a state of emotional stress. Indeed, she almost wondered herself if she were behaving sensibly. She had slept badly and felt sick from having drunk too much sherry without taking any food. She was more angry with Günter, too, than at first, when she had been preoccupied with how his leaving her would affect her personally. Now, self-pity had given way to anger at his apparent desire to see her upset. She bitterly condemned what she saw as his egoism: not satisfied to indulge a shallow preference for another woman, he also required reassurance that his wife was missing him.

Coffee and scrambled eggs restored her sufficiently to allay her own fears that she was not fit to drive, though she decided not to add to her mother's anxiety for her safety on a long car journey by telling her truthfully what had caused her to change her plans. When she got through, Mrs Quinn's voice sounded almost hostile: she disapproved of expensive international telephone calls quite as much as she hated people to change their arrangements.

'But I still don't see why you have to bring the car.'

'I've told you, I've decided to stay a couple of weeks.'

'What about Günter? I thought he couldn't manage without you for more than forty-eight hours at a time.'

'He's going to a seminar in the States next week. He won't even be here.' Catherine was pleased at her own inventiveness: the lie carried conviction.

'That still doesn't explain why you need a car.'

'It'll make it easier for me to get about.'

'You can use your father's car.'

'I thought he'd changed his insurance.'

'Yes, well, he would drive you anywhere you wanted to go.'

'Oh, mother, don't go on. I've booked now and I'll be with you before lunchtime tomorrow.'

'That's what you hope. The party's tomorrow, remember.'

'I'll be there. Please don't worry.'

'I'm not *worried*. I just think you're crazy.'

Catherine said goodbye and hung up, oppressed by the coldness she sensed in her mother's attitude. She felt suddenly nostalgic for the comfort which, for the first twenty-odd years of her life, she had been able to take for granted: whatever problem she had had to face, she had known implicitly that her mother was on her side. She wondered now if her perception of her mother's support had been mistaken: had it perhaps only seemed unquestioning because she had never tested it? Had it been a fluke that its withdrawal, once her marriage had settled down, had come so late? Or had the fault really lain with herself for assuming that, in her mother's eyes, she could do no wrong? She went upstairs and finished packing, then called on her neighbour to leave the key and instructions for Frau Keller. She repeated the lie that Günter was in America and left the date of her own return uncertain.

It was a bright, clear September morning and by the time she reached the Autobahn she was already experiencing some of the exhilaration that comes from going on a journey. At least while she was on the move she could enjoy the illusion of being cut off from her cares. She had never before driven so far entirely on her own and she found herself filled with a ridiculously childish sense of adventure. Though not inclined to speed, she made good time and stopped just outside Brussels for an early lunch.

As she sat down to her tough steak and greasy chips she looked at the other customers, idly speculating on what had brought them there. There was little mystery about any of them: travelling businessmen, truck drivers, British Army of the Rhine personnel going on leave. Then she noticed that the man sitting at the next table, though he wore no wedding-ring, bore a telltale band of white flesh on his third finger. She could not recall whether Günter had been wearing his ring the previous night. His wanting to wear one at all had been among the many niggling things to which her mother had taken exception: Mrs Quinn considered that no self-respecting man would ever choose to wear jewellery. At the time, Catherine automatically accepted her mother's view and tried to talk Günter out of his ring. While she was growing up she had invariably followed her mother's lead: perhaps she had unconsciously conceded the right to form her own taste in return for so much indulgence in everything else.

It had come as something of a shock to her when, a few years after her marriage, she had found herself disagreeing with her mother on a quite trivial matter of interior decoration, but she had not backed down and gradually the realization had dawned on her that she actually knew better than Joyce how pictures should be hung and furniture arranged. This led to other discoveries of maternal fallibility and even to a feeling, which she kept to herself, that her mother's moral judgements were not always sound. It is odd to live to twenty-five before finding much to criticize in a parent, but once Catherine had broken out of her mental subjection, disillusionment came quickly. Then why on earth was she so anxious to return home now? She had reacted with the reflexes of twenty years ago without for a moment being able to become again the daughter she used to be. The trouble was, she was totally unused to coping alone: she had never even lived by herself and she had gone from the bosom of her family into a marriage which she had allowed to dominate her life. She had not worked for the past five years, but even before that her job had been peripheral and she had formed no close friendships in Germany. Her flight to Liverpool was in a way a refusal to accept her solitary condition, even if she could not reasonably expect to find there the company she required. 'I just don't want to be alone,' she thought sadly as she drank her coffee, before leaving the restaurant as quickly as possible. The need to concentrate on her driving would, she hoped, distract her from this ominous train of thought.

Her journey continued smoothly. Her cabin, designed to accommodate three people, seemed almost spacious. She was roused from a fitful sleep a little before six o'clock the next morning by a banging on her door and a cheerful northern voice offering her tea. Obediently, she got up and dressed, though it was nearly three hours before the ship berthed and she was driving out of Hull docks. She stopped at a motorway café and lingered over coffee, reluctant to arrive at her destination before her mother expected her. In the end, it was just past noon when she reached Liverpool. She drove first to the little group of shops near her parents' house. They seemed dingier than when she had done errands there as a child and the pavement was strewn with litter. Catherine went into the flower shop. In a corner on the floor was a pile of bouquets, laid out like corpses and tightly sealed in cellophane, waiting to be delivered. The flowers for sale consisted of artificial blooms, some gladioli and a few tired carnations. The assistant, a surly girl of about eighteen, was on the telephone, recounting to her friend what had happened in the pub the night before. After Catherine had waited a couple of minutes she said, 'Eh, Julie, I've gorra go. A customer's come in.'

'I suppose you haven't anything else in the back?'

'No, that's the lot.'

'Then I'll have seven gladioli, please.'

'Seven? They're 65p each.'

'That's all right.'

'D'you want some fern?'

'No, thank you. I don't think fern goes with gladioli, do you?'

'Dunno. Burrit's free with orders over £3.50.'

The girl bundled the flowers into two sheets of patterned wrapping-paper, took the money and resumed her conversation with Julie before Catherine was out of the door.

The Quinns' house was one of the smallest semi-detacheds in the neighbourhood. Joyce was a fanatical housewife and kept her net curtains and doorstep ferociously clean. She greatly resented Catherine's occasional remarks to the effect that the Germans were cleaner than the English, and it was true that no individual German housewife could be more meticulous than Joyce. What struck Catherine, however, was more a failure of public spirit: an indifference to the stray sheet of newspaper or plastic bag that wrapped itself around a lamp post; a refusal to attack the weeds that grew abundantly between the paving-stones; and a startling tolerance of animal excrement. The cars were an eyesore, too, since so many households possessed two or even three and, as many of the garages were needed as general storage space, they stood all day in the road.

The front door opened as Catherine walked up the path. 'You're earlier than I expected,' said her mother. 'I suppose you drove very fast.' She kissed Catherine perfunctorily and took the flowers, saying, 'You shouldn't waste your money on this sort of thing. And we have better glads in the garden.'

'Where's Daddy?'

'At his prayers! Didn't you know he's got religion all of a sudden? He goes to church every day – to make up, I suppose, for all the Sundays he missed in his youth. But he should be back any minute.'

Catherine followed her mother into the kitchen where, knowing better than to offer help, she watched with mute disapproval while Mrs Quinn made a white sauce that was certain to be lumpy. It was to go on some baked fish that had long been in the oven. Potatoes and peas were also being kept warm since Mrs Quinn's wish to have the pans cleaned and put away before the meal began took precedence over the superior taste of freshly cooked food. Catherine heard a key in the door and went out to greet her father.

'Hello, darling, have you had a good journey?' Mr Quinn embraced his daughter warmly.

'Wash your hands now, if you want,' called his wife. 'It's all ready.'

They sat down and Catherine began to chatter inconsequentially about her journey. Her mother was not interested and changed the subject.

'I suppose I should have given you sherry or something first,' she said. 'You all seem to booze all the time these days. I've known Peter and Anthea to drink wine with steak and kidney pie. One thing laughing at the other, I'd say.'

'There are cheap wines.'

'Well, of course, Anthea wouldn't buy an expensive one.' Although a frugal housekeeper herself, Joyce had never forgiven her daughter-in-law for refusing to put on a spread when entertaining her husband's parents: you might eat hot pot when you were on your own but you bought a roast for visitors.

'And what's Sarah's fiancé like? You hadn't met him when I was last here.'

'He seems a nice enough lad,' said Tom, speaking quickly before his wife had time to put the disapproval evident in her expression into words. 'Very quiet, though, compared to Sarah.'

Mrs Quinn brushed aside her husband's comment. 'Sarah is affected and spoilt and she has even less sense than her mother. The boy is a fool, too, but because he went to some third-rate public school they think he must be a great catch.'

'She seems to have a good job.' Catherine remembered her brother's proud account of how well Sarah was doing since she had moved to London.

'She's only a secretary.'

'Oh, but a bit more than a typist, surely.'

'Well, she likes to call herself a personal assistant. Just as she likes to call this do tonight an engagement party, when to all intents and purposes they've been married for months.'

'But you can't get too upset about that sort of thing these days – all young people do it,' said Tom, soothingly.

'I'm not upset about *that*,' retorted his wife contemptuously. 'People were sleeping together before they were married when *we* were young, even. What I object to is all the fuss about getting engaged, then all the build-up to a great white wedding in a year or two. Either they should be honest about flouting convention or they should at least *pretend* to respect it.' She started to clear the plates, refusing Catherine's offer of help. 'Help to carry three plates, indeed!'

'You look a bit tired, love,' said Tom, when he and Catherine were alone.

'I'm not used to driving so far on my own.'

'Is everything all right at home?' It was one of his endearing traits always to refer to her house in Germany as her 'home'. For her mother, home was where your parents lived. She was on the point of answering, with at least a hint of the truth, when Mrs Quinn returned.

'I haven't made a proper pudding,' she said, putting down a bowl of stewed plums, 'as I expect we'll have to eat all sorts of muck tonight.'

'You don't seem at all in the party spirit. Has Peter done something to make you cross?'

'Oh, I'm not cross with Peter. I'm just sick of hearing

how marvellous Sarah's in-laws are. I didn't bring up *my* children to be impressed by a bit more money or a southern accent.' Catherine reflected that this, at least in her own case, was quite true. She could not recall ever having been particularly impressed by superior social standing or wealth as such and when she first went to live in Germany she had vigorously disputed German assertions that Britain was an incorrigibly class-ridden society. Later, however, she had come to see what they meant and she put down her own impunity to snobbish distinctions to her mother's having instilled in her from birth a confidence that she was at least as good as anyone else – if not actually better.

'How's Jennifer?'

'Overworked as always.' Jennifer had four children of whom the youngest was only twelve and in addition, for most of her married life, she had held a full-time teaching job. Mrs Quinn, while believing that women were fools to marry at all, was highly critical of those who tried to 'have their cake and eat it': once married she considered it essential that they stay at home and devote themselves to their families. To her chagrin Jennifer seemed to have coped well with her double role: her children were neither delinquent, unhappy nor mentally subnormal. She therefore told everyone that her daughter was suffering from constant exhaustion and premature ageing, clear evidence that the way she had arranged her life was mistaken.

'And are the children all well?'

'Oh, I expect so. They're past the measles and mumps stage now, you know, by a long chalk.'

'And have you no news, Catherine?' Tom looked a little anxiously at his daughter.

'Not much.' Catherine shrank again from communicating the real news in front of her mother. Then, sensing that her reply sounded ungracious, she smiled and said, 'I think perhaps the journey has taken more out of me than I thought. I didn't sleep very well on the boat.'

'Well, no,' said her mother, 'I don't suppose anyone does. You should have flown.'

'Would you mind if I went to bed for a couple of hours?'
'Of course not. I think it would be very sensible.'
Catherine moved as though to help clear up first.
'Don't bother with that,' said Joyce, peremptorily, 'you'll want to be properly rested for tonight.'

Catherine went up to the room that had been her bedroom from earliest childhood. Until she was thirteen, she had shared it with Jennifer and her sister's bed still stood there, occupied from time to time by Günter. The furniture had been bought on her eleventh birthday and, dignified by the name 'suite', seemed very grand compared to the 'utility' wardrobe and second-hand beds it replaced. It had not worn particularly well. All Mrs Quinn's efforts had been unable to remove the stains on the dressing-table left by Catherine's school exchange partner from France who had liked to douse more than just herself in eau de Cologne each morning. Time had taken its toll of the wardrobe doors, too, and they no longer hung quite right. The bed squeaked as Catherine lay down. She thought how much nicer her own house was, but hardly supposed that the near intolerable oppression which had overcome her was aesthetic in origin. She would willingly give up her elegant taste in all externals if only she could feel at ease again in the little house with its flower-strewn carpets and patterned wallpaper.

Sleep was impossible. Outside, a clock struck three, chimes that she had heard for years from her bed, this bed. The sound, reinforcing the unchanged appearance of her bedroom, took her back to a Christmas vacation twenty years ago when she had been equally unhappy, after the experiences of her first term at Oxford had revealed a new discrepancy between what she was and what she wanted to be. What she was, was an industrious mouse who scarcely ventured outside her college, an ugly, soulless building at an indecent distance from the centre of Oxford; what she wanted to be, was what American feminists were later to call a sex-object, though they gave to the word a pejorative connotation which Catherine, in the early 1960s, would certainly not have recognized.

She had attended a sedate girls' grammar school, at which the senior mistresses belonged to that inter-war generation of liberated women who had consciously chosen a career in preference to marriage, and had found the choice exhilarating; they had never struck Catherine either as self-pitying or as bitterly resentful of men. From them – and her outstanding academic record, coupled with perfect manners, had made her a great favourite – she had imbibed the general principles of female equality and these, reinforced by the domestic experience of a strong-minded mother, protected her from ever doubting that her sex could hold its own. While she was at school, she had little contact with boys and it was not until she got to Oxford that she learned that confidence in her own intellectual powers was of no use whatsoever in establishing satisfactory social contacts. Early in her first term another Liverpool girl took her to a staircase party in Merton where she sat in a corner, miserable and shy, until seized upon to dance by a loutish youth with acne and a Bradford accent. His choice of her as a partner wounded her deeply: she accepted that convention still gave boys the initiative but she was offended that such an appalling young man should have supposed her to be on his level. Subsequent tentative efforts to become involved in undergraduate societies quickly foundered; everywhere she felt herself to be doubly inhibited, by confident upper-class girls on the one hand and by brash state-school products on the other, the latter all flaunting regional accents far stronger than the faint trace of Merseyside which lingered in her own speech.

So she retreated sadly to her college, keenly aware that she was missing the best of university life but unable to do anything about it; she envied the girls who turned heads at lectures – not so much by their beauty as by their self-assurance – and she envied those who quickly acquired boyfriends who could introduce them to wider pleasures than were to be obtained inside a women's college that bore more resemblance to a boarding-school than to a place of higher learning. True, she could have found some partner who was happy enough to have her, presentable as she was, but her instincts told her that he would not be good enough: she had her own definition of acceptable sex-object. Fearful that, if she ventured into mixed company, she would be doomed to suffer the pain of rejection by the boys she would have liked to attract as well as the humiliation of attentions from those she despised, she increasingly concentrated on her work and sought company only in a safe little group of girls who, while by no means freaks, shared her own shyness.

Together they struggled to acquire a taste for Tio Pepe while polishing their epigrams before going down to cheerless dinners in Hall. Years later Catherine looked back on this time with regret that it had always been tinged with melancholy; they had all been so anxious to lead a different sort of life in Oxford that they had underestimated the very real pleasure of their own conversation, which was varied, intelligent and often witty. They formed perhaps one of the least militant groups of women the University had known, coming as they did after the first great battles had all been won but before the new ones had even been thought of. In answer to the hypothetical question, 'Which would you rather take with you when you go down, a first or an engagement ring?', they were unanimous in preferring the latter.

In the event Catherine was the only one to get a first, though two of them, settling at the last minute for grey men from Keble, got their engagement rings. Catherine's tutor had told her some months before Schools that she was likely to do well, at the same time expressing a hope that she would stay in the college to do research. When she went on to suggest that a possible subject for her thesis might be a sixteenth-century writer who had produced a sort of early literary criticism entirely in Latin, Catherine said little, but privately she was shocked that her own devotion to scholarship could be so drastically overestimated. With horror she saw her whole life as a continuation of school: in a closed, female society she would pass from successful examination to substantial thesis and respected contributions in learned journals. But for what did a first in English qualify her, if not for the academic world? At the end of her last summer term she returned to Liverpool muddled and uncertain about everything except her decision not to go back to Oxford.

Her mother then had been tireless in comforting and reassuring her. Mrs Quinn, having married too young and – for all her conscientious application to maternal duty – having felt imprisoned by marriage, had been more than just proud of Catherine's success: she had wholeheartedly shared it, vicariously achieving through her daughter all that she had been denied herself. Made to leave school at fourteen because her parents needed her help, for next to no wages, in the shop, she had been determined that her children would reap all the benefits of education. From an early age she had told them that of course they would win scholarships to the grammar school and, once they had done so, she had been equally emphatic that they would go to university. Her relentless ambition had paid off and all her children took degrees, though only Catherine attained the excellence her mother craved. Even so, when Catherine confided in her that her disappointments at Oxford were of a social, even sexual, nature and had nothing to do with her work, Mrs Quinn was full of sympathy. She knew how much her daughter needed a boyfriend, at the same time fully understanding Catherine's scruples about accepting 'anything'. Women, she believed, should aim high and the disdain she had long felt for her own husband made her all the more eager that Catherine should find a worthy boy for herself. She did not realize that Catherine's yearning for a partner had virtually displaced all other ambition; had she done so she would hardly have hit upon the idea of sending her daughter all the way to Germany to find the social recognition which had eluded her at Oxford.

How bitter her mother must have been, thought Catherine, when, on top of the disappointment of her favourite marrying abroad, she had had to bear the ultimate responsibility herself for bringing her together with her future husband. Catherine recalled very clearly how Joyce, while helping her to pack for that fateful holiday, had hinted at the advantage of moving in *adult* company: the boys at Oxford had been too young, too immature for her, she had probably frightened them off. Whether or not Mrs Quinn was right, the fact that Günter was seven years older had greatly increased his attractiveness in Catherine's eyes: having felt herself rejected by boys, she was all the more flattered by the attentions of a man. Even now she was in no doubt that her marriage had been inevitable, so desperate had she been to secure a husband.

Why? Catherine was sceptical of feminist assertions that conditioning alone made women seek the role of home-maker. Not only did she credit herself with the power to resist conditioning in an unacceptable direction, she questioned whether she had personally been exposed to all that much pressure to conform to feminine stereotypes in the first place. While never having felt inferior to men, she had nevertheless believed herself to be incomplete as long as she remained single. Her impatience to marry sprang from a need deep within herself; it had nothing to do with how she perceived the role society required of her. Perhaps if she had met with social success earlier, if she had only been able to mix naturally and easily instead of feeling weighed down by her own gaucheness, she might not have been doomed to marry the first man who asked her.

Doomed? Catherine was too honest to accept such a word. Her marriage had not in itself been tragic or even regrettable: it had brought her years of happiness and in the course of it she had, in her own opinion, become more confident and attractive, more at ease with herself. The heartbreaking, futile 'ifs' which were crowding her mind should not concern what had happened all those years ago – 'if only she had not been the pathetic, unliberated sort of girl who needed a husband' – but what had only just occurred: 'if only Günter had not taken up with Anna'. She would not call it 'falling in love'; never having experienced such a 'falling' herself, she chose to believe that it did not actually happen all that often.

But she was beginning to feel that she was to blame for its happening at all. All the effort she had put into making her marriage secure, in creating an environment in which she and Günter could both live free from the stresses and conflicts which bedevilled the unions of less single-minded women, had resulted in total failure. She might be angry with the details of Günter's behaviour but the fundamental fault was hers for, having taken it upon herself to ensure their happiness, she had ultimately misjudged the means of achieving it. She heard her mother calling up the stairs that tea had been made and got up to join them, a sense of failure added to her sense of hurt.

Five

Peter and Anthea Quinn lived in a large Victorian house in a fashionably mixed neighbourhood of Birkenhead. They had anticipated the vogue in old houses and, twenty years before, had paid only a few hundred pounds more for their ten rooms and extensive garden than Jennifer and her husband had paid for a slightly larger version of their parents' semi-detached in Liverpool. Although for years it had had inside a bare and underfurnished look and it was still intolerably cold in winter, Peter was inordinately proud of his house. His pride stemmed only in part from the property as such and had far more to do with his elation at having demonstrated, through the purchase, that he had broken away from the *petit-bourgeois* limits of his parents' home. He would never convince his mother that it was more chic to shiver among shabby sofas in a vast hundred-year-old room than to be warm and snug in a pre-war suburban estate, but in his heart he knew it to be true. He was grateful to his wife for giving him this insight and also for having the courage to believe that they could afford such a large house at a time when they were still struggling to make ends meet on Peter's basic salary as a secondary-school teacher, long before he had got his present, better-paid job lecturing in a teachers' training-college.

Peter had met Anthea at an amateur-dramatics society. She was the daughter of a doctor and, in the early days of their courtship, had rashly given her future mother-in-law the impression that she believed herself to be the Quinns' social superior. Now Mrs Quinn was not so much egalitarian as convinced that her own family was better than any other and she ruthlessly attacked Anthea's social pretensions by emphasizing her academic inferiority. Anthea, an only child, had been sent to a private school, but though she repeated the 'O' Level course three times, she left in the end with only two passes – in Art and Scripture – to her credit. When she got married, she at once gave up her job in the typing-pool of a large firm and devoted herself to being a housewife *par excellence*. In theory, it should have pleased Joyce that her only son had found so conscientious a helpmate; in fact, she had from the beginning poured scorn on Anthea's domestic accomplishments. There was, she maintained, an affectation in Anthea's flower-arranging and soft furnishings, and she had scant admiration for her cooking – her daughter-inlaw's culinary masterpiece, she was fond of saying, was a sort of Greek shepherd's pie. Over the years, Anthea had singularly failed to win either approval or affection from Mrs Quinn.

Nevertheless, relations were kept up through regular visits and phone calls. Jennifer, who cared deeply and equally for all the ill-assorted members of her family, had been tireless in ensuring that no one lost sight of anyone else. Catherine, from being abroad so long, was ignorant of most of the ups and downs in the relationship between mother and son and son's wife, but she never went to Liverpool without marvelling at Jennifer's success in preserving ostensible harmony. As they drove through the Mersey Tunnel – her father tensely gripping the steering-wheel and hugging the kerb in the slow lane – her mother talked uninterruptedly about Anthea's manyfaceted folly, as she perceived it. 'Her latest craze,' she said, 'is doing up old furniture. She goes to what she calls a restoration class and then rummages round junk shops for flea-ridden settees and chairs that she re-covers in material bought cheap at Birkenhead market. Peter raves about the results.' Was it the activity itself, wondered Catherine, or the fact that Peter 'raved' about it, which drew her mother's scorn?

As the Quinns were the sort of people who took the time on an invitation card literally, they were the first to arrive, apart from Sarah's fiancé and his parents, who were staying in the house. Anthea opened the door to them and greeted them breathlessly. She pecked each of them on the cheek and ushered them into the room which, to Mrs Quinn's open derision, she had recently taken to calling the 'drawing-room'.

'Peter's just opening the wine,' she explained. 'I'll go and get him.' She left them alone and an icy look settled on Joyce's face. Catherine sat down on what was clearly a restored chair, found it very uncomfortable and stood up again. Her father was peering, as he always did, at the bookshelf, though Peter rarely bought any new books: as Anthea said, he could get anything he really needed from the college library. After a few minutes Sarah came in, followed by a thin young man of nondescript appearance. 'Hello, hello!' she gushed, 'how super to see you again. Catherine, meet my future husband; Charles, meet my aunt. "My aunt" – doesn't it sound funny?'

Catherine shook hands with Charles and murmured some words of congratulation.

'It's awfully nice of you to come so far,' he said, giggling nervously. 'Sarah says you're an awfully close family.'

Joyce had still not spoken but at this she said, 'It's not so easy to be "close" to Catherine – or Sarah, either, for that matter, with all those miles between us.'

'Grannie thinks people must be *mad* to leave Liverpool,' explained Sarah.

'Oh, is that so?' said Charles. 'I thought *everyone* was leaving Liverpool these days.' Sarah, recognizing the attempt at humour, laughed loudly; Catherine and her father smiled weakly and Mrs Quinn shot Charles such a poisonous look that he blushed.

The door opened and Charles's parents joined them. Sarah introduced them, to her grandmother's bewilderment, as 'John and Laura'. John seemed rather aloof but Laura, a well-covered woman in her mid-fifties wearing an expensive dress that was just a little too youthful and a little too tight, fell upon Mrs Quinn and said in a loud Home Counties voice, the sort that inevitably grates on northern ears, 'Oh, *you* must be Grannie – we've heard *so* much about you!'

Mrs Quinn stood up. 'Well,' she said, 'I'm sure I'm not *your* Grannie. And now I think it's time someone went to see what Peter's doing. If he's been opening wine since we arrived, he must have sold the car to pay for it.' Tom, as Joyce left the room, took the *Oxford Book of English Verse* from the shelf and opened it at random. Laura turned to Catherine: 'I suppose that that was an example of the famous Liverpool humour,' she said.

'It's my mother's humour,' said Catherine, feeling sudden sympathy for her mother's open rudeness in face of this stranger's uncouth confidence. Her sympathy was fleeting: she was herself never one to behave badly in company. She pulled herself together and asked sweetly, 'Did you come up by car?'

It was just the right question. Not only had they driven, they had come in their new BMW and John soon became even more eloquent than his wife on the subject of the car's speed and comfort.

'You really have to hand it to the Germans,' he concluded, 'whatever else you may think of them – as people, I mean – they *do* know how to make jolly good cars.'

'Darling, do remember this lady is married to a German.' Laura turned to Catherine, insincerely apologetic. 'Johnnie's awfully tactless sometimes.'

'Not tactless at all,' mumbled Johnnie, then, looking at Catherine directly, 'and d'you actually live over there – all the time?'

'Yes, not far from Bonn. It's a very pleasant area.'

'Nice scenery and that sort of thing?'

'Quite nice, yes, and the little town we live in is not without charm.'

'Oh well, of course, they always did keep everywhere very clean, didn't they?'

Other guests were beginning to arrive: Anthea's parents, schoolfriends of Sarah's (most of whom seemed to be called Emma), friends of the family and a few neighbours. Peter had at last appeared with a tray of seven half-filled wine glasses, not nearly enough to go round, and Anthea was inadequately introducing people. Tom was immersed in 'Il Penseroso'.

Catherine found herself listening to a neighbour relating at some length how his holiday – a Rhine steamer cruise – had been ruined by the food. She must have answered his first questions automatically, for she really could not recall what had started him on what was clearly a much-practised diatribe. 'Even the mashed potato was unrecognizable,' he was saying, 'more like semolina pudding, I thought. I don't know how you put up with it.'

'I don't eat on steamers very often,' explained Catherine. He saw her point and chortled immoderately.

'Ah, no, well you wouldn't, would you? Silly of me, really. Ha, ha!'

'I think my sister's just arrived,' said Catherine. 'Do you know Jennifer?'

'Jennifer? The one with all the children? Of course I know her, we meet every Christmas at Peter and Anthea's drinks party. But do go over and say hello yourself – don't mind me. I'll go and see if there's a chance of a drink anywhere.'

Catherine moved towards the door where Jennifer was apologizing for their late arrival: Bob's car wouldn't start and they had had to push it off the path to get Jennifer's ancient Mini out of the garage. Then they had had to push Bob's car back on to the path and then they had needed to wash their hands. Anthea emphasized that their lateness really did not matter, strongly implying that their absence had not even been noticed. But Jennifer never took offence: indeed, the consistently uncritical affection she showed her sister-in-law was precisely what Anthea 'didn't like about her'. Catherine joined them and was greeted enthusiastically. Jennifer, who always bought her own clothes, for every occasion, at Marks and Spencer's, invariably began conversations with Catherine by admiring whatever she was wearing. There was no envy in her compliments: she could remember her little sister's delight, at the age of four or five, in a new party frock, and assumed the grown woman's vanity to be undiminished.

'Have you lost weight?' she asked, after doing full justice to Catherine's silk dress.

'No, my weight stays pretty constant.'

'Gosh, I wish mine did! I've put on pounds this last year, but I tell myself that once you get to fifty you should accept plumpness with a good grace.'

'You certainly look fit – mother was saying you looked tired.'

'Oh, dear old Mum! She's always saying that. By the way, where is she?'

Catherine explained in a very few words the circumstances of Joyce's retreat to the kitchen, but Jennifer at once understood every nuance. She was about to go and find her mother 'to talk her round' when Mrs Quinn appeared, carrying a two-litre bottle of Frascati. In passing, she said 'hello' to her older daughter, took in with a frown that the buttons of her dress were pulling slightly over her bust, and launched herself on a group of guests. 'My son doesn't seem to notice when glasses are empty,' she said, 'let me fill you all up.' The bottle was quickly emptied and, before Peter had realized what was happening, his mother had fetched another and was continuing her genial progress through the party. At last, satisfied that everyone had been served, she attached herself to a group that contained none of her close relatives and soon had them laughing at her own jocular assessment of her chances of getting a job as a barmaid. Having once decided against spending the evening nursing her anger in the kitchen, she was determined to be the life and soul of the party. Catherine, who had in recent years seen only the sour and critical side of her mother's character, the side she turned to her husband and wayward children, was baffled by the change.

'Is she often so jolly?' she asked Jennifer.

'Only with strangers and the few young people she approves of. She gets on very well with our kids nowadays.'

'Have any of them come tonight?'

'No. Sally really is too young to enjoy this sort of do and Carolyn's still in France, but I'm afraid the boys just don't much care for Aunt Anthea and Cousin Sarah and have, like Oscar Wilde, pleaded a subsequent engagement. You'll see them tomorrow – Mum insists we come to lunch in your honour, though I worry that it's getting to be too much for her.'

Catherine found herself absurdly touched. Her mother had been giving family dinners for her – unripe melon, overcooked beef and leathery apple pies – ever since she had left home but this one now, when unhappiness had heightened her sensitivity to kindness, took her by surprise. She could not speak immediately and was pleased when Peter joined them.

'And how are my little sisters this evening?' he asked, putting an arm round each of them. 'I trust our mother has seen to it that you have enough to drink?'

'Yes, Peter, thank you.' Jennifer ignored the edge in her brother's voice, or perhaps she did not even hear it. 'The party seems to be going very well.'

'Do you really think so?' Peter sounded anxious. 'I'm a bit worried about John and Laura: they've got cornered by that awful man from next door and I'm sure he's boring them to death. But there'll be something to eat soon and then I'll have to try and propel somebody more *simpatico* in their direction.'

Anthea, who had disappeared some time ago, now reappeared and began urging her guests to fetch themselves something to eat. As is usual at parties, nobody showed the slightest inclination to obey the hostess's injunction. With increasing desperation Anthea, joined now by Peter, pleaded with people to go 'before it got cold'. Gradually, the trickle to the buffet began. As the dining-room was situated in a bay-windowed room jutting out on the front of the house and was thus at the farthest possible distance from the kitchen, the food would, likely as not, have been cooled already on its way to the table. Nevertheless, everyone entering the room made enthusiastic noises of appreciation for all the trouble Anthea had gone to.

It was a spread notable mainly for its variety: pizzas and quiches; coleslaw and beef stew; chicken salad and ratatouille. Mrs Quinn was heard saying to her husband as she put a piece of quiche lorraine on his plate, 'Of course you'll be able to eat it: it's only a posh name for bacon-and-egg pie.' Catherine, having helped herself to what she considered a restrained assortment of dishes, went to look for somewhere to sit down. Chairs had been placed round the walls of the two downstairs sitting-rooms and although no attempt had been made to split them into sociable clusters, Anthea had ensured that there would be a chair for every guest. Catherine sat down in a corner of the back room where the family watched television. She felt weary and miserable but at the back of her mind there was a conviction that it was better to be here than brooding alone somewhere.

A man of about twenty-seven, with spectacles and a red face, sat down beside her. 'Anthea really does do this sort of thing awfully well, doesn't she?' Catherine, looking with inward distaste at his plate, on which the sauce from the stew mingled with the mayonnaise and tinned pineapple of the chicken salad and both encroached upon the pizza, agreed vociferously. The obligatory questions which followed established that he was one of Peter's colleagues and seemed to be greatly in awe of the older man. Catherine could not understand why: for years now she had found her brother snobbish and dull.

'Peter told me you got a first at Oxford,' the young man remarked, *à propos* of nothing at all. Catherine nodded, astonished that Peter should think it worthwhile trying to impress people with something his sister had done so long ago. 'He says you've never really done anything with it,' the man went on. 'He can't get over that you're content just to be a *Hausfrau*.' He used the German expression, as so many English people do, as though it contained a depth of pejorative meaning which the English word 'housewife' lacked.

'No doubt he thinks it would have been of more use to mankind if I'd written the definitive interpretation of some little-known fragment in Middle English.'

'That sounds very scathing. Do you think all scholarship is pointless, then?'

'No, of course I don't. I just worry that some of our assumptions about what constitutes a useful life may be a bit wide of the mark.'

'So would you say that the "Three Ks" are what really matter for a woman?'

'"*Kirche, Kinder, Küche*"? They hardly apply to me: I never go to church, I have no children and, although I can cook well enough, I'm not the sort of housekeeper a sensible, old-fashioned *Biedermann* would have been looking for. I'm much too extravagant and I haven't a clue about preserving fruit and making jam.'

'Then what is important for you?'

'Clear thinking and kindness.'

'You answered as though you'd given the matter a lot of thought.'

'Perhaps I have. But I'm afraid my reply was not original. Bertrand Russell said it first. And he went on to say there's precious little of either commodity about in the world today.'

'And has that been your own experience?' The young man looked at Catherine with a degree of earnestness that seemed to imply a right to probe her experience. She felt irritated by what she considered his impertinence; at the same time she feared that she was just too old for this sort of conversation.

'It really depends what mood I'm in,' she said, lightly, and then, seeing Anthea had come in to urge people to get their pudding, she suggested they do the same. Sensing a brusqueness in her tone, he obeyed without another word. Perhaps he had not, after all, been as interested in what she was saying as she had supposed.

On the way to the dining-room they met Jennifer, carrying a pile of plates into the kitchen. Catherine decided to be helpful, too, and, in being so, to escape the risk of further interrogation over the cheesecake. She followed her sister, collecting a few dirty dishes on the way. In the kitchen they found Anthea's daily help stacking the dishwasher. 'Gosh,' said Jennifer, 'you are well organized.'

'Oh, yes,' said the woman, 'Mrs Quinn's got everything under control. She's hardly left anything for me to do.'

'It certainly doesn't look as though there's much *we* can do,' said Catherine, moving towards the door. Jennifer, however, remained a while chatting pleasantly about the amount of time and energy a dishwashing machine *really* saved. Although not particularly eager to eat Anthea's meringues, Catherine felt that politeness demanded she fetch something more to eat. In the dining-room she found her father. He was alone, helplessly surveying the débris on the table.

'Can I get you some pudding?' Catherine knew that, as her mother always put out her father's dinner – rather as she might have put out a child's – he would be reluctant to help himself.

'I was just trying to decide what,' he replied. 'There doesn't seem to be anything ordinary like fruit salad, does there? Perhaps I'll try some of that chocolate one, if you don't mind.'

Catherine put the serving-spoon into a dish of mousse and it met with unexpected resistance. 'Oh, that this too, too solid mousse would melt ...' she murmured and was surprised at the guffaw with which her father responded. Affection for him welled up inside her and she longed to say something which would indicate that affection. Instinctively her mind reached back to her childhood, to a time before her mother's contempt for Tom had become evident to her and imperceptibly begun to affect her own attitude. 'Were you reading Tennyson before supper?'

she asked. He was her father's favourite poet and when she was about four he had recited 'Morte d'Arthur' to her until she wept. Joyce had thought it cruel to upset a little girl with such morbid verse and Catherine herself had hardly felt it to be consistent with the extreme gentleness which otherwise characterized him. Nevertheless, she appreciated this early introduction to poetry and she could still quote more Tennyson by heart than many another poet of whom she was more fond.

'No,' he said, 'I was trying Milton again. I know I'm missing something, but I've never really been able to warm to him. Perhaps it's that I can't be bothered looking up all the allusions, or maybe I've been put off by learning what sort of a person he was – he can't have been at all nice to live with.'

'And that matters?'

'Oh, yes, very much.' Tom thought a moment, then added, 'But I'm afraid I'm not always consistent. I shouldn't think Dickens' wife thought *he* was very nice but I like him too much to let it bother me.'

Mrs Quinn now came in. 'Oh, there you both are! I've been looking everywhere. I think it's time we were going.'

Tom obediently put down his unfinished pudding but Catherine said, 'Don't you think we ought to wait for coffee? And then perhaps Peter wants to propose a toast to the young couple or something.'

'I doubt it. I have a strong suspicion they've run out of booze. Nobody's had his glass refilled for half an hour. Anyway, it's nearly half-past ten and it'll be after eleven before we get home and your father's never liked driving in the dark.'

Clearly, there was to be no argument. Catherine sought out their hosts, while Joyce waited in the hall for them to come and say goodbye to her. When Anthea at last came, Joyce managed to convey a meaning quite the opposite of the one apparently contained in her speech of thanks. 'Thank you so much, dear. I've had a lovely time and the food was really very nice. Tell Sarah that I hope she and Charles will continue to be very happy together.'

She was as voluble on the way home as she had been going. She deplored the 'far-back' way Sarah spoke and what she called John and Laura's 'complete lack of real class'. Anthea's catering had, as always, been woefully inadequate and her son had made no effort to introduce his mother to his other guests. Jennifer had looked a sight in a blouse that was miles too small and her own husband had disgraced her by keeping his nose in a book for most of the evening. Catherine said little but was dismayed to find herself inwardly agreeing with much of what her mother said, while at the same time wishing she hadn't actually said it. She too was critical of the hodge-podge called supper and of Peter's shortcomings as a host, but she preferred to keep these views to herself. She wondered if such restraint was a mistake, all part of the sham that led to her seeming, to Günter at least, intolerably self-controlled. Perhaps she kept altogether too much to herself: most obviously just now Günter's leaving her, of which she had still not said a word to anyone.

When they got home she sat with her parents in front of an electric fire drinking weak instant coffee made with hot milk. In spite of the taste, which was execrable, the drink was marvellously comforting and she began to feel more at ease than she had all day. It was nice that Jennifer and her family were coming tomorrow; perhaps she would tell her sister what had happened and then again, she thought, perhaps she would sit on her secret a little longer.

Six

Friday was a busy day for Günter and, although he needed a good deal of extra attention – in the form of aspirins, coffee and mineral water – from his secretary, he was glad to have so much to occupy him. When at last he came to clear his desk, he was surprised to find that it was past seven o'clock. He wondered how Anna would receive him tonight. Perhaps she would be out again at one of her damned meetings. Perhaps she would wish to take him to task for being drunk the night before. He realized with a shudder how very little he really knew about her. He was attracted to her, certainly, and not just sexually. He was attracted to her youth, to her freshness, to the enthusiasm which she brought to her pet causes. And then there was the vulnerability which he perceived beneath all the tough assertions of independence and equality. It was ironic that Catherine, the stay-at-home, had for years seemed robustly independent, in no way in need of his protection. Recalling his encounter with her the previous evening renewed his hostility. Even her offer of help with his packing, he thought, had sprung not from kindness but from contempt for his ineptitude; how long had he felt that she looked down upon him? Anna, he was sure, did not, but the spontaneity in her which he so admired would mean that he might have to accept more alterations to his routine than Catherine would ever have suggested. It was a price he was willing to pay. If Anna really were not at home again, then he would not sulk and he definitely would not drink; he would go out to a restaurant for a meal and do his best to take a proper interest in her news when she eventually did return. If he met her in the right spirit, then surely there would be time in the course of the weekend for them to enjoy just being alone together.

Anna, meanwhile, was feeling slightly uneasy. It did not occur to her that mere pressure of work was keeping Günter, and she began to fear that he was perhaps angry that she had stayed out so late – even that he did not intend coming back at all. She too reflected that she had little idea how Günter would behave. She did not in the least regret having gone to her meeting but still she did not want to fight with him about it. The vulnerability which Günter had sensed was there; there was something which the older man could give her which she cherished and which she had never before experienced. For Anna, an only child, had known little love and even less wholehearted approval. Her mother had married her father when they were still students and the pregnancy which had brought forward the wedding date had also brought to an end her own hopes of a degree. As a baby, Anna had been looked after by a mother who resented her, with help from a grandmother who was ashamed of her very existence.

At first, the young family had lived in their in-laws' house but, after completing his doctorate, Anna's father took a job with a big mechanical-engineering firm and the next years saw a steady increase in their prosperity, as he successfully climbed the managerial ladder. The higher her husband's prestige, the more Anna's mother enjoyed her role as his wife, and she threw herself into supporting him: by which she understood wearing only the very best clothes, consorting with the very best people and relentlessly accompanying him on every business trip. Anna's grandmother, ever an unwilling babysitter, gradually withdrew and Anna was left increasingly to her own devices. At thirteen she was already used to spending her evenings alone, with only an Alsatian dog for company.

Wolfgang, though he was not the first boy she had slept with, was certainly the first one she had really loved and she desperately wanted him to return her love. He did not. He took her liberated talk at face value and thought it very convenient that her liberation made the gratification of his desire so straightforward. He showed that he considered her his equal by treating her as casually as he treated his male friends, and she was far too afraid of appearing old-fashioned to admit, even to herself, that red roses and candlelit dinners might, occasionally, be nicer than paying for her own drinks in a crowded bar where Wolfgang was always meeting friends whose conversation he evidently enjoyed more than hers. His eventual jilting of her had been as matter-of-fact as the rest of his conduct and when she tried, incoherently, to explain the depth of her own emotional involvement he told her callously that she should have mentioned it before: he would not, then, have allowed the affair to continue as long as it had. His own conscience was clear since he had never pretended that it was likely to become a long-lasting attachment.

After he had left her, Anna realized how terribly alone she was: she had many casual girlfriends but no single close one, and to seek comfort from her mother was out of the question. In desperation she had gone to the Hemmersbachs as the only people, outside the student circles where she might bump into Wolfgang, who could offer her an escape from total, wretched loneliness. She had hardly expected much comfort but Catherine was a gracious host and the wine – she usually drank very little – loosened her tongue. On the drive home, she sensed in what Günter was saying about his work that he too was unhappy and she wanted to show her gratitude for the way in which her troubles had been listened to by listening a little longer to his. She invited him in.

The conversation moved on from Günter's personal criticisms of his soap-makers to the global sins of multinationals. Anna was soon telling him how many babies in the Third World were killed each year because their mothers had been bamboozled by altogether improper advertising into giving them powdered milk instead of nursing them themselves. The deaths did not stop with the babies: the tobacco industry was mounting huge advertising campaigns in the poorest countries and when the people got cancer the pharmaceutical firms were there too, dumping the drugs that they were not allowed to sell in the West ... The charges were not new to Günter but it was the first time that they had been put to him personally, spoken from the heart by a young girl who not only saw the problems in the simplest terms of industrial villain and exploited innocents, but who also had no doubts about the ease with which they could be solved, if only people were taught to care enough. He listened to her spellbound. Anna was very quickly aware that she had never before had an audience quite like this: her father would have argued with her, quoting statistics to prove how foreign investment in poor countries improves the quality of life for even the poorest inhabitants; and her student friends would long ago have interrupted to give their own superior analysis of the same problem. But Günter just listened, apparently for the sheer pleasure of listening to her, a look of tender admiration in his eyes.

Up to then, the act of going to bed with someone had not, in itself, held any very great significance for Anna. Her mother's advice on the subject had stressed the importance of contraception and touched, with some distaste, on the possible dangers of infection. The boys whom Anna knew all regarded it as a routine part of any close relationship with a girl, and Anna might be forgiven for not realizing how very differently Günter regarded his first adultery. For him, the sex was far from routine and there followed from it daily tokens of affection – flowers, unexpected telephone calls to ask how she was, gifts of every newly published book he thought she might want to read – which delighted her by their novelty. She had begun to think that she might even one day love him as much as she had loved, perhaps still did love, Wolfgang, when she found that she was pregnant.

Waiting for Günter now, anxiously watching the clock as it got later and later, she wished from her heart that she had not been so careless, for it was clear that Günter did not see abortions in the same positive light as she did. Certainly her pregnancy had, if anything, increased his loving solicitude towards her but, while enjoying such attention, she feared that it was not quite all she wanted from life. All the same, if he did not come back, she would be miserable. She thought of her unloving parents and of Wolfgang: perhaps she was always going to be rejected. Self-pity had brought tears to her eyes when Günter at last arrived. She ran to the door and threw her arms round him. As he had been more than half expecting an empty flat, he was especially touched by the warmth of her embrace.

'Good heavens,' he said, 'you look as though you've been crying. Whatever has upset you?'

'I thought you weren't coming back.'

'Not coming back? To you? What could have given you such a monstrous idea?'

'It's very late. And I was out last night when you wanted us to go out for a meal.'

'But I wouldn't just desert you because of that. Actually, I thought you might have been cross with me for getting so drunk. I assure you it's not something I do all that often.'

'Then your doing it last night means that you were put out by my absence?'

'Not put out exactly. But, yes, I was a bit disappointed. I needed you. I'd called on Catherine on my way here – just to get some more clothes – and she was insufferable.' He paused. This was the first time he had directly criticized his wife to Anna and he was torn between wanting her to sympathize with him for all the years he had spent with so unfeeling a woman and his own instinct that, after all, he still owed that woman some loyalty.

'Insufferable? What do you mean?' Anna, remembering her own grief when Wolfgang left her and assuming that Catherine would be reacting in the same way, began to fear that Günter, like Wolfgang, disliked his women making a fuss once he had had enough.

'Well, she was so icy calm. When I arrived she was drinking sherry – God knows what gourmet delight she had waiting for herself in the kitchen – and she treated me as though I were a virtual stranger. There was no sign at all that she'd even noticed her husband had left home. And when I couldn't stand sitting there any longer making conversation in this utterly forced way and I went upstairs to pack, she followed me. I was so upset by her attitude that I suppose I was making a mess but she asked me if she should pack for me as though I were some backward child who still hadn't learned to tie his shoelaces: she'd do it for me this once, but it really was about time I learned to do it properly for myself.'

'And so did you let her pack for you?'

'Certainly not. She was reading the paper when I left – I think she'd forgotten I was even in the house.'

Anna's thoughts were racing. She saw Günter's visit to his wife as a sign of his general solicitude: yes, he was a kinder man than any she had known. But what would he have done if he had found Catherine in a state of suicidal despair? She could hardly believe her own good fortune: it appeared that she was to be allowed to keep Günter without even a pang of conscience; perhaps Catherine had actually been wanting him to go. She kissed him tenderly, and then again, wisely refraining from joining in his disapproval of Catherine's behaviour. He relaxed.

'What are we going to do about supper?' he asked, after a while.

'I'm afraid I haven't got much in.' She giggled with a self-deprecating sweetness that had been quite missing from her assertion, two nights before, that a meagre meal in the evening was good for the figure. 'I'm not really any sort of cook.'

'You don't have to be. But it's Friday and I'm afraid it's too late to get a table anywhere decent. Is there somewhere near where we could get a bite?'

'There's a Yugoslavian restaurant but I've never been

to it. And there's a take-away pizza place.'

'Do you like pizza?'

'Yes, actually I do, quite a lot.'

Günter was delighted. The shop sold not only hot pizza but Chianti and salad as well and as they sat eating it – he insisted on candles only – he felt that the meal had greater charm than any he had eaten in years. After it they sat listening to records, his arm resting round her shoulders. They spoke little but their mood was so full of harmony and contentment that Anna did not wish to break it, even in order to switch on the news.

Günter was the first to wake next morning. He felt happier than he had for years. Anna, still deeply asleep, looked, without her glasses, younger than ever. He noticed particularly how lovely and clear her skin was. She had a dark complexion and never wore any make-up, so there was none of the nocturnal pallor in her face which Catherine's had after it had received its bedtime cleansing and oiling. He got up quietly and dressed quickly; he would go out to buy fresh rolls for their breakfast.

Waiting in the queue at the baker's – it was obviously getting-up time for half the neighbourhood – he studied the faces of the other customers, mostly men, pitying what he took to be the dullness of their lives. Nobody smiled or used more words than necessary in ordering their bread and there were a number of cross exchanges about alleged queue-jumping. Anxious not to be involved in one himself – nothing should be allowed to cloud his good temper – Günter let several people take his place. At last the girl behind the counter took pity on him and said, 'Surely it must be your turn?' Grateful for her attention, he wanted to buy up the shop: rolls, croissants, wholemeal bread and a plum tart. They sold coffee, too, and he had a pound freshly ground. 'Do you sell butter?' he asked. The girl pointed to a refrigerated display behind him and he bought butter, cheese and milk. Then he noticed preserves on another shelf and bought three sorts of jam. On his way back to his car he saw a flower shop and bought red roses. He was nearly home when he realized that there was probably nothing to make the coffee in; he returned to the shops and looked for a hardware store. Armed with a Melitta jug, filter and filter papers, he set off once more.

Anna was still in bed but she stirred slightly as Günter opened the door. He began to potter about, tidying up last night's dishes and laying the table. The noise he made, for all his efforts to be quiet, finally woke her. She got up and came to him, bewildered by the mountains of food on the table.

'Where did all this come from?'

'I've been out. The rolls are still warm and the water's boiling. It's time you learned how to make coffee.' He smiled and kissed her as he said this but she reacted irritably to the presumption of his last remark.

'Perhaps I don't want to learn,' she muttered. 'And I've got to clean my teeth.'

Günter got on with the preparations alone and by the time Anna, wearing jeans and a tee-shirt, returned, breakfast was ready.

'The flowers are lovely,' she said. Günter had already put them in water; early in their relationship he had thoughtfully presented her with a couple of vases.

'Did you think to buy a paper?'

He laughed. 'No, I can't say I did. But I do think I deserve some praise for thinking about absolutely everything else. I even got a coffee pot and filter.'

'We didn't hear the news last night.'

'Does it matter?'

'Of course it does. I want to know what's happening.'

'I'll go and get you all the papers you want after breakfast.'

'The rolls really are very good,' said Anna and caught Günter looking at her with evident relief that she had stopped sulking. Unused to anyone else's happiness being so dependent on her own mood, she felt chastened, but also a little frightened by her new responsibility.

'My mother always goes out to get rolls when we stay with her. Catherine loves them and they're one of the few things my poor mother puts on the table which Catherine can honestly praise.'

'Do they get on well?'

'They're both very well-behaved. But they tend to do everything so differently that over the years there may have been a bit of submerged friction. Catherine's a great wow with all the old men, though. My father idolizes her.'

'I suppose that doesn't endear her to your mother, either.'

'I think what my mother doesn't like is Catherine's utter imperviousness to any suggestion that there may be a better way of doing something than the way she has chosen. It isn't that she takes offence or argues with you, she just completely ignores what you've said. She *knows* she's right.'

'Do your parents have any idea about me?'

'No. I should ring them up some time. Catherine always sees to it that we get in touch over the weekend. But I doubt I'll be able to tell them over the phone. They'll have to meet you for themselves.'

Anna smiled. 'I'm not at all certain that will help.'

'They'll enjoy having a grandchild. I think they've cared more about Catherine not being able to have babies than she has herself – though maybe that wouldn't be very hard.' Anna said nothing but looked uncomfortable. 'What's the matter? You always look sad when I mention the baby.'

'Perhaps it makes me sad.'

'But why on earth should it?'

'I don't think I'm ready to be a mother.'

'Oh, darling, every woman feels like that and you're still so young. But when the time comes, you'll find that you are ready really. I'm sure of it.'

Of course Anna had not meant that she just had a few doubts about her ability to learn the basics of infant care. She tried once more. 'I mean I wonder if I should have the baby at all.'

'Oh, Anna, my love, don't talk like that. I know you said something about an ...' he hesitated over the word, '... about an abortion at the beginning, but that was just to make it easier for me, I know, until you could be certain I'd want to marry you.'

Anna was startled by this novel interpretation of her motives. A new twist indeed to the boundless egoism of a man! But how could she make him see it differently? She shrank from doing anything too final, anything which would send him, disgusted, back to Catherine.

'It's a lovely day,' he said. 'Shall we go out somewhere?'

'Yes, why not? But I want to get the papers first.'

For the first quarter of an hour in the car, Anna was absorbed in her reading, only pausing to inveigh against the opportunism of politicians. 'They don't seem to care what people think of them,' she said of the FDP which was now, having left the Schmidt government, involved in negotiations with the opposition, 'just so long as they hold on to power themselves.'

'But isn't that how you expect politicians to behave?'

'Oh, Günter, don't just accept without question that politics can't be anything but a cynical, self-seeking business. It's got to be something more. The problems we face are so huge, our situation is desperate.'

'Is it? I would have said we were doing rather well.'

'Well? How can you say that? Nearly half the world's population doesn't have enough to eat, our natural resources are being squandered, the environment is being ruined and we may all be blown up tomorrow. I'd hate to hear your scenario for doing badly.'

'Of course you can make it sound grim if you like. But I still don't think it's quite that bad really. We've come a hell of a long way in the last forty years.'

'Oh, you mean that we as Germans have? You mean it's better now that the fascism is all conveniently beneath the surface and our leaders all pretend to be impeccable democrats?'

'Come, come, Anna, that's a silly way to talk.'

'How dare you tell me I'm silly, just because I don't agree with you?'

'I didn't call *you* silly, but the way you were talking. And it *is* silly not to distinguish between the monstrous evil of Nazism and the occasional opportunism of democratically elected politicians.'

'"Monstrous evil" rolls off your tongue very easily, doesn't it? I suppose it makes you feel good to condemn what happened before you were born and when you were still a baby. It was all terrible, but it had nothing to do with *you*, all *your* generation are model citizens.'

'And what do you want me to do? Say that it *was* all my fault?'

'Not your *fault*, no. That would be ridiculous. But there's got to be some connection between what the Germans did then and what they're doing now. You want to let everybody off too lightly.'

'On the contrary, I want the reality of fascism to be clearly remembered, and it won't be if the word is constantly used to describe everyone whose politics you personally don't care for.'

There was a silence. Anna found herself close to tears. Günter had never argued with her before and she was hurt not only because he seemed to have had the last word but also because his tone implied a superiority of knowledge and experience which she wished to deny. Günter, too, was ruffled by the exchange. Anna's confused accusations, while easy enough to deal with as mere debating points, had touched a raw nerve. The trouble was that he *did* feel, along with many of his generation, that he was to blame for Hitler. Especially while he was growing up, the burden of knowing what Germans had done had been almost unbearable. As a teenager, he had come home from school after being shown films of Auschwitz, longing to ask his parents what they had thought at the time, what they had done and what they had failed to do. But the fear of learning that, even in the smallest part of their minds, they had condoned anti-Semitism, kept him silent. Instead, he would force himself to ask what he would have done in their place. His older brother had been born in 1935. Was it fair to expect his parents to have taken a heroic stand? One that would have endangered their lives and left their baby defenceless? But because everyone thought of his own skin first, crimes had been committed to trouble the collective conscience for generations. Inevitably, as he got older, the agonized questioning became less urgent, leaving him only with an expectation, rarely disappointed, that foreigners would not like him much, because he was a German. Catherine, he realized, had helped him to repress his anxieties: she gave him credit for possessing sound liberal views, insisted that evil was a universal phenomenon and steadfastly refused to spoil her own good relations with the older members of his family by dragging up the past. Anna, he feared, might well revive in him all the old feelings of vicarious guilt.

'What speed are you doing?' Anna asked, suddenly.

'One hundred and sixty. Why?'

'Surely even you know how dangerous it is to drive so fast?'

'I'm sorry. Are you frightened?'

'Not for myself. But your car is pumping out poison that is lethal. There'll be no forests left standing in a few years' time. And the faster you drive, the more poison you produce.'

'All right. I'll go a bit slower if it will make you any happier.'

'Not because it will make *me* happy! Acid rain isn't something that only affects *me*.'

'No, of course it isn't.' Günter spoke soothingly, stretching out his hand and laying it on hers. 'You're absolutely right about speed. And it's a waste of petrol, too.'

Anna said no more. She felt that there was an element of humouring in Günter's ready acquiescence but she appreciated the reassurance conveyed in the pressure of his hand too much to take offence.

'I thought we'd go to Bad Münstereifel,' he said, as he

shortly afterwards turned off the motorway. 'There's no point wearing ourselves out driving for hours.'

They approached the little spa down a curving road through the woods. 'My father used to come here for his cure,' said Günter, 'but he prefers to stay nearer home these days. Catherine and I always visited him a couple of times during his stay and he'd take us out to a café and stuff us with huge portions of cream cake.'

'All part of the cure?'

'For him it was. He certainly went home looking fitter than when he arrived. But I suppose that may have come from the rest and the change of air as much as from the treatment. The English are always very scathing about water cures, and I suppose it does look a bit ridiculous: all those elderly people taking off their shoes and socks in the middle of a stroll in the park to paddle in cold water.'

'At least it can't do them any harm.'

They parked the car just outside the medieval city wall and entered the old part of the town through one of its fourteenth-century gates. They walked along a cobbled road with the river on one side and pretty little shops on the other, holding hands. 'Some of the shops really seem quite smart,' said Anna.

'Yes. I thought we might buy you a dress.'

'Buy me a dress? Whatever for?'

'Because I've never seen you wearing one.'

Anna was about to retort that if she felt more comfortable in jeans, then that is what she would wear, when she caught again the look in his eyes which reminded her how anxious he was to please. 'OK,' she said, though without enthusiasm.

Inside the shop, they made an odd pair. The fashionable, middle-aged assistant did her professional best to hide her disapproval of the sloppily-dressed, sulky girl and her foolishly besotted escort; Anna did nothing to hide her disapproval of a shop selling cotton frocks for upwards of three hundred marks. In the end they settled on a full skirt in heavy powder-blue poplin with an edging of white lace round the hemline and a blue and white patterned blouse. Günter insisted on an Italian sweater as well.

'My mother always shops in places like that,' said Anna with a shudder as they left. 'Only the ones she goes to are probably even more expensive.'

'There's nothing wrong with wanting to look nice.'

'Isn't there? She pays a terribly high price for it and I'm not sure that she could ever succeed in looking "nice" anyway.'

'Why do you dislike her so much?'

'Because she never did anything to make me like her.'

'Surely you can't mean that.'

'Oh, but I do. I spoiled her fun and limited her freedom by being born and she's never really been able to see me in any other light.'

'How very sad.' Günter spoke with such an intensity of feeling that Anna felt obliged to qualify her last remark.

'Oh, it doesn't bother me that much any more. I don't even think of her all that often, now I'm living away from home. It was only that shop and the cow of an assistant which reminded me.'

'Then I'm sorry I took you there. But I do think you look lovely in the dress. We must buy more pretty things for you, and you'll be needing different shoes, too.'

Anna sighed. His compliments and his own delight in her altered appearance did not offset the presumption of his wanting to change her in the first place.

'Let's go to the Kurhaus restaurant for lunch. They're sure to have vegetarian food there and it's a nice walk up the hill – though perhaps it's too far and you'd rather take the car?'

'No,' said Anna, a little wearily, 'I'll enjoy a walk.'

The Kurhaus proved to be farther away than Günter had thought and the path up to it was very steep. The sanatorium buildings, sturdy and functional, stood in neat gardens and commanded a fine view of the old town. The entrance hall contained an informative display of therapeutic teas and curative water could also be drunk there. The dining-room, with its clinically white tablecloths and serried rows of tables, had a institutional look which was at odds with the appearance of the diners, who were mostly plump and well-dressed, out to enjoy themselves rather than to improve their health.

Anna looked at the menu which was divided into sections: for 'normal diet', 'diabetic diet', 'low-fat diet' and, tucked in at the end, 'meat-free diet'. Günter looked at the 'normal' food. The calorific content of each dish appeared next to the price, but otherwise the selection was very much what it would have been in any other *gutbürgerlich* eating place.

'I shall have venison and dumplings.' he said. 'Catherine disapproves of dumplings and has never taken to anything with a gamey taste. A pity, really, when she's such a good cook.'

'I think you're just as keen on food as she is. You don't seem to be able to go for more than a couple of hours without thinking about it, anyway. I'm not like that.'

The waitress came and took their orders. Anna, apparently choosing at random, said she would have eggs florentine. Günter could not persuade her to have a glass of wine. 'I drink hardly any alcohol,' she told him, irritably.

'So I've noticed. You're really quite a puritan in some ways.'

'Is that meant as a criticism?'

'Not at all. I love you so much because you are so different.'

'You mean different from Catherine?'

'Perhaps that is part of it, yes. You mustn't forget that there haven't been all that many women in my life – I can't help comparing you with the one I've known longest.'

'It's odd she hasn't made more fuss.'

'Fuss? She doesn't believe in making a fuss, but I confess that I hadn't expected her to live up to her principles quite so successfully in this particular situation.'

'Perhaps she's wanted to be free for a long time. It can't have been much fun for her stuck in the house all day.'

'She wouldn't have agreed with you on that. After all,

she did have a job for several years, and she insisted that she never for one moment regretted giving it up. She says it's a perversion of civilized standards to believe that work is what gives life its purpose.'

'Somebody has to work, especially if they want to enjoy Catherine's standard of living.'

'She didn't dispute that and she claimed to be very grateful to me for making her leisure possible. It just annoyed her that a lot of people would pity her for having given up her chances of a career; she said it was me who was to be pitied.'

'I wonder what she'll do now?'

Günter shrugged. He did not want to talk about Catherine any more. 'How is your spinach?' he asked.

'It's all right. I really don't care what I eat. I wouldn't have minded skipping lunch altogether.'

'Oh dear, it looks as though I shall soon be very thin! Perhaps you'll indulge me a little – couldn't you try cooking the sort of vegetarian food which would make me positively want to give up meat too?'

'I'm not vegetarian because vegetables taste better, but because I don't believe in killing animals for food, or in breeding so many unnecessary animals in the first place and wasting precious foodstuffs fattening them up for the kill.'

'Please don't let's argue.'

'I didn't know we were arguing.'

'Well, you seem so cross. I just want us to have a harmlessly enjoyable day out and you're determined to find fault with everything I do. I drive too fast, I eat too much meat – what will it be next?'

Anna made no reply but turned her head away. Günter realized that she was crying. 'Darling, don't cry!' he pleaded, mortified. 'Come on, we'll get out of here. This wasn't the right place to bring you, I see that now.'

The waitress, skilled in avoiding her customers' eye, did not bring their bill for several minutes, and by the time Günter had paid, Anna had fought back her tears. They went out into the garden and sat on a bench beside a wood and iron sculpture of obscure symbolism. Günter put his arm round Anna. She sat up straight, as though to be rid of his arm, and then flopped back on to it.

'I can't bear to see you looking so sad,' he said earnestly.

'Then you mustn't try to change me all the time.'

'Me change you? I wouldn't dream of it. I thought it was the other way round, actually, and you wanted to make a good ecologist out of me.'

'But you've been on at me all day. I have to learn how to make coffee; I have to wear pretty clothes; I have to cook fancy vegetarian food for you – probably the very same courgette soufflés and onion tarts Catherine used to make me eat when I came with Wolfgang. I refuse to turn myself into your creature in this way.'

Günter laughed. 'How you exaggerate everything!' He kissed her cheek. 'But I find you altogether irresistible.'

Anna, though not altogether happy with what Günter had just said, could not help being touched by the admiring tenderness of his caress. Of course she was right: he would increasingly want her to change to suit him, however much he protested the attractiveness of her independence. With a sinking heart, she realized that she would find it easier to fight him on specific plans for her transformation than to resist the protective comfort of his love. She had never felt so loved before; if only she could believe herself capable, in the long run, of behaving in such a way that she would not forfeit his love.

They walked slowly back to the car and returned to Bonn. Günter drove at an exemplary 100 kilometres per hour and said nothing more about food for the rest of the day. Anna relaxed, gratefully perceiving the effort he was making to please. In the evening, they sat again listening to records and Anna, though she said little, seemed unable to let go of him. He found her clinging to him agreeable and even when they went to bed, she fell asleep holding his hand. He lay awake a long time, reflecting on the way her mood had changed in the course of the day. He did not yet take her outburst in the park all that seriously: he was confident that he would succeed in calming her fears that he wanted to change her fundamentally, while after all persuading her to alter some little details. Nevertheless, he was aware that coping with Anna's emotional demands upon him was going to be a good deal more strenuous than marriage had ever been. He eventually went to sleep firmly telling himself that it was the very effort involved in making Anna happy which most beguiled him.

Seven

Joyce Quinn was up early on Sunday morning, peeling mountains of potatoes and making pastry for her pies. Although she was far from regarding cooking as a creative art, she took pride in the sheer quantity of food she set before her children and grandchildren. They did not visit her nearly as often as she would have liked. True, Jennifer, who lived near, called several times each week, but these were flying visits to see if her parents were 'all right', and sometimes she did not even have time for a cup of tea. Joyce was a woman of great energy and drive but circumstances had forced her to concentrate her efforts on her children and sublimate in them all her own thwarted ambition. Inevitably the satisfaction she could derive from their successes grew less as they grew older: their adult achievements were modest and their own families increasingly removed them for their mother's direct influence. Joyce seemed almost to resent the happiness of her children's marriages: it made her feel superfluous when by nature she liked to be the centre of attention. It was not that she wanted to be treated with obvious respect or sentimental cosseting, but rather that she needed to be needed, and her pride was hurt that both her son and daughters had proved more than able to organize their lives happily without there being any clear role left for her to play.

In addition, her own experience of marriage had

jaundiced her attitude to it as an institution. For fifty years now she had been asking herself why she had married Tom. Ironically, in view of the fact that her parents had disowned her because of him, it was Joyce's own mother who had brought the young people together. Mrs Stewart had been fond of Tom: he was a good-looking boy with a ready smile and he presented his mother's excuses for not paying the bill that week after all with something approaching charm. It saddened her that the brightest of the family should be forced to leave school early, his prospects blighted for the sake of a brother who wanted to join the priesthood. With a father who drank and an ostentatiously devout mother worn out by childbearing, the Quinns embodied many of Mrs Stewart's prejudices against Catholics. When she took it upon herself to find some sort of work for Tom, it was in the hope that, through her own influence, she would be able to redress some of the disadvantages inherent in his upbringing.

Since leaving school Tom had led an aimless existence: sleeping late each morning, then walking down to the Picton Library, where he read voraciously but without direction, and ending up most evenings playing cards, either in somebody's house or at a public whist drive. It was a bad time to find work, even if the seeker were more determined in his quest than the easy-going Tom Quinn. But eventually Mrs Stewart succeeded. A commercial traveller told her about a door-to-door tea-selling venture which was desperate for salesmen. Wages would be paid solely on a commission basis: Tom was free to work as much or as little as he liked. Ruefully, he agreed to give it a try and he was as surprised as anyone when he proved to be a born salesman.

Naturally, he spent his money as he earned it: his first purchases were a pair of shoes for himself and silk stockings for his mother; then he showered the younger children with sweets and comics; finally he took Joyce Stewart to the pictures. They sat in the best seats and, as they went in, he presented her with a pound box of Nestlé's Home Made Assortment, encouraging her to eat the entire top layer before the main feature had even started. Joyce, who had been brought up to think that eating a Fry's chocolate cream bar in one go was reckless self-indulgence, felt that Tom was leading her into a new world. They went to a dance together, a Saturday-night hop at the local Co-op, and it was not long before Mrs Stewart, who had hitherto had only praise for Tom, was making disapproving noises and urging her daughter to stop going out with him. 'It wouldn't do to get too serious,' she said, ominously. Perhaps Mrs Stewart, by anticipating a desire to marry, actually created one: her warnings put the idea of marriage into Joyce's head and soon she and Tom were considering setting up house together. Both of them regarded marriage as an escape: for Joyce an escape from the drudgery of the shop and for Tom an escape from the overcrowded little house where he could not even read in peace. But they underestimated the strength of their parents' disapproval: the Stewarts immediately washed their hands of Joyce and the Quinns rejected Tom as soon as it was plain that his bride would not be 'turning'.

The young couple found cheap rooms over a shop in Islington, the rent reduced in return for their acting as caretakers. At first, things went well. Joyce joined Tom on his rounds and sold almost as much tea as he did, for their selling techniques were wonderfully complementary: when Tom's soft talking proved resistible, Joyce would win the customer over by her no-nonsense, woman-to-woman approach. In spite of an early pregnancy, Joyce worked with a will until, three months before Peter was born, the law caught up with the man behind the whole enterprise (he had been promising customers who bought in bulk expensive gifts which never materialized) and they were both out of work. From then until the war they were desperately poor. Tom eventually took work as a newspaper canvasser, setting off each Monday morning by train on a workman's ticket to a different town in Wales or the north west where he and three or four other men would trail the streets trying to convince people, who were themselves often out of work, that what they most urgently needed was a subscription to the *Daily Express*. Joyce went out cleaning, taking her babies with her, her bitterness at the way life was treating her much increased by the insolence of the would-be genteel women who employed her.

The qualities which had in courtship endeared Tom to Joyce became in married life a source of mounting exasperation. A gift of expensive chocolates could bring her no pleasure when, for the first time in her life, she had holes in her shoes. The values which had imbued her childhood reasserted themselves, but repeatedly her efforts at frugal management were frustrated by Tom, who would put their last two shillings on a horse or enter into ruinous hire-purchase agreements for luxurious toys which the children were too small to appreciate. In response to her angry complaints he would only smile, shrug his shoulders and go out, leaving her fury without an outlet. His religion also tended to exacerbate the tensions between them because, while putting no pressure on her to become a Catholic, he doggedly refused to repudiate his faith. True, he was not very devout in those days, but still he would never give her the satisfaction of agreeing with her strictures against the evils of Rome. After their babies were born, he took them, without her consent, to a priest to have them baptized, and for this she never forgave him.

The war brought immediate relief to Joyce. Tom was called up and she had money coming in which she was free to manage in her own way, so that even before her parents' death, she had brought a certain order into their previously chaotic finances. By leaving her all their money the Stewarts not only enabled Joyce to move into a house of her own in a suburb full of neat gardens and tree-lined roads, they also strengthened her conviction that she was the superior partner in the marriage. The difference, moreover, which their posthumous generosity made to Joyce's material circumstances was matched by the difference it made to her memory of them. She forgave their decade of neglect and was half inclined to consider their action reasonable: she really should not have married Tom and she began to ask herself if it would not have been better to leave him long ago and return home penitent. But the role of dependant did not suit Joyce, neither as wife nor as daughter. She dreamed of freedom.

It was to remain a dream. Tom returned safely from North Africa, agreed that she had got the house looking very nice (though personally he didn't much care where he lived), and before his leave was over she was pregnant. Increasingly, Tom led his own life within a household which his wife dominated. After the war he held on to enough of his teacher's salary to pay for his modest gambling and his books; Joyce did as she liked with the rest. That her daughters, in particular, had both been so eager to get married, was still a source of wonder to her. If only she had had their chances, their education, then she would certainly have never dreamed of tying herself to any man. Her sons-in-law impressed her almost as little as her husband did.

Jennifer's Bob, indeed, rather reminded her of Tom, though without the vices: he did not gamble and he was very busy in the house and actively involved himself in bringing up the children. Her dislike of Günter was stronger. He had taken away her pet and then, as far as she could make out, treated her as a doormat. Joyce seethed with rage when she thought of Catherine spending her day doing domestic chores, waiting submissively for her husband to return. It was useless for Catherine to remind her that Frau Keller did all the hard work and that she positively enjoyed cooking: her mother knew better that getting the dinner ready day in, day out, and clearing up the dirty dishes – whether or not you had a machine for washing them – were part and parcel of the very enslavement which she had hoped *her* daughters would escape. 'Catherine seems happy enough to me,' Tom would say after each visit and Joyce would explode that happiness – in the sense of not being obviously *un*happy – was not the criterion by which she judged her daughter's fate. She had wanted to see – she was fond of the metaphor – her child's 'name in lights'; it wasn't happiness that counted but liberation from the humdrum.

Now, as she rolled out her pastry, Joyce muttered to herself about the impression Catherine had made the day before. She detected some strain; she was less talkative than usual. And it was odd that she should be staying so long. After so many years of resolutely short visits, Joyce was sceptical that her daughter had decided to prolong her stay just to please her mother. In Joyce's opinion, Catherine had ceased to do things 'just to please her mother' long ago. She paused in her work and put the kettle on. She would make tea and take a cup up to Catherine. But before the water had boiled, Catherine was down, wearing a dressing-gown and looking pale without any make-up.

'Hello,' she said surveying the pans full of vegetables and the half-made pies, 'it looks as if you've been up half the night.'

'I like to have everything ready when they arrive. And they sometimes come as early as half-past eleven. They probably will today as they'll want to have a proper talk with you.'

Mrs Quinn made the tea and they sat down at the kitchen table to drink it. 'And they'll all be coming except for Carolyn?' Catherine felt the need to say something and her mother's thoughts appeared to be miles away. In fact, Joyce was trying to decide whether her daughter really was less buoyant than usual and whether the drawn look about her eyes was just part of the natural process of ageing. Catherine, she remembered, was getting on for forty. How absurd that the child she still considered her 'baby' should be so old!

'Mmm, that's right. Carolyn's staying on in France until nearer the beginning of term. She was in Italy at Easter and talks of learning Danish next. She'll be forgetting her English soon, with all these foreign languages.'

'And why on earth Danish?'

'She thinks she might try for a job in the EEC after she's taken her degree.'

'What a pity she dropped German, then. She did it to O Level, didn't she?'

'Oh, yes, but it was the one language she never took to. And then she had a very bad experience with her exchange family. They were terribly German, no sense of humour at all, and she was only fifteen – a very impressionable age.'

'I thought she was supposed to be a bright girl. And whatever she may have felt five or six years ago, I don't think it's very intelligent of her to harbour a prejudice against the entire nation *and* its language just because of one rotten holiday.'

'Now don't be getting on your high horse! Even though you might like living there, you've got to admit it wouldn't suit many English people.'

Catherine opened her mouth to speak but then only sighed. Over the years she had had to put up with so many slighting remarks about the Germans. Perhaps she would not have minded as much if the vague prejudice of so many English people, even those as young as Carolyn, had been based on the acknowledged crimes of the Nazis, but these were hardly mentioned. Indeed, Catherine had heard remarks about her family's Jewish neighbours in Childwall which made her hair stand on end. No, what she disliked was the apparent assumption that the English were not only altogether better than the Germans, but that they had a positive right to flaunt their superiority and indulge their hostility.

'Well,' said Joyce, getting up, 'I can't sit here all day. If you want a bath you should go now, before your father gets up.' She sounded brusque but that was to mask her growing certainty that Catherine did indeed look tragic, far more so than disappointment at a niece's unwillingness to learn the language of her adopted country could justify. But this was not the time to go into it. Today she was host and she was determined that her party would be an unqualified success.

As expected, Jennifer and her family arrived well

before noon and quickly imposed their own cheerfulness upon the household. Stephen and Andrew, now nineteen and seventeen, flattered their grandmother outrageously and she responded to their attentions with a good humour she rarely showed towards Tom. Their affection for her had not developed until they were well into their teens. Joyce disapproved too much of the way Jennifer was bringing up her children for the relationship to be close while they were still small. When Jennifer had made it plain that she would take as little leave as possible from work, her mother had angrily warned that *she* would never be prepared to look after the babies in order to enable her to hold on to her job. She regarded double incomes as a twofold evil: they betrayed greed on the part of those who drew them and they would, as they became more common, lead to a general erosion of men's pay, so that soon all mothers would have to work, whether they wanted to or not, and all children would suffer. In fact, Jennifer had never intended to use her mother as a daytime babysitter but the strength of her mother's views made her shy of bringing her babies at other times as well and they tended to come only on formal family occasions. Mrs Quinn misunderstood her daughter's reserve and assumed that she was afraid of exposing her children to their grandmother's influence. Only when they grew old enough to walk over and see her on their own did they properly get to know each other.

The boys, calling at first out of a sense of duty, soon found that they really liked Joyce. They liked her outspokenness and the unpredictability of her opinions: one minute she would be attributing juvenile delinquency to so many women going out to work and the next she would be saying that the world would never improve until women had more say in running it. She also threw herself wholeheartedly into the boys' enthusiasms, whether it was the peace movement or Liverpool FC. When they had their ears pierced or their hair permed, she did not pretend to like it but she invariably modified her disapproval by saying that 'you're only young once'. Sally was more her grandfather's pet: she was quiet and studious and shared his appreciation of Victorian poetry. The day therefore could not help but go well and Catherine found herself very content to listen rather than talk, quietly enjoying the obvious harmony of her sister's family life. She felt it would have put an unforgivable blight on the atmosphere if she had interrupted the good-humoured general conversation with an announcement that her marriage had broken up. So once more she put off making the inevitable disclosure.

They sat on round the lunch table until four o'clock and then the whole family attacked the chaos in the kitchen – not, it is true, with Mrs Quinn's usual systematic efficiency, but with speed and a lot of laughing. Then sandwiches had to be made, scones buttered, and they sat round again, drinking pots and pots of tea. It was eight o'clock before the party broke up and by then Joyce was clearly tired. She declared that it would do them all good to relax in front of the television, by which she meant that she intended to go to sleep. It was not long before she and Tom were both snoring gently.

Catherine was not sorry to be relieved of the obligation to make conversation. She was even hopeful that she might find something worth watching, since distance had lent enchantment to her view of British broadcasting. In Germany there was little on offer apart from poorly synchronized American rubbish and plodding, homemade documentaries and she fondly imagined that the English had a rich choice, night after night, of drama, comedy, instruction and escapist entertainment. Tonight she would have liked nothing better than to watch something amusing and undemanding, but she was doubly unfortunate: first came a variety show with unfunny comics and unmusical singers, and then a play, professionally and convincingly acted, to be sure, but much too near the bone to make for comfortable viewing. A successful, middle-class couple's ten-year-old marriage was breaking up. The situation was not identical to her own: it was the woman who had fallen desperately in love and the husband who had to be told that the happiness which he had thought secure was in fact illusory; but still Catherine watched with horrified fascination to see what happened to them. At the end she found herself crying her heart out as the cameras switched from a picture of the woman walking joyfully through the park with her lover to one of the husband washing down an overdose of sleeping-pills with a bottle of whisky.

It was not that, even for a moment, she saw herself contemplating suicide: on the contrary, she was dimly aware of a flickering optimism that told her she would eventually emerge from her crisis more or less whole, even though she had no idea as yet of how she would go about ordering her new life. Nevertheless, her sympathy for the man in the play was undoubtedly increased by the similarity of their situations: it was not to Günter's credit that she happened to be tougher. While unable to identify herself with the degree of the deserted husband's despair, she could recognize in the self-justifying egoism of his wife's attitude some of Günter's own arguments. The play over, she stopped crying but went on thinking about it as though the characters had been real people, until she found herself as angry with them as she was with Günter. She rejected the wife's assertions that she had a right, a duty to *herself,* to seize her opportunity for greater happiness with another man, irrespective of the cost in terms of her husband's unhappiness. Catherine doubted if there were even such a thing as duty to oneself: for duty to have any meaning at all it must surely be unselfish. As her reflections became increasingly censorious, she began to feel slightly ashamed of herself. She had never been religious and her general views on moral issues had been formed in the 1960s atmosphere of obligatory liberalism: in principle she was still totally in favour of what might be called a humane divorce law. But while wanting the law to remain liberal, she suspected that she wanted individuals to live up to the uncompromising ideals of the marriage service. She shook her head at her own lack of realism, doubting that there had ever been a time when 'for better or worse' had been taken literally.

Joyce was waking up. 'Have you been crying?' she asked, sharply.

'Oh, yes, but only at a play. It didn't have a happy ending.'

'I thought you would have grown out of that sort of thing by now.'

'I don't think you grow out of anything much really. It's only your outward appearance that changes. Shall I make you a drink?'

'That would be nice. Can you bring yourself to make milky Nescafé?'

Catherine smiled. 'Just about. Actually I rather enjoyed it myself last night.'

When she returned with the coffee her father was also awake. Unlike his wife, he was a little ashamed of having slept so soundly. 'We really must be getting old,' he said. 'Did you at least have something good to watch?'

Catherine outlined the play in a couple of sentences. Tom regretted that there had been nothing light-hearted for her; her mother expressed scepticism that anyone would kill himself just because his wife had left him. But then, she added, she never had been able to understand suicides. The conversation moved to people they had known personally who had killed themselves: only the other week a neighbour's brother had been found dead in his garage, poisoned by exhaust fumes.

'He'd just lost his job,' said Tom, 'and of course there's not much chance these days of getting a new one. Everything's closing down.'

'Liverpool's a dying city. It's a wonder there aren't riots all the time.' Mrs Quinn spoke with even more than usual ferocity. 'And when I think how it used to be! I remember walking down the Dock Road when there were so many ships you couldn't count them.'

'But there were hard times, then, too, my dear.'

'I'm not saying there weren't. But the place was still *alive*. Now all the young people with any nous get away to London as soon as they have half a chance.'

'You used to say you'd like to live in London.'

'I didn't know what I was talking about.' Joyce smiled mischievously. 'I didn't know then that it was full of people ...' she paused before bringing herself to utter the Christian names which denoted a degree of familiarity she preferred to withhold, '... like John and Laura.'

'They really did manage to get under your skin, didn't they?'

'I wouldn't have minded them so much, if Peter and Anthea hadn't been falling over themselves to make such a fuss of them.'

'Surely they were only trying to be hospitable.'

'Oh yes, they're always very hospitable, aren't they? Putting us in a room on our own for half an hour and not bothering even to get drinks for half their guests.'

'Well, I didn't have much conversation with them myself ...'

'You didn't have much conversation with anybody, as I remember, because you were too busy reading.'

'... but they seemed pleasant enough people. Her voice was a bit loud, but that may have been due to nerves.'

'Nerves! And what, may I ask, could have given her "nerves"?'

'Oh, I don't know. A lot of strangers to meet – she may even have sensed some hostility.'

'Oh, so what you really mean is that actually *I* was to blame for her loud voice and rude manners. I must say I find it very touching after all these years that you'd still rather take any old stranger's side than agree with your wife.'

'No, no, I don't want to take anybody's side ...'

'Exactly, that's just what's the matter with you.'

'But mother,' Catherine protested, 'you were just complaining that Daddy was always taking the *wrong* side. You can't have it both ways.'

'No, of course not. *I* can't have it *any* way. You're all against me.' Joyce put the cups together on the tray and left the room. Catherine could think of nothing to say which did not imply a disloyalty to one or other parent.

The sympathy she felt for her father in face of her mother's sarcasm was partially offset by her unwillingness to see her mother withdraw into resentful isolation. She took refuge in the lateness of the hour and said she was going to bed. By the time she had reached the door, her father had taken up his book and was reading serenely. In the kitchen Joyce was noisily rinsing the cups, indifferent in her anger to the danger of chipping them. Catherine took up a tea-towel and began to dry them.

'You must be tired,' she said, 'you put on a marvellous meal today, and it was a big crowd for you to cope with all on your own.''

'Do you really think so? Well, praise from you is praise indeed.'

The dishes having been put away, Catherine kissed her mother goodnight and escaped upstairs before Mrs Quinn's bitterness had a chance to reassert itself.

Next morning Catherine dressed with her usual care, although she had no idea how she could usefully occupy her day. For years now, her visits to Liverpool had been squashed into a few days, just about long enough to see Jennifer and Peter, but short enough for her mother to reproach her for wanting to be off again before she had had time to unpack her suitcase. Sometimes she had felt mean about leaving: her mother was much alone for, even when her husband was in the house, he spent more time reading than talking to her. Catherine wondered if the conversation, when they did speak, always took such a bitter turn as it had the night before. Could she perhaps, by her presence now, help to create a happier atmosphere between them? The irony of seeking to restore harmony to her parents' fifty-year-old marriage while recovering from the wreckage of her own amused her.

'Do you have any particular plans while you're here?' asked Joyce after breakfast.

'Not really. I just thought it would be nice not to be in a rush for once.'

'Well, it's certainly a treat for *us*. Would you like to come into town? I have to get a birthday present for Carolyn. Of course, Lee's isn't open on a Monday, but Lewis's is quite nice these days, and it's very handy to the bus.'

'Won't we go by car?'

'Oh no, there's no point. You can't park anywhere and I travel free with my pass.'

'Surely there are plenty of multi-storey car parks?'

'Yes, but they're not safe.'

'Not safe?'

'No, Mrs Roberts from number 74 was mugged in one.'

Catherine was about to question the validity of arguing from this one instance that all multi-storey car parks were not safe but she stopped herself. Her mother would not be convinced and it would be fatiguing to them both. She might as well agree to go by bus, especially as she knew that if she held out about the car, her mother would sulk all morning.

The bus was empty when they boarded it. The driver seemed to know Mrs Quinn, who insisted on paying Catherine's fare. 'I like that one,' said Joyce, as they sat down. 'Some of the younger ones are very surly. But of course it's not like it used to be when they had conductors. I don't know why they had to get rid of them – just putting even more people out of work. Many of them were really funny, too. I remember once a woman asking if the bus stopped at the Pier Head and the conductor replied, "Jesus, Missus, I hope so!".'

Catherine laughed and Mrs Quinn, pleased with the success of her joke, launched into her repertoire of 'scouse stories'. Catherine noted with something like envy the obvious affection her mother had for her city. 'I have no roots like hers,' she thought. As they left the relative affluence of the outer suburbs, more and more passengers go on. Catherine was shocked by the evident poverty of their appearance and regretted being so elegantly dressed herself. A young woman, painfully thin, squashed into the seat in front of them with her three small children. The two oldest jostled for the space by the window. 'Will yer stop that, you two?' said the mother. The children took no notice. 'If yer don't stop, I'll belt yer.' The woman's tone was quiet and monotonous and her sons ignored her. After a couple of minutes' more squabbling, she took each child's wrist and slapped it hard enough to make a bright-red mark appear. The older boy shrugged but the younger one howled. His brother took the opportunity to establish triumphantly his right to the window seat. The howling grew louder. 'Oh, for Christ's sake, Barry, shut up! Or d'yer want another one?' Still the howling continued. His mother began to rummage in her shopping-bag, a shabby affair in imitation leather, the handle much mended. She fished out a bar of chocolate and shared it between the children. The howling subsided.

'That was where the Rialto used to be,' said Joyce, as the bus pulled up at a traffic light with a piece of waste land to the left and decaying slave traders' terraces, relics of Liverpool's belated Regency blossoming, ahead of them. 'It was completely burnt out in the riots.'

'I remember it very well,' said Catherine. 'I always used to find myself saying, "Signor Antonio, many a time and oft on the Rialto, you have rated me about my monies and my usances," as the bus went past. And wasn't there a murder there, too, years ago, when it was still a cinema?'

'No, dear, that was the Cameo. Of course, the Rialto hadn't been a cinema for a long time. It was a bingo hall for a while and then ended up as a carpet warehouse. I heard the owner had some sort of arrangement with the Social Security and it was dissatisfied customers – of course, round here nearly everyone is on supplementary benefit – who set fire to the place. But I suppose he was well insured. It's always the wrong people who suffer.'

Catherine marvelled at her mother's sturdy anarchism. How shocked Günter's parents would be if they could hear her! The riots of the previous year in Liverpool had been much dwelt on by German newspapers and television. Her in-laws had actually telephoned specially to ask if her parents were 'all right'. Oddly, she had herself never feared for their safety and her complacency was founded on more than her superior knowledge of Liverpool geography. But on what? British phlegm? Or was it mere ignorance of how street violence develops? She looked at the faces in the bus, many of them black or half-caste. They showed above all resignation: she could not imagine them being whipped into any sort of passionate commitment by a mob orator. Yet a year ago, they – or at least their teenage brothers and sons – *had* gone on the rampage. It was time to get off. A lot of people were standing up and moving towards the door. Catherine, wedged tight in the crowd, noticed the smell of unwashed bodies, a smell she hardly knew. She was not so much disgusted as distressed that these people should not yet have caught up with the cleanliness of the rest of the Western world, and she felt a sudden ache of pity for the shoddy cheapness of their clothes, the imprisoning limits of their lives.

The bus stopped just outside Lewis's, a few yards from the entrance which, a quarter of a century before, had been so sensationally adorned with Jacob Epstein's bronze figure of a naked man, powerfully thrusting his way out of the bombed ruins of the old store. Then, all Liverpool had tittered at the sculpture's nakedness but now, if it was noticed at all, it struck the observer more by its idealized vision of the whole human body than by its incidental exposure of the private parts. Mrs Quinn ushered Catherine along the pavement towards the front entrance leading straight to the perfume counters.

She was delighted to have her daughter accompanying her again on a shopping jaunt. As a child 'going to town' on Saturday had for Catherine been as regular a weekly observance as going to church on Sunday had not. In those days they had shopped mainly at Henderson's, where, according to Joyce, customers were made to feel ill at ease if they were not smartly dressed. There was no doubt in Catherine's mind that her mother had regarded this inhibition on democratic shopping with complete approval; was it then not at odds with her present sympathy for rioters? Henderson's no longer existed: it had changed hands, tried to improve business by moving downmarket and finally closed altogether. Joyce, bitter at what she considered the destruction of her city's pride, a process which she perceived as having been imposed entirely from outside, increasingly identified herself with the dispossessed.

'I thought I'd get her some good perfume,' she told Catherine, 'something she wouldn't be able to afford for herself. I can't buy her clothes at her age and she says she'd rather have a parcel to unwrap than the money or a gift voucher.'

They went to the corner devoted to French perfumes. There was no sign of an assistant. 'This really does annoy me,' Joyce began irritably. 'The shops are just too mean these days to employ enough people, even though they pay the staff they have little enough.'

Catherine looked round. At the next counter, a girl was leaning against the till, gazing with deep interest at her fingernails. 'Excuse me,' said Catherine, 'we'd like to buy some perfume. Do you think you could help us?'

'French perfume?'

'That's right.'

'Sorry. I'm only Revlon. She won't be long, though, she's on her break.'

'Oh, really!' Mrs Quinn was now very vexed. 'Then we'll have to think of something else.'

'Couldn't we go and get a cup of coffee while we wait?'

'Oh, all right, though all the really nice cafés went long ago. But the place here on the top floor is quiet and it does have waitress service.'

They made their way across the floor towards the lifts. As they approached the stationery counters, they saw a boy of perhaps twelve or thirteen being led off by a security man. The little bunch of women waiting for the lift were discussing what had happened. 'The nerve of him!' said one. 'Just stood there, bold as brass, saying he'd never touched her purse.'

'He was very cute throwing it into the bin so quick,' said

another. 'The assistant said it isn't the first time they've nabbed him.'

'He should be at school, anyway. But they only go when they feel like it these days. And you can't blame the teachers – they're not allowed to lay a hand on them, whatever cheek they give.'

'Bring back the birch, that's what I say. A good hiding'd do them all the good in the world.'

As they got into the lift, Catherine found that she was very nearly crying. She had only caught a glimpse of the boy but it had been long enough for her to take in both the bright-scarlet blush spreading up his neck into his cheeks and the wretched state of his footwear. He was wearing dirty pumps with holes in them where his toes had worn through. Her impression had been that he was trembling with fright; she had seen nothing of the hardened criminal so apparent to the other witnesses. Joyce was still grumbling about the perfume counter and seemed not to have taken in anything else. When they reached their floor and found that the restaurant did not open until noon, she became even more irate. 'There's a coffee bar somewhere,' she said, 'but it's not the same.'

'Let's try it anyway.'

'Are you dying for a drink, then?'

'Yes, I'm quite desperate. Come on, the escalator will be quicker.'

When at last they sat down with their coffee at a little white table and Catherine had moved the half-full ashtray while her mother wiped away a puddle of tea with a paper handkerchief, Joyce said, 'Are you feeling all right? You seem to have gone a bit strange all of a sudden.'

Catherine felt the tears coming into her eyes as she answered, 'That poor boy upset me.'

'What poor boy?'

'The one they'd caught trying to pinch somebody's purse.'

'He sounds to me like a naughty boy, not a poor one.'

'But he *was* poor. He'd never had a chance. And all the

old hags in the lift could say was that he ought to be flogged.'

'Yes, well, that's what a lot of people think. But he won't be flogged, you know, so you needn't get too upset about it.'

'I wish he'd stolen my purse, instead. He'd have been welcome to it.'

'What a very silly thing to say! That would only encourage him to go on stealing purses.'

'But perhaps he really needed the money.'

'And you, of course, do not. That's the difference between you and the poor woman whose purse he actually did take. *She* needed the money, and it happened to be hers by right. Not many people here have your fat bank balance to make up what thieves take off them. But I really cannot see why you should *cry* over it.' Catherine had given up trying to restrain her tears and was now quite openly wiping her eyes.

'I'll be all right in a minute,' she said.

'Do you remember the gateaux in Henderson's?' Joyce wanted to restore the agreeably nostalgic mood of their conversation on the bus.

'Yes, they were lovely,' replied Catherine, with an effort. 'I think I liked the cream buns best.'

'I remember asking you once how many you thought you could eat before getting sick and you said you'd never had enough to get anywhere near finding out.'

'No wonder I was fat.'

'You were never fat. It was just that when you were at Oxford, the fashion was all for Belsen victims.'

'I don't think the mini-skirt did much for anyone, really.'

'But you had to wear it. You might as well be out of the world as out of the fashion when you're young.'

'I don't think girls today are quite such slaves to fashion as we were. Don't you agree they seem to wear whatever they fancy?'

'Carolyn does, certainly. She hasn't got a clue how to dress – just like her mother.'

'You're very hard on Jennifer.'

'I don't like the way she's letting herself go. She'll be really fat soon.'

'But does she even want to be thin and smart?'

'Of course she does – every woman, if she's honest, wants to look nice.'

They had finished their coffee and reluctantly Joyce agreed to try the perfume counter once more; she had no other ideas for a gift and it would only be cutting off her nose to spite her face if she went home without anything. The assistant, refreshed from her break, was one of those loquacious, middle-aged types who call all their customers 'love' and assure them blandly that every article they pick up is *precisely* what they are looking for. Catherine, used to the trained competence of German shop assistants, was irritated that her mother could receive no informed reply to her question as to which fragrance was most suitable for a young girl. In the end, after being liberally sprayed with samples, they made their own decision and went to find wrapping-paper for their purchase.

'Could they not have gift-wrapped it at the counter for you?' asked Catherine, thinking of the pretty parcel which her cosmetic shop in Bonn would have made up.

'Oh, no, I shouldn't think so.' Joyce selected her paper, rebuked the girl at the till who crumpled it getting it into the bag, then announced that she would go to the food hall to get 'a bit of boiled ham' for their lunch. Catherine said that she would go and buy some chocolates and meet her mother at the door.

'Don't go wasting your money on expensive chocolates for me, now. I think I'm going off them anyway.'

'Aren't there any at all that you like?'

'No, not really. I've had too many lately. Jennifer's always bringing big boxes – it's her guilty conscience for not coming more often and staying longer.'

'Well, Daddy likes them, doesn't he?'

'Oh, yes, *he* does. You can buy them for him, if you want.'

Catherine found what she wanted and joined the queue

for the till. In front of her stood an elderly woman clutching a bag of sweets which still had to be weighed. As she came to the till, she handed the assistant a handful of copper coins and said, 'I don't know whether I'll have enough for all of them, dear. Will you take a few out for me if you need?'

The girl sighed, just perceptibly, and raised her eyes to heaven, before starting to count the change. 'You've only got 22½p 'ere. The ½p's no use to you.' She weighed the sweets. 'They weigh over five ounces.' There was a note of accusation in her voice.

'Well, just give me what you can. That's all the money I've got left.' As the girl proceeded to remove all but five or six sweets from the bag, the old woman turned to Catherine and said, without bitterness, 'It's awful what you've got to pay for a few sweets these days, isn't it?'

Catherine, holding her two boxes of chocolates worth nearly £10, nodded her head vigorously and tried to smile agreement. She could not bring herself to say anything at all. She wanted to shovel a heap of sweets on to the scale until the finger swung out of its upper weight limit, present them to the old woman and, for good measure, shake the surly girl at the counter for her lack of feeling. But she did nothing. As she mutely handed her own purchases over to be wrapped, she watched the woman, who had carefully put her paltry bag of sweets into a string bag, walk slowly away. Once more, she found herself close to tears.

'Catherine, you're weeping again!' said her mother as soon as they met up. 'Are you sure you're all right?'

'I'd like to go home.'

'Very well, we'll go and get the bus.'

'Couldn't we get a taxi?'

'Certainly we *could,* but it seems a bit unnecessary when the bus stop is so handy.'

Almost as soon as they had joined the queue, an empty taxi approached: the town's taxi-drivers now did most of their business ferrying people from the city centre to their homes in Liverpool 8. Many of their fares were would-be bus passengers who had got tired of waiting. Catherine flagged down the car and firmly ushered her mother, still grumbling, into the back. In less than a quarter of an hour, they were home.

Eight

Mr Quinn was at mass when they arrived. Catherine had not spoken since they'd got into the taxi, except to give the driver directions. Joyce had made a few desultory remarks about the traffic but failed to engage either her daughter or the driver in conversation. As soon as they were in the house, she said, 'And now are you going to tell me what all that was about?'

'There was an old woman in Lewis's who had no money left for sweets.'

'So was she trying to shoplift?'

'No, of course not. Why do you ask?'

'Well, isn't it usually the criminal classes who get the lion's share of your sympathy?'

'I wanted to buy her some.'

'And did you?'

'No. I didn't do anything. That's the point.'

'And does it surprise you?'

'It disappoints me.'

'Hmmm. Well I must say if I'd known how distressing a trip to town was going to be for you, I'd have suggested a walk in the park instead.'

Tom had just come in. As he joined them, he asked, 'And did you have a nice time, then?'

Catherine at once said yes, it had been very nice, until... but she had hardly finished telling him about the young delinquent before she was crying again. Her father was concerned but her mother remained only puzzled and sceptical.

'Really, Catherine,' she said, 'I don't see what there is for you to cry about. It's not even as though you were going to do anyone any good with your weeping.'

Catherine said nothing. Her thoughts were very confused. The two little incidents, on top of the bus ride, might well have provoked her tears but deep down she suspected that she was only in part crying for the boy and the old woman: for the most part she was crying for herself. Her father came over and sat next to her on the settee, putting his arm round her. It only made her cry even more and Joyce, feeling excluded, said irritably as she went towards the door, 'Well, by all means have a good cry, if that's what you feel like. I'll go and see to lunch.'

For a few moments they sat in silence, then Catherine said, 'Mother, of course, is right. It's not just the poor downtrodden people of Liverpool I'm crying about. Günter's left me.' At last she had said it and, as if by saying it she had finally removed it from the realms of bad dreams and turned it into unalterable fact, she cried even more.

Tom did not speak at once, although he pressed his daughter closer to him. Then he said, 'I thought something was wrong from the minute you arrived – you've been very brave keeping it to yourself so long.'

'Or very cowardly.'

'And how long have you known yourself?'

'Only since last Tuesday. But it seems ages ago.'

'And may I ask why he's left you?'

'Oh, he's fallen in love with some girl and she's having a baby.' As she said the words 'fallen in love', there was something of her mother's sarcasm in her tone. Her tears had quite subsided.

'And had you no idea beforehand that something like this was going on?'

'Not that there was "another woman", no. He'd been a bit moody but I thought he was just fed up at work. I'm not very good at understanding strong emotions.'

'Now I don't believe that for a moment.'

'The funny thing is, I had no intention of telling you in a flood of tears. I really thought that I was on the point of coming to terms with it. After watching that play last night, even though I bawled my head off over it, I felt sure that I would be able to cope.'

'It wouldn't be human not to be upset. And it wouldn't be good for you to repress your feelings altogether and kid yourself that you *were* completely in control.'

'I am ashamed, though, of taking myself so seriously. Even with Günter gone, aren't I infinitely better off than the boy in Lewis's?'

'Perhaps in some ways you are. But I don't think you should even try to compare your present unhappiness with his deprivation: they're altogether different. But being unhappy yourself may make you more sensitive to other people's troubles.'

'You flatter me. Mother sees it more clearly: shedding tears over little boys being taken off to Borstal is mere self-indulgence. And naturally I'm much nearer solving my own problem than I am to doing anything to lessen anybody else's.'

'And for the moment your own problem is quite big enough. I'm glad you came home with it.'

'So am I,' said Catherine, and at that moment she meant it. 'There was really nowhere else I could have gone.'

Joyce returned to tell them that lunch 'such as it is' was ready. She had overtaxed her culinary powers the day before and for today they would be eating very modestly. 'I'm glad to see you've stopped crying at last,' she added. Tom frowned slightly but Catherine smiled.

'I've got a secret off my chest,' she said. 'Günter's gone off with a girl half his age.' Instinctively she was telling her mother what had happened in the words she could already hear Joyce using when, in turn, she told other people.

Simultaneously with the news itself, Mrs Quinn took in that Catherine had first confided, not in herself, but in her husband. She was hurt and said, with some intention to wound, 'Really? Well, I can't say I'm altogether surprised.'

'Joyce, what on earth are you saying?' Tom felt for his daughter but was inadequate to the task of remonstrating with his wife in front of her. Catherine, touched by her father's ready sympathy, was tempted to cry again but, gradually dissatisfied with the instability of her emotions, restrained herself.

Joyce, meanwhile, realized that she had been unkind. 'Oh, I only meant it's the sort of thing men do all the time. I'm really very sorry for Catherine.'

'And I should think so, too.'

'Shall we have a drink?' Joyce, still unable to find the right words of comfort, hit upon a gesture that was neither appropriate to herself, a lifelong teetotaller, nor to the very limited alcoholic stores in her house. But both Catherine and her father, sensing her embarrassment and wanting to ease it, agreed enthusiastically. Mr Quinn came off best for there was some whisky in the cupboard and he liked whisky. Catherine did not and was left with a choice between a sweet sherry which her mother kept for making trifle, and Southern Comfort, won two years before in a raffle. She chose the sherry.

'Of course I know you only drink "Tio Pepe" as a rule,' said Joyce, proud that she had remembered the brand. 'I meant to get some in for you, but the shop at the top had sold out. They had another which they said tasted just the same, but I didn't like to risk it without asking you first.'

'This is fine,' said Catherine.

They sat for a minute or two in awkward silence. Catherine, having at last confided the fact of Günter's desertion to her parents, felt disinclined to say more. A part of her mind seemed to have distanced itself from what was actually happening and to be observing the little group in the Quinns' sitting-room dispassionately. Tom, whose placid and amiable temper had been maintained largely by his refusing ever to acknowledge anything distressing, was at a loss as to how to comfort his daughter beyond offering her repeated assurances of his own love.

His wife, although she had been caught off balance both by the actual news and by its not having been communicated to herself before anyone else, was now gradually regaining her composure and was, typically, the first to speak.

'And don't you want to tell us more about it, love?' Her voice, more hesitant than usual, was soft and her eyes were anxious.

'I don't really know. There's not a lot to tell, anyhow. Her name's Anna and she was Wolfgang's girlfriend.' Catherine remembered the difficulty her mother always had sorting out Günter's vast family – his parents each had half a dozen brothers and sisters – and quickly explained which cousin was Wolfgang's mother. 'He ditched her and she turned up at our house one Sunday to cry on our shoulders. I suppose it went from there pretty much by itself.'

'And why should she cry on *your* shoulders? Has she no parents?'

'Yes, she has, somewhere – they don't live in Bonn, she's only at the university there.'

'She'd probably had her eye on Günter all the time. And he, of course, would be flattered because she's so young.'

Catherine found this suggestion ridiculous. 'I'm sure she didn't fancy him at all. On the contrary, she was very obviously in love with Wolfgang, even though I always thought he treated her a bit roughly.'

'Then how does she come to be having Günter's baby?'

'How can I possibly answer that? Perhaps they both long for a child. Perhaps it was just one of those tiresome "mistakes". The main thing is that Günter's over the moon about it now that it's happened.'

'Huh! I bet the girl isn't.'

'Why ever shouldn't she be?'

'Because girls very rarely are in such cases. Things haven't changed all that much, you know, and it's still no way to start married life – even if you don't have to begin by getting rid of the first wife. Still she got herself into the mess and she will have to get herself out of it. It's you I'm worried about. I think you'll just have to force yourself to look on the bright side.' Mrs Quinn's tone, no longer so openly solicitous, had become cheerfully businesslike. Catherine felt that it would not be long before she was being told that losing her husband was the best thing that could have happened to her. Irritated by such optimism, she said nothing. Joyce continued, 'Of course it's a pity you ever married him in the first place, but you're still just about young enough to make a fresh start. It'll be hard for you to begin with but we'll all rally round. You'll get over it in no time.'

Catherine stood up. 'I'm sorry,' she said, 'but I don't think I'm quite ready for such bracing words.' She went out of the room and upstairs.

'I don't think, Joyce,' said Tom when she had gone, 'that you should have let her see quite how glad you are that her husband's treated her in this way.'

'Well, really! I'm sure I'm not glad. But it may still be good for her in the long run. I hated to see her turning into a vegetable.'

'You just hated to see her happily married.' Her husband picked up his newspaper, on which he had written the names of the horses he'd chosen for the day's doubles. Catherine was best left alone for a while and he was anxious to put his bets on before the first race. He went into the hall to telephone the bookmaker. Joyce took no notice, her thoughts now fully occupied with the task of rehabilitating Catherine. She decided that she was not, after all, so very tired from the previous day's entertaining and that she would try to get Jennifer and Peter to come round that evening for a bit of supper. Perhaps she could arrange for them to come without Bob and Anthea: that would be so much nicer.

Upstairs Catherine was lying on her bed, miserable but dry-eyed. She marvelled at the confidence of her mother's reaction: once she had absorbed the initial shock she had known exactly what advice to offer. Probably, thought Catherine, there was much to be said for a robust refusal to give in to grief – if only it were as simple as her mother seemed to think. Joyce, having disapproved of the marriage all along, naturally saw in Günter's present behaviour a vindication of her own disapproval. She had never believed in Catherine's happiness and the fact that Günter had now left her proved that she had been right to deny that her happiness was ever real. Catherine saw it differently: whatever her own failures and whatever Günter's weaknesses of late, there had been a long period of contentment for which she continued to be grateful.

She was fully aware of the rejuvenating effect which her misfortune was likely to have upon her mother. She supposed that she had had some inkling that it would be like this when she first began to doubt the wisdom of rushing home to Liverpool. Nor could she blame her mother for taking her decision to return for a prolonged visit as a plea for protection and an implicit readiness to accept maternal guidance. It is a commonplace that in the eyes of their parents, children are never fully grown up. The years away from home and her mother's influence had profoundly changed Catherine but to Mrs Quinn she was still the clever but pliant daughter she used to be. Her marriage had been an aberration and now that it was finished they were free to take up where they had left off. Catherine knew that her mother's assumption of the right once again to direct her life was absurd, but she knew equally well that Joyce would never see the absurdity. She might resist Joyce's advice to the point of quarrelling with her but she would never convince her that she was no longer the person she had been before she left home. In anticipation of the struggle to come, Catherine felt weary. She lacked the energy to take herself off altogether, to try and cope alone, but still she was far from being able to acquiesce quietly in whatever Joyce might plan for her.

She got up. She could not spend the day in bed, as though she were an invalid. She washed her face and put her make-up on again, forcing herself to take, if anything, more care than usual. She was pleased with the result: the signs of the morning's tears were all but obliterated.

'That's better,' said Joyce, when she went downstairs. 'Now you look more like my little girl again.'

The wording of the compliment jarred on Catherine but she only said, 'I think I'll go for a walk. Can I bring you anything back from the shops?'

'No, thank you. Your father will drive me up to Allerton Road later. Aren't you going to have anything to eat?'

'No, I'd rather not, thanks. I never eat much in the middle of the day.'

'As you like. It's no wonder you've gone so thin. Are you going for a walk in the car?' Catherine had picked up her car keys and handbag.

'I thought I'd drive to Calderstones Park and walk there for a bit.'

'Yes, that's a good idea. Though you won't find it as nice as it used to be. All these cuts have meant they don't have the money for the gardeners or the gardens any more. It's a disgrace.'

The park was only a mile away. Catherine left her car near the main entrance and walked towards the great stone gateway, past the circle of grass in the middle of the road where the 'Calder Stones', big, rough-hewn lumps of sandstone of great antiquity and alleged pre-Christian religious significance, had stood until the polluted air from the ring-road traffic had threatened their survival and they had been removed to the museum. As a child, Catherine had often come here for walks with her father, walks on which he had encouraged her to learn how to spell rhododendron, antirrhinum and chrysanthemum, according to the season. In the spring, there were daffodils growing wild in the fields which stretched from the formal gardens to the lake and her father had quoted Herrick, with a predictability Catherine loved. At primary school she had herself learned 'I wandered lonely as a cloud' off by heart, winning a prize for her recitation at a speech contest, but her father did not care for Wordsworth and she adopted his prejudice without question, just to please him. He knew many of the sillier ballads by heart and they would giggle together over the leech-gatherer and, 'Oh, no, sir, we are seven.' It subsequently came as a great surprise to her to discover that the same poet had also written 'Tintern Abbey'.

Her mother had never accompanied them, asserting that she was far too busy and leaving Catherine with the impression that only men and children had time for leisure activities. But it was Joyce who had told Catherine that the park was undoubtedly 'the finest in the north of England', perhaps she had claimed that it was 'the biggest outside London' as well. Certainly, the information she had given Catherine about her native city had all tended to superlatives: 'the longest underwater tunnel in the world', 'the only floating landing stage', the unfinished Anglican cathedral had 'the highest interior' in – was it the world or just Britain? It did not really matter, any more than it mattered whether all Mrs Quinn's statistics were strictly accurate. What mattered was that Liverpool was a place to be proud of; as soon as she could read the labels on their groceries, she had even been encouraged to take pride in the number of products which were manufactured there – matches and sugar, jam and biscuits. No wonder, thought Catherine, that her mother was now so bitter.

The park, however, was not quite as run-down as Joyce had implied: the bank of autumn flowers which Catherine remembered as a mass of rich colours, lovingly selected afresh each year, seemed sparser than it used to be, and there was more uncollected litter about. But still it was pleasant walking there, the noise from the road now very distant and the layout conveying a sense of spaciousness, an illusion that the heavily built-up suburbs were worlds away. Catherine had gone to school very near and had often walked home through the park. She sat down on a bench in the rose garden and thought nostalgically of those days when her life had been so straightforward, when there had been no tension either within herself or with the people close to her. In her marriage she had done her best to ensure harmony but it had involved a conscious effort unknown to her when she was young, and the harmony itself had further cast a shadow over her relations with her mother.

Catherine got up to walk again. She would go round the lake once before returning to her car. It was nearly four o'clock and the children were coming out of school. She noticed that a little group of girls coming towards her were wearing a uniform that was just recognizable as the one she had worn herself: the badge on the blazer was the same, as were the navy skirt and striped blouse. There the resemblance ended: these girls were hatless and tieless and two of them were wearing coloured ankle socks. With a shock, Catherine realized that they were smoking. She was sure that such a thing would have been unthinkable in her own day; she was not merely making the common middle-aged mistake of seeing everywhere a falling off from the standards of her youth. She looked at the girls a little harder and longer than was quite polite and one of them, catching her stare, said loudly to her companions, 'What's up with 'er, then?' Catherine walked on quickly.

When she got home, her mother had the kettle boiling but was holding up tea for her. 'You seemed gone a long time,' she said, 'and I know there's no café in the park any more. You must be dying for a drink.'

It seemed to Catherine that her mother, while kindly offering her tea, was also declaring her right to know how she had spent every minute that she had been away. 'I just walked round once,' she said. 'It didn't occur to me to look for a café.'

'No, well, I suppose you're not much of a tea-drinker anyway. Would you rather have coffee?'

'No thanks, tea will be lovely.' Catherine took the cup and accepted a piece of sticky bun which her mother – anxious perhaps to provide something extra-nourishing – had liberally spread with salty butter.

'I've been busy while you were out,' announced Joyce, after pressing her to eat a second piece of bun. 'I rang Jennifer and Peter and they're both dropping everything to come over this evening. Fortunately Bob's got night school but I'm afraid Anthea insists on tagging along as well.'

'Why shouldn't she come?'

'Oh, I just thought that under the circumstances it'd be nicer for us to be on our own. You mightn't feel you can talk so freely with her there.'

'I don't know that I want to talk very much anyhow.'

'Oh, I know how you feel, but it'll do you good to get it out of your system. You've been bottling it all up for far too long.'

'It's not a week since he told me.'

'That's as may be. But you must have had your worries before that. It can't have taken you completely by surprise.'

'But it did.'

'Now you're not going to tell me that Günter was the loving husband one day and leaving you the next.'

'No, that's true, but it never occurred to me that he had someone else – I had never thought of him as that sort of man.'

'They're all that sort of man if they get the chance.'

'And when are they coming? I thought you were tired still from yesterday.'

'I'm never tired in a crisis. They're coming for their meal. I insisted. I went shopping while you were out and I think I can put on a very nice little dinner. Nothing fancy, of course, but that's not my style.'

'Won't you let me help you?'

'Not today, thank you. You go and put your feet up. There are plenty of books in the house for you to read – your father buys more than ever since he's retired.'

Catherine did as she was told; it was the easiest thing to do. For the next hour she sat dipping into her father's new books, trying to find something that would take her mind off herself. She lacked the willpower to concentrate enough for a biography of Mussolini and a fat edition of Mrs Gaskell's letters failed to grip her. She ended up with David Lodge, undemanding and amusing, if ultimately unsatisfying. At half-past six her mother came in with a tray of glasses and a bottle of Tio Pepe.

'You must have a drink,' she said. 'You'll be getting withdrawal symptoms the way you're going on.'

'You're very good, but I hope you don't really think of me as an alcoholic.'

Just then the doorbell rang and Joyce went to answer it. Jennifer, without taking off her coat, came straight into the room where Catherine was sitting. She threw her arms round her sister and said, 'Oh, my poor love! What can I say? It's awful. I'm so sorry.' She seemed about to cry. Catherine found herself oddly unmoved; perhaps she had cried herself out in the morning. She smiled but said nothing. 'You must still be feeling numb from it all. Mum said he only told you last week. I can't believe it. You seemed so happy. What sort of a girl can she be?'

'You'll find Catherine can't – or won't – tell us an awful lot about her,' said Joyce. 'Why don't you have a drink? I bought gin and tonic as well, in case you prefer it.'

'Gosh, you did go to town!' Jennifer poured herself sherry. As she raised her glass to her lips she looked towards Catherine, who obediently raised her glass in reply. 'Cheers,' she said, feeling that the word was even more inappropriate than usual.

'I have to go and see to the chicken,' said Joyce. 'No, I don't need any help. Perhaps, Jennifer, if you're planning on staying, you'd like to give me your coat.'

'She is marvellous, isn't she?' said Jennifer when they were alone. 'The way she rises to an occasion when she has to, no one would ever think she was turned seventy.'

'My divorce will be the making of her, I'm sure.'

'Oh, Catherine, I didn't mean it like that. But you must find it a relief to be home with the people who love you.'

'I can't help wondering if she really does love me. She loves the youngest daughter that I used to be, but I'm afraid that if she bothered to get to know the person I have now become, she might not much care for me at all.'

'What a funny way to talk!' Catherine shrugged her

shoulders and Jennifer, who could not bear to sit in silence, went on, 'Is Peter able to come?'

'Oh, yes, everybody's "rallying round". Anthea is coming too. Mother, of course, is very put out about that.'

'Poor Anthea! Oh, I think I hear their car. I'll go to the door.'

Catherine remained where she was and soon Anthea's voice was heard saying loudly, 'We've brought flowers and champagne – well, it's sparkling hock, really – the flowers are for mother-in-law and the champagne is for everyone. You left on Saturday before we got round to drinking it.'

'That's all right, then,' said Mrs Quinn, 'so long as it's left-overs. Are the flowers from the garden?'

'Yes, freshly picked only half an hour ago, just before we left. Shall I put them in water?'

'No, I'd rather do it myself, thank you. You'd better go into the sitting-room and have a drink. The potatoes are nearly done.'

Peter and Anthea entered the room together. Catherine stood up to receive their embraces. Peter, with a simpering smile, remarked that the news had taken him completely by surprise. 'You were so very much your composed and charming self on Saturday,' he said.

'It would hardly have done for me to put a blight on the engagement party.'

'Oh, Catherine, how awfully sweet of you to think of it like that.' Anthea squeezed her hand. 'And sherry, how super! It really must be quite the most civilized drink in the world.'

Tom, who had been listening to the racing results on the radio in his bedroom, now joined them. Jennifer kissed him, Peter and Anthea greeted him in a rather more offhand way.

'Will you have sherry?' asked Peter.

'Thanks, son, whatever's there.'

'But I thought you didn't like sherry,' protested Jennifer.

'Well, no, I don't really.'

'There was some whisky in the cupboard this morning,' said Catherine, 'I'll go and get it.'

'Why didn't you say you don't like sherry?' asked Peter.

'Well, it's not that important, is it?'

Catherine returned with his drink. 'Did you back any winners?'

'Ah, now I was really very unlucky. I got the first one in my doubles up and the next one came in second. The third one finished nowhere but the fourth won and then the result was overthrown by a steward's enquiry. Pity, because it was 7-1 and with the first winner I would have more than cleared my stake.'

Joyce appeared at the door to announce that dinner was ready. 'You're not talking about your horses, are you?'

'Daddy was very unlucky with his doubles,' said Catherine.

'Unlucky! I'd like to know when he's ever told anyone that he'd won. I assume that he does sometimes, of course, or we'd have been in the workhouse long ago.'

They moved into the dining-room. Joyce, whose first-course inspiration was strongly influenced by what she had seen on restaurant menus, had bought paté from the fish shop and arranged it on lettuce leaves with a slice of tomato. Toast for so many being, she claimed, beyond her, there was French bread to go with it. 'I'll see to the wine,' she said firmly as they sat down. 'The men in this family can't be trusted to do it properly.' She moved round the table, filling the glasses almost to the brim. 'Of course I don't understand these things myself, but at least this didn't come from the supermarket.'

There was a general chinking of glasses and knives and a murmur of appreciation for the hostess. 'I can't take any credit for the meal so far,' insisted Joyce, 'the paté came from a shop.'

'It's still very good,' said Jennifer.

'I never *used* to make my own, either,' said Anthea, 'until Peter bought me the food processor – but now it's so incredibly easy, and you save *so* much money that I think it's more than worth it.'

'But isn't it true,' Joyce looked at Catherine for confirmation, 'that these fancy machines take all the juices out of the meat? Of course, you won't think too harshly of me for not having chopped the liver by hand *today* – after all, I didn't decide to invite you until two o'clock this afternoon.'

'It's all lovely, Mum,' said Jennifer. 'I think you're marvellous.'

'Yes, dear. I know you do.'

It was some time before all the dishes for the main course had been brought in and passed round. Joyce, while open to innovation for the starter, was adamant that a roast must be accompanied by two sorts of potato and several vegetables. Chicken in addition required bacon and sausage to garnish it. At last everyone's plate had been heaped to the satisfaction of the hostess and the repeated compliments on how lavish a feast she had provided died away. There was a silence and then, both anxious to break its awkwardness, Jennifer and Tom started to speak at once, only to give way to each other almost immediately, with assurances that what they had been going to say was of no importance at all. Catherine, feeling responsible for the general embarrassment, forced herself to say something: 'I began reading that new David Lodge this afternoon. It's quite fun, but I don't think it'll make me laugh as much as *Changing Places* did.'

'We haven't read it yet,' said Anthea. 'We're waiting for the paperback.'

'You could have had my copy, dear,' said Tom. 'It's not the sort of book I'd read twice.'

'You are sweet! But, of course, we'll wait now till Catherine's finished.'

'I think it's amazing,' said Peter, 'how he finds time to write all these novels – even if a lot of them do derive from his work.'

'He must be terribly well organized,' said Jennifer, 'I picture him a bit like Trollope, conscientiously writing so many words each day.'

'Are we going to spend the whole evening discussing books?' asked Joyce, challengingly.

'Why do you ask? Don't you want us to?'

'It's not exactly what I had in mind when I invited everyone, I'm sure.'

'I thought,' said Tom, a trifle disingenuously, 'that you just wanted a quiet family evening. And it really is very nice to have you all here; the chicken is lovely, too, Joyce. It's one of my favourite dishes.'

'You sound as though you have forgotten what Catherine told us this lunchtime.'

'Of course I haven't forgotten. But if Catherine would rather talk about books with us, then I think that's what we ought to talk about.'

'I'm sure none of us wants to pry,' said Anthea, 'but I have found – and I have, sad to say, a couple of friends who got divorced – that talking really freely about it can help tremendously.'

'You're all very kind,' said Catherine, 'and naturally you want me to tell you everything. It's just that in my case "everything" is not very much.'

'Do you not think,' said Jennifer, 'that it may be a flash in the pan, and that they'll get tired of each other and go their separate ways again? It's rather more than a seven-year itch, I know, but still these things can happen without necessarily ruining the marriage.'

'I hope,' said Joyce, 'that Catherine would not be so foolish as to take him back.'

'Would it be foolish? I don't know. But it's unlikely to happen if she has the baby. It wouldn't be fair to the child for me even to want it.'

'Goodness, you are saintly! But do you think she won't have the child?'

'I don't imagine she has any moral reservations about abortion, if that's what you mean. She's a very modern young woman: utterly against missiles and the death penalty and all for mercy killing and abortion. But Günter is anxious to have the child and I am altogether in the dark about her attitude to him. He is sure that he loves her, but it will all depend in the end on how much she loves him.'

'I really would never have thought,' said Jennifer, 'that he was the sort of man to lose his head in this way.'

'I always found him a bit of a cold fish,' said Anthea, 'though I suppose he makes a different impression in his own language. The Germans always speak such funny English.'

'I was hardly ever able to get him interested in a proper conversation,' complained Peter. 'I would make some remark about, say, arms control and he would reply with a balanced judgment on the lines of "on the one hand the Americans consider and on the other hand it appears to the Soviets..." It was quite impossible to find out what he himself thought – if, indeed, he thought anything at all.'

'He was probably afraid of offending you by saying the wrong thing. Poor man, I don't think he ever looked very comfortable when he was here.'

'That was his own fault,' said Joyce. 'I'm sure we did everything in our power to make him feel welcome. But he would not put himself out – he didn't even bother to learn the language properly. I don't believe he understood more than half of what we were saying.'

'But he goes to the States on business all the time, so his English can't be all that bad.'

'Well it wasn't good enough for this family!'

Catherine felt herself withdrawing from the conversation. Part of her wanted to argue, to defend Günter: his English was more than adequate to their table talk but he had grown up in a family where shouting about politics was simply not the sort of thing you did when you met up with your relatives. She would also have liked to challenge her family on the way they had received him: had they really wanted to make him welcome? But was it sensible, having kept her criticisms to herself for so long to bring them into the open now, when none of them was likely ever to see Günter again? She remained silent while they went on, dredging up occasions when her husband had proved himself to be lacking a sense of humour, brusque in his treatment of his wife, wounding to English sensibilities, or just generally too reminiscent of any number of Gestapo officers in the countless war films they had seen.

Jennifer helped her mother to clear the table for the next course. Mrs Quinn had bought Brie, Stilton and Cheshire and was offering fancy ice cream and tinned fruit to anyone who didn't care for cheese. 'Have you thought what you are likely to do, Catherine?' asked Peter, when they were all served.

'Of course I've thought, but I've not reached any conclusion.'

'Might you return to the academic world?'

'"Return to the academic world" is choice! You make it sound as though I once had an established place there.'

'Well surely it would only have been a matter of time before you had – if you'd stayed at Oxford.'

'I couldn't say. It's all too long ago.'

'Perhaps you could get a job where your German would be useful. I saw one with Amnesty International advertised only the other week which specified "fluent German and an ability to formulate well in English".'

'And how about teaching? Though nowadays you would have to get your teaching certificate first.'

'I can't see Catherine being happy teaching in a school for the rest of her life,' said Mrs Quinn, firmly. 'She made the mistake once of setting her sights too low, we must see that she doesn't make it again.'

'Now, mother, don't knock the teaching profession. It's been your family's bread and butter for long enough.'

'Catherine can do better for herself.'

'You're beginning to talk about me as though I weren't here. Shall I go and make the coffee?'

'It's already made. I put it in thermos jugs. I did not want *any* of you messing in my kitchen this evening. We'll go into the other room to drink it.'

Once they were all settled, Peter again pressed Catherine to talk about the future, but she refused to do so. 'I appreciate your concern,' she said, 'but if you go on, I shall have to leave.'

This time, in the silence that followed, Tom was more successful in introducing the subject of books. Had they read about the phenomenal success of *The Name of the Rose?* He was looking forward to the English translation coming out. Since Catherine was the only one who could recall anything at all about the book, the conversation was in danger of dying, when Tom brought up the question of what exactly semiotics was. His dictionary said 'the study of sign language', which made him think of semaphore, but that, surely, was an improbable field for scholarship. Peter began to explain, Catherine's thoughts drifted away and Joyce appeared uncertain whether she should take a nap or start up a rival topic of her own. Jennifer, sensing that the real business of the evening was over and that her mother was tired, stood up and, with apologies to Peter for interrupting him, said that it was time for her to go.

'Come round any time,' she urged Catherine. 'I promise I'll only talk books – though I don't get much time to read any – if that's the way you prefer it.'

'Thank you. I will come over.'

'And don't forget, I'm at home during the day as well,' said Anthea, 'or at least I can always arrange to be, if you ring beforehand.'

'You might find it easier to talk one-to-one,' said Peter.

'Are you going to start the dishes?' Catherine asked her mother, as soon as they had left.

'No, for once in my life, I'm not. You can help me in the morning, if you like.'

'Right, it's a deal.' She kissed her parents good night and escaped to bed, taking the David Lodge with her. Before she went to sleep, she had finished it. Clearly, she must try to get many more such books for the coming weeks.

Nine

The weekend had, after all, ended on a sufficiently harmonious note for Günter to be able to settle to his work on Monday morning with all his customary energy. Anna, on the other hand, had nothing to do during the day which commanded her full attention. She went to a lecture in the morning and then joined a group of friends in the 'mensa' for lunch, but her thoughts remained firmly centred on her own very personal situation. She increasingly felt a need to confide in someone and an equally strong reluctance to go back to the flat and wait, alone, for Günter's possibly late return. So when Steffi, a girl she had known since her first semester, said that a boutique behind the Münsterplatz was selling off a bargain lot of jeans, she jumped at the chance to go with her and look at them.

The pedestrian precinct was full of midday shoppers and the little back streets were too crowded for much conversation to be possible. On their way they collected leaflets from Turkish and Iranian dissidents and were accosted by a well-dressed young man who asked them if they believed in God. Anna was on the point of saying 'no' when Steffi answered firmly for both of them with 'Yes, thank you, we're very devout Roman Catholics.'

'It's no use getting involved,' she said to Anna, walking on more briskly. 'And they usually give up when they hear you're a Catholic.'

The jeans were something of a disappointment since the popular sizes and colours had already sold out. 'Are you interested in looking at anything else?' Steffi asked.

'Not really, but if you fancy an ice cream or something, I wouldn't mind going somewhere to talk.'

'OK. Anything rather than work.' They went to an Italian ice-cream parlour and, in the gloom at the back, sat down on hard little chairs at a formica-topped table and ordered *cappuccino*. Steffi took out cigarettes. 'Do you still not smoke?'

'No, kill yourself.'

'That's a nice thing to say, I'm sure.' She lit a cigarette and, as Anna seemed disinclined to start the conversation she had requested, asked, 'Haven't you properly got over Wolfgang yet?' Anna shrugged. 'I saw him in Bonn again the other day with Silke What's-her-name – you know the tall, blonde one who's supposed to be so clever.'

'Well, of course, I'd expect there to be somebody else by now. I haven't seen him for months.'

'Really? How time flies. But you still look awfully miserable. Is something else the matter?'

'I'm having a baby.'

'You're *what*? It can't be Wolfgang's, can it?'

'No, of course it can't. I've been seeing someone else. He's much older.'

'And married?'

'Yes, but he's left his wife.'

'So the baby wasn't a mistake?'

'Well, yes, it was really. I don't really think I want it.'

'And he does?'

'Yes, very much. In a way, it's rather touching. He seemed awfully keen on me from the start but it was only the pregnancy that finally made him break with his wife.'

'So why are you unhappy?'

'I'm frightened. I don't love him like I loved Wolfgang and if I marry him I know he'll expect things from me which I'm just not prepared to give. He claims to be all in favour of equality but deep down I think he'll want me to stay at home all day and have the supper ready when he comes in.'

'Then why don't you give him up?'

Anna hesitated. How could she explain how comforting it had been to feel herself so loved, and how unwilling she was still to forfeit Günter's approval and affection? At last she said, 'I don't suppose I really want to give him up, not completely.'

'Then you are in a bad way! You don't think you really love him, you don't want his baby, *and* you don't want to give him up!'

'I should never had told him about the baby.'

'Then why did you?'

'Oh, why does anyone ever tell anything? Things slip out and then that's it. You can't un-say them. Maybe I wanted to test him, to find out how he'd react – whether he'd be horrified and just see it as an inconvenience for himself, or whether he'd be more concerned for me. How could I know he'd think it was the best thing that had ever happened to him? I didn't even know till after *I* was pregnant that he and his wife had wanted children and she couldn't have any. He says now that he was more cut up than she was when they found out.'

'And are you quite sure you don't want the child?'

'I'm as sure as I can be. Once you have it, it's there for life, isn't it? I look round at the unsmiling women in the street, pushing their prams, babies crying. I see them in the supermarket, harassed with trying to get all the shopping in, and the child whining about sweets he's not supposed to have. I think of nappies and broken nights and myself going under beneath the self-centred claims of husband and child, and maybe having more children. And it terrifies me – I haven't even begun to live my life yet.'

'And can't you have an abortion without telling him until afterwards and hope he'll understand?'

'Mmmm, that's probably what I'll end up doing. But I know he won't understand.'

'How can you know that? If he really loves you, he must understand.'

'He'll see me as a murderess.'

'Oh, come off it, Anna, what sort of freak is he?'

'Well, I will be killing his child, won't I?'

'His child!' Steffi snorted with exasperation, giving particular emphasis to the first word. 'It's *you*, not him, that's having it. It's your belly that will get fat with it and you who'll be stuck with it when it's born. He's had his affair with you in spite of having a wife already, so how do you know he won't have more affairs while you're at home nursing the baby? And, anyway, it's just ridiculous to talk about it as a *child*; it's nothing like a child, yet. It's just a little cluster of cells which even in the ordinary course of nature might never come to anything.'

'But I won't be leaving it to the "ordinary course of nature" if I have an abortion, will I?'

'For Christ's sake, Anna, you're beginning to sound like the Pope. If basically you really agree with all the pro-life cant, I don't see that you've got a problem. You just get married and live happily ever after. And if you're lucky your baby will be the sort that doesn't cry much and your husband will take a turn changing its nappy.'

'I wish it was as simple as you make out. The point is, I won't live happily ever after, whatever I do.'

'No, well, I don't suppose anyone does, except in fairy tales.'

They sat on a little longer, talking more generally. Steffi, for all her irritation at what she considered mistaken scruple, could see that Anna was deeply distressed and in need of help. Steffi was not sure what help to give but, before they separated, she had told her the telephone number of another student acquaintance who had had an abortion earlier in the year. Anna, for her part, did feel some slight relief from having put what she had been thinking into words for somebody else to hear, even though doing so imposed on what she said a finite form which was absent from the endlessly shifting nature of her thoughts. She had been unable to tell Steffi what it was that really made her hate the idea of losing Günter because she shrank from admitting that he was the first person in her whole life who had made her feel loved.

Perhaps in unconscious compensation for this omission, she had overstated the case against an abortion. Her views, in fact, were much the same as Steffi's, and she was not concerned with the morality of abortions in general but with the particular effect which her undertaking one would have on Günter's attitude. While speaking to Steffi, she had become increasingly certain that he would condemn her, even though they had not really discussed the matter. Wistfully, she wondered if she were perhaps attributing sterner opinions to him than he actually possessed.

He came home that evening in cheerful mood. He was pleased to hear that Anna had been to a lecture, he had thought for a long time that she was not sufficiently serious about her studies. 'But why should it matter to you whether I get a degree or not?' she asked. 'Don't you want me to stay at home and look after the baby?'

'You'll have to take a semester off, I expect, but then I'm sure we can get someone to mind it for a few hours each day while you go to lectures and the library.'

'I can't believe it's ever going to happen.'

'What?'

'Anything – the baby, my degree. I wonder sometimes if this whole affair with you is even real.'

'And do you think of it as a pleasant dream or a nightmare?'

'Mostly pleasant, but I have a feeling that at any moment it may all turn into a nightmare, and I'll never wake up from it.'

'Poor Anna! I wish I could exorcize all your fears. Why can't you just trust me to make you happy?'

'Did you make Catherine happy?'

'She always said she was happy.'

'And did it have anything to do with you?'

'I thought it did once, but not any more.'

'I sometimes think nobody ever makes anyone else happy: happiness is something you're born with – or, more likely, you're born without it. Though God knows other people can make you *un*happy.'

'I hope I will never do that to you.'

'Not intentionally anyway; I'm sure you wouldn't want to make me unhappy.'

'But you still feel you'll be unhappy in the end. How can you be so sure that happiness is not for you?'

'It's not an easy thing to be happy in the world we live in.'

'Oh, is it only global problems that weigh you down?' Günter smiled. 'I think I can cope with them.'

'By pretending they don't exist?'

'By keeping them in their place.'

'I hate a world where everything is supposed to have its place.'

'Hate it or love it, you've got to live in it. Take your place in it beside me and let me protect you from all the nasty things outside.'

'Oh, how I wish that you could!'

'And what makes you think that I can't?'

'Oh, just some awful certainty inside me that things will never go right.' Günter was dismayed by the force of Anna's depression but still he took it to be a passing mood, if not one that could be conquered by argument alone. He drew her towards him and stroked her hair. 'You must learn to be happier with yourself,' he said, 'learn to love yourself a little more and then perhaps you won't hate the world so much.' Anna sighed. It was good to feel him so close but the shadow cast by the decision she would soon have to make did not go away.

The next two days brought so much work for Günter that he was obliged to stay at the office until well past seven o'clock. Anna, having been reassured the previous Friday that such lateness was not likely to mean that he had left her, greeted him with resentment rather than relief when he eventually did arrive home. 'I don't seem to be seeing any more of you awake that I did before you moved in,' she complained.

'I'm sorry, love,' he replied placidly, 'it's not always

like this.'

'Just nearly always?'

'I'll make it up to you at the weekend.'

'Oh, are we to go joy-riding again?'

'We can do whatever you wish.'

'Well, in that case you mightn't see me at all. I've half arranged to go down to Hesse for the last day of the state election campaign. And then I'll probably stay on for the special meeting of the party executive on Monday.'

'I didn't know you were on the executive.'

'Every party member is automatically on the executive. We mean what we say about our party being the only genuinely democratic one.'

'It must make coming to a decision more difficult.'

'It may take a bit longer, but it's much more satisfactory in the end.'

'And where will you stay?'

'Good lord, I've no idea. I'll take a sleeping-bag and sleep on somebody's floor, probably.'

'I could drive you down and we could stay in a hotel.'

'Thank you, but that wouldn't suit me at all.'

There was little Günter could do. He suspected that Anna's sudden impulse to go away on her own sprang more from a desire to punish him for coming home late than from any perception of her duty as a fully-paid-up 'Green' to add another voice to her party's democratic deliberations. He therefore made an effort to get home early on the Thursday and, remembering the success of their improvised meal at the weekend, brought pizza and Chianti in with him. But she was not there. He looked in vain for a note telling him where she was and then sat down to his pizza alone. At least drinking a bottle of Chianti by himself was less injurious to his liver than drinking most of a bottle of whisky had been.

When he had eaten, he changed into slacks and a sweater and settled down in an armchair with the remains of the wine. He was still trying to decide whether to watch a television documentary on the church in Poland or to start reading an old John Le Carré which he had found among Anna's books, when the door opened and she came in. 'Oh,' she said, sounding surprised. 'You're very early. I've brought some friends with me.' A girl and four young men followed her into the room. The girl had naturally blonde hair, cropped short at the back and falling in a heavy fringe over her face. It was her only striking feature and her clothes, like Anna's, appeared to have been chosen to attract as little notice as possible. The boys were all extremely tall, dressed with a sedate casualness that seemed to say they had no need of mere sartorial protest. Günter was glad that he was no longer wearing his office suit but still felt awkward about meeting them. They seemed, however, not to share his embarrassment and after giving him a perfunctory 'Hi', they settled themselves on the remaining chairs and the floor as though he were not there at all.

The conversation dwelt at first on the election in Hesse. A couple of the group had been in Frankfurt the week before canvassing and had come back impressed by the breadth of the Greens' support. 'It's fantastic,' said one. 'Housewives are coming to us in droves. I stood outside a hairdresser's shop in a dull little suburb and half the women coming out, their hair all stiff with lacquer, took my leaflets and wished me well.'

'My great-aunt is going to vote Green,' said another. 'She says the economic miracle didn't make anyone any happier, just greedy and discontented.'

'An awful lot of people are mad about the airport extension. Even those who don't get excited about nuclear reactors springing up near where they live hate the noise of aeroplanes all day. They've admired us for protesting and risking arrest – perhaps in a couple of years they'll be joining us in fact, not just in spirit.'

The boy sitting next to Günter was offering him a cigarette. 'Thank you, I don't smoke,' he said. He toyed with the idea of remarking on the inconsistency of agitating about industrial pollution while voluntarily poisoning your own body, but thought better of it. It was enough that he should look old enough to be the father of everyone present without behaving as though he was as well. The boy, however, seemed to have been so well brought up that he was now hesitating before lighting his own cigarette. 'Maybe,' he said, 'it's not really fair to Anna. After all, she has to sleep here.' The possibility that Günter might also be sleeping there suddenly occurring to him, he added, 'Have you known Anna long?'

The question took Günter by surprise. Had Anna, he wondered, been as secretive about him as he had been about her? He did not know what to answer. 'Actually we're engaged to be married' sounded absurdly old-fashioned and, moreover, inappropriate to a man still married to another woman. But how else could he put it? The word 'boyfriend' would stick in his throat and he lacked the panache to say simply, 'We are lovers'. As he struggled to find a reply, light dawned on his companion. 'You're not the man she mentioned, are you? The one who picked up the pieces when Wolfgang ditched her?'

'You could put it like that, yes.'

'Gosh, somehow I'd pictured you altogether different.'

Günter had no wish for the boy to elaborate. He turned his head to the other side of the room, to where Anna was sitting. Talk had moved to the Middle East. The massacre in the Palestinian camps in West Beirut the previous week had shocked them all. Anna, her voice full of emotion, was recounting a report she had read of how some of the victims' bodies had been mutilated.

'It makes me sick,' said the young man next to her. He was well built and very fair and when he spoke he showed a mouth full of dazzling, perfect teeth. Günter thought, however, that there was something arrogant, verging on the cruel, about the set of his jaw. 'The Jews,' he went on, 'only suffered twelve years under the Nazis but they've been making the Palestinians suffer for decades.'

'Israeli imperialism wouldn't be possible without American support,' said another. 'Why do they go on pouring in arms and money?'

'Because of the power of the Jews in the States, of course. There are more of them there than there are in the whole of Israel.'

'But there aren't that many as a proportion of the population as a whole.'

'Yeah, but they have the power, they have the best-organized lobby and as soon as anyone objects to supporting Zionism, they throw up their hands and squeal about anti-Semitism.'

Günter was feeling increasingly uncomfortable. Had such opinions been uttered by any of his own contemporaries, he would already have spoken up, but the sense that he still had of being an elderly intruder held him back.

'It wasn't actually the Israelis, though, was it,' said Anna, 'who did the killing in Sabra and Chatilla?'

'Oh no, not personally. They were stationed all of fifty metres away. And yet we're supposed to believe that they heard and saw nothing – or only what was compatible with a military exercise to flush out guerrillas. The people who lived round Auschwitz and Bergen-Belsen haven't been permitted such conveniently partial sight and hearing.'

Günter could restrain himself no longer. 'I find your analogy very distasteful,' he began, wishing that he did not sound so pompous. 'A vicious civil war has been raging in Lebanon and the Palestinians and Phalangists have been perpetrating atrocities upon each other on a tit-for-tat basis for years. Perhaps the Israeli units could have stopped the massacre and perhaps they couldn't – it's not for us to say. But you must not forget the outcry there has been in Israel itself – the people there are quite as shocked as you are.'

'Are they? Well, I suppose *some* are, just as there were *some* Germans who didn't like the Nazis. But they're not numerous enough to make Begin or Sharon resign, are they? And for all the shock-horror noises from Reagan, he's not going to stop supplying his protégé with the means to continue oppressing and terrorizing its neighbours, is he?'

'The parallel you draw between Israel and the Nazis is most offensive. There's no doubt that what happened in West Beirut is very shocking, but there is equally no question of its being genocide, nor indeed of the Israelis being directly responsible.'

'Ha! The Christian militias have all been trained and encouraged by Israel, and their commanders are personal friends of Sharon. Moreover, if it hadn't been for the Israeli invasion, they wouldn't have been able to go into the camps like they did in the first place. I hope you're not going to say you approved of the invasion as well?'

'Not altogether, no. But I understand how peculiarly anxious Israel must be about the security of its frontiers and I believe that we, as Germans, have to take some responsibility for that sense of insecurity which Jews, anywhere, may feel. It was us, after all, who made the world such a deadly place for them and it's reasonable that they want to make the haven they have now found as safe as possible.'

'The Germans were hardly unique in their anti-Semitism.'

'But they were unique in the thoroughness of their persecution.'

'And this uniqueness means that just because we're German we have to be blind to everything that is wrong with the State of Israel?'

'I think it ill becomes us to shout about it, yes.'

'And so you don't care at all about truth or objectivity or being fair to the Palestinians?'

'Quite frankly, I doubt that Germans are even capable of objectivity where Jews are concerned. It will take many, many more years for the sins of my parents' generation to be erased.'

'I think that argument stinks! Don't kid yourself that you are doing the Jews – or anyone else – any service by being so mealy-mouthed. To refuse ever to say a bad word about a Jew *on principle* is just an inverted form of the old anti-Semitism. When you deny Jews the right to be judged by the same standards as everyone else, you set them apart with your blanket approval just as surely as if you put yellow armbands on them again. But it fits in well enough with the hypocrisy that you find everywhere in this bloody country. Making money is the only thing that really matters and it's very convenient to excuse opting out of politics and tough decisions with pious references to the sins – as you sentimentally call them – of our fathers. I say it's time we took control of our own destiny again and made our own foreign policy; it's time we stopped all this American arse-licking and thought twice about the humbug we call our free democracy.'

'Our present freedom is not to be sneezed at.'

'No? Well, tell me what it really amounts to, then. The privilege to be the first to be blown up because we have the most American rockets pointed at Russia on our soil? That's certainly a freedom that's worth having!'

'We can't help our geography and we can't undo our history, but at least the balance of power in Europe has kept the peace here for nearly forty years.'

'It's a lousy sort of peace.'

'But better than any sort of war, surely?'

'Fear of war shouldn't make cowards of us to the extent that we do not even try to make a proper peace with the other Germans.'

'And do you suppose that the Russians would let them make peace with us, even if they wanted to?'

'Oh, you're going to bash the Russians as well, now, are you? I can't even be bothered arguing if it means having to listen to how naughty the Communists are – I get enough of that from my father.' The sneer as he said this made Günter shudder but he decided to say no more. He found a youthful flirtation with Communism, however misguided, easier to tolerate than the sort of militant anti-Zionism which bordered on anti-Semitism. But how he wished they would go away! As long as they remained, he felt obliged to sit there; to announce that he was going to bed would, he imagined, draw attention to his relationship with Anna in a way which might embarrass her. He toyed with the idea of saying that he was going home – Catherine was away and he could, if necessary, make some excuse, privately to Anna as she saw him out, about needing to fetch something. But then he recalled her distraught state the previous Friday when his lateness made her think he had deserted her: might she not fear the same now, if he suddenly left at nearly midnight? No, he would have to sit on and hope that the party would soon break up of its own accord. The talk returned to specifically 'green' problems. *They* all knew that, sooner rather than later, people would have to stop driving cars and go by bus or bicycle, but how could the idea be sold to the average German, who loved his car more tenderly than his wife, let alone to the thousands whose livelihood depended on car manufacture? Günter could no longer keep awake. Aware that his eyes were closing and that he had no power to stop them, his last conscious thought was a prayer that he might not snore.

The noise attendant upon people standing up and taking their leave woke him, but nobody took much notice. Only the amiable boy who had refrained from smoking passed him the compliment of saying that it had been nice meeting him. When they had gone, Anna stretched and said, 'God, I'm tired. I wish I could have gone to sleep, too.'

'Why didn't you send them home earlier, then?'

'Well, one doesn't, does one? Is that the way you and Catherine used to treat invited guests?'

'We were not above giving gentle hints, when it got past our bedtime, certainly.'

'And what is your bedtime?'

'I like to be in bed by about eleven during the week – don't forget how early I have to get up, or how hard I have to work.'

Günter had spoken with perfect good humour, but Anna was incensed.

'Christ! I hope you don't expect me to sympathize with you for having to work so hard. Because I promise you I won't. 'If you work hard it's because you want to and because you enjoy the satisfaction of earning more and more money, far more in fact than is decent, and certainly more than anyone is worth.'

'Now you're exaggerating again. It's a sign you need to

get some sleep. Come on, let's go to bed.'

'I won't have you take that tone with me!'

'What tone?'

'That "come on now, little girl, I know better" tone. I'm sick of you dismissing my opinions as mere childish silliness.'

'Do I do that?'

'Don't pretend that you don't know that you do! You even had to lecture my friends on their foolish misconceptions this evening, though you more than met your match in Holger.'

'Oh, his name's Holger, is it? Well I must say that's a good old Germanic name for a clean-cut Aryan lad. He would have gone far in the Hitler Youth.'

'How dare you say that?'

'Dare? It doesn't take any daring at all. I may spend too much time at work and too little time attending political meetings, but I still have enough energy left to form an opinion about the Holgers of this world – and so far the courage to voice it.'

'Just because he didn't let you have it all your own way when you were arguing doesn't mean that you're entitled to slander him. His views are a hell of a lot clearer and sounder than yours will ever be.'

'They probably are clearer but they're far from being sounder. People like him terrify me. They're so sure they're right and so full of contempt for anyone who disagrees with them. I just hope they never get any real power. And for that reason it's to be hoped that your party continues to attract their support, since as Greens they really aren't all that likely to do much harm. You'll be lucky to scrape your five per cent.'

'Oh, you really are letting me have it, now, aren't you? I don't know how you can have kept quiet for so long about what you really think.'

Günter, seeing too late that Anna was on the verge of tears, realized that he had gone too far. Her defence of the detestable Holger had provoked him to extend his criticism of the person to Greens in general. 'I'm sorry,' he said, inadequately. 'We're both overtired. I can't help it if I love you more than I like your friends.'

'I wish I knew just what you meant by loving me.'

'Then you would know more than most people – even the mistresses of great poets – usually know.'

'You say it so often that I sometimes think it's yourself you're trying to convince, not me.'

'And you don't say it at all.'

'Don't I?' Anna became defensive. 'Perhaps that's because I think it should go without saying.'

'And *is* your love for me of the kind which "goes without saying"?'

'I'm just not used to people wanting me to tell them I love them.'

Günter laughed. 'There's nothing unusual in that. Old-fashioned romantics might even say that true love only comes to anyone once in a lifetime. In fact, I rather think it's a rule that applies to me.'

He looked at her so tenderly that, in spite of herself, she was touched. Rationally, she might want to dismiss what he had said as sentimental nonsense, but the part of her which for so long had been deprived of affection could not help but respond. She moved towards him and they embraced. Later, in bed, Günter said quietly, 'But you still have not said it.'

'I love you,' she said, and he had to be satisfied.

Ten

Catherine's refusal to discuss her future, indeed to talk at all intimately about her own concerns, suggested to Joyce that she had perhaps been premature in inviting Peter and Jennifer to offer their comfort and advice. She should have left Catherine to herself for a bit longer, while indirectly, with a bit of old-fashioned maternal spoiling, reassuring her daughter that she was among the people who loved her most. The day after her improvised dinner party she permitted Catherine to help her with the dishes but kept the conversation on strictly neutral themes. Catherine was content to talk about the pros and cons of dishwashing-machines and the number of neighbours whose houses had been broken into in the last few months, although the absence of any intrinsic interest to herself in such topics increased the impression she had been gaining that she was only biding her time and no longer properly belonged in these surroundings.

The dishes finished, they sat down to the inevitable cup of tea. 'Can I do any shopping for you?' asked Catherine.

'No, thank you, dear, I got in plenty yesterday and we didn't eat all the chicken. Are you going for a walk again?'

'Perhaps, but it rather looks as though it will rain.'

'The weather forecast said it would,' said Tom. 'I think I'll go to mass in the car.'

'May I come with you?' Catherine did not know what

had put such an idea into her head; she usually only visited churches to admire their architecture.

'If you like.' Tom showed neither surprise nor enthusiasm. 'But we'll have to be leaving in a minute or two.'

As she saw them to the door Joyce said, 'Well, you really are breaking out in fresh places.'

'If it does me no good, it'll do me no harm,' said Catherine, lightly, and they left.

Mr Quinn's parish church was, for the older members of the congregation, a shockingly modern structure. About a dozen years before it had replaced a much loved sub-Gothic building which, with its brightly painted altar and abundant plaster statues, had in their view been a 'proper' place for prayer. The new church, purpose-built to accommodate the reformed liturgy and owing more than a little of the inspiration for its design to Liverpool's Metropolitan Cathedral, was altogether too austere: why, with its whitewashed walls and Stations of the Cross stripped of all pictorial content, you might almost think you were among Protestants! Catherine, who had years ago occasionally accompanied her father to church, was impressed by the change: she appreciated the new airiness and welcomed the removal of a particularly lurid statue of the Sacred Heart with its chest slit open to disclose a Valentine-card heart. In those days Tom's devotions had been very irregular: if, for example, they had chanced to be out walking and passed a church where people were just arriving for mass, he would suggest they go in too and afterwards she would be dimly aware that his spirits were oppressed. Once or twice he had commented on the 'nice little families' seated near them and she detected a wistfulness in his voice, a regret that his own little family, though nice enough in its way, never went to church together.

The improvement Catherine perceived in the architecture was not, she felt, matched by any improvement in the liturgy. True, she had not, as a teenager, been able to recognize in the priest's mumble much of the Latin she was learning at school, but still she recognized a solemnity in the proceedings and caught something like a dramatic climax at the moment of consecration. Now, the remoteness had been replaced by a language that was altogether too casual, and full participation was called for. The service began with a procession from the back of the church: the priest followed by two middle-aged women with trays in their hands bearing the Communion wafers and the water and wine. At the altar they made perfunctory little bows and then took their places in the front pews. The priest greeted his congregation: 'Good morning, everyone!' he said. To Catherine's astonishment the elderly men and women around her – there were not all that many, this being a weekday service – replied, like well-drilled infant-schoolchildren: 'Good morning, Father!' The mass then proceeded at a smart pace, a droning dialogue between priest and congregation devoid of all expression. When the time came to receive communion, Catherine found that she was the only person to remain seated.

'I hadn't realized quite how much it had all changed,' she remarked as, barely twenty minutes after arriving, they drove away.

'Oh, yes, it's changed all right. Not everyone likes it, of course, but I think all that Latin really must have put a lot of people off.'

Mrs Quinn, exercising a quite extraordinary degree of forbearance, refrained from making any comment when they got home. Indeed, as the day wore on, Catherine began almost to regret her mother's self-control, for the effort required of so outspoken a woman not to mention the subject which occupied all her thoughts, while at the same time contriving to appear far more sweet-natured than usual, was so great that the atmosphere became quite charged with the current of her restraint. It was not that Catherine felt at all ready to embark upon the long and detailed analysis of career opportunities which the rest of the family seemed to consider so pressing. She told herself that it had still only been a week since Günter dropped his bombshell. Perhaps, she thought, she might have been spared the tension which now existed between her own wish to do nothing and their wish to sort everything out as quickly as possible, if she had been more obviously devastated by what had happened. Had she collapsed under the strain, then her family's solicitude would have been channelled into first restoring her equilibrium and she would, quite naturally, have been permitted a long period of recuperation. She smiled at the possibility of feigning a nervous breakdown: of course it would not do. She felt too desolate to jump at the chance of belatedly catching up on all the opportunities she had forfeited by her early marriage, but not desolated enough even to pretend to have lost her grip altogether.

The next couple of days seemed to pass very slowly. She helped a little in the house, browsed among Tom's books, watched television and tolerated, from her mother, a good deal of harking back to the successes of her childhood and youth. Joyce had a phenomenal memory for detail and Catherine marvelled at how clearly she remembered events which had happened twenty, or even thirty, years before. Letters which she had written home from a school camp at the age of ten, school magazines full of her contributions, glowing reports, all were fetched to corroborate the picture her mother was painting of a brilliant little girl. If there had been anyone else listening to it all, Catherine would have been embarrassed; as it was, she was more inclined to sadness, for what came through all the reminiscences even more strongly than pride in a clever child was the treasured memory of a very close relationship. Until meeting Günter, Catherine had shared everything with her mother and, unlike herself, Joyce had never forgotten in the intervening years how precious their closeness had been.

At lunch on Thursday, Tom said, 'I was thinking of going to see Gerard this afternoon.'

'Gerard?' queried Catherine.

'The brother who's a priest out in Crosby. Your father's got very thick with his family over the last year or two.'

'I thought perhaps you might like to come with me.'

Tom turned to Catherine. 'It'd be a change from sitting around here all day.'

'Oh yes,' said Joyce, drily, 'they say a change is as good as a rest.'

'Well I'm certainly not in need of a rest,' said Catherine. 'I've hardly slept so much in my life as I have these last few days. But, yes, I would like to come with you. Will you be coming, too?' She asked the question more to show Joyce that she had no wish to exclude her than out of any conviction that she was likely to join them.

'Of course not. As they wouldn't speak to me fifty years ago, they're hardly going to want to now.'

'Now there I think you're wrong. Gerard would be very pleased to see you. I've often thought it would be nice to invite him over some time. He's been a bit lost on his free day since Agnes died.'

'Really, Tom, what do you take me for? But if Catherine is curious about her long-lost relations, then by all means take her with you. It's time I got on with the ironing, anyway.'

Catherine was not altogether happy leaving her mother but the appeal the outing had for her was very great. While she was growing up, an almost total silence had been maintained about her father's relatives. As always, Joyce had set the tone: on the one hand she still nursed her slight at their rejection of her as a suitable wife for Tom and on the other she believed them all to be 'much too common' to mix with her own aspiring children. Nor was Tom very forthcoming: his childhood recollections, or at least the ones he chose to share with his own children, were few and tended to be of a very general nature – how many sweets you could buy for a penny, his first visit to a cinema, the Jesuits' way of enforcing discipline, and the hours of pleasure he had had reading 'penny dreadfuls'. At a time when the possibility of her own mother's dying constituted her worst nightmare, Catherine had tried to find out more about her father's feelings for his own mother. Had he really gone for years without seeing her? It appeared that he had. Catherine listened, in unbelieving horror, to his account – on a day when he was being unusually confidential – of how they had once bumped into each other in town, only to go their own ways again, after the first look of embarrassed recognition, without speaking. She had also pressed him to tell her more about growing up in such a big family, but his powers of description, which could be very vivid indeed when it came to less personal matters, invariably failed him, and he rarely went beyond saying they 'rubbed along all right, for after all they were not used to anything different'. Catherine was, therefore, fascinated by the fact of this reconciliation with his own so late in life and looked forward to meeting her new uncle with a pleasure made even sweeter by the expectation of being 'taken out of herself' for a while.

'You had better tell me at least the names of your brothers and sisters,' said Catherine, as soon as they were on their way. 'I shall feel silly knowing so little.'

'Will you? Oh, I know they say blood's thicker than water but I've never been quite sure myself. If you lose touch with your family for a long time, then when you do meet again, they really might as well be total strangers – and not even strangers you're sure to like.'

'But you must have cared a little, or you wouldn't have bothered to re-establish contact at all.'

'Oh, that! It was more a coincidence, really. There was a poor old lady I used to see at mass every Sunday who was crippled with arthritis, and I started giving her a lift. Well, of course, we got chatting and it turned out that her daughter had married one of my nephews. So then it got back to them that I'd returned to the fold and *they* got in touch with me. I get on quite well with Gerard – he's turned out very nice. He was scarcely more than a child when I left home, you know, and anyway he'd been at the seminary since he was twelve.'

Catherine found this explanation completely in accordance with her father's essential passiveness. It would indeed have been strange if he had exerted himself in the matter, but it was equally consistent that, once his brother had found him out, he should judge him favourably. 'You were a huge family, weren't you? How many are still in Liverpool?'

'Seven,' said Tom, with a mischievous grin. ' "Oh, yes, sir, we are seven." And to avoid any Wordsworthian confusion, I shall make it clear at once that three of us now lie in Anfield Cemetery. Of the other four, there's Gerard and myself, then a sister, Teresa – she can be a bit heavy-going – and another brother, Joe. He went into the police but he's retired now. They've none of them done too badly, really, all things considered. I think your mother pictures them all still crammed into a tiny terraced house with an outside toilet and no bathroom.'

'And haven't you told her that it's not like that?'

'No, I don't really talk about them at all to her. She's not interested, you know.'

'But if you find that you get on well with your brother, perhaps she would enjoy his company, too.'

'Yes, I've often thought that. But you saw how she reacted when I suggested having Gerard round. She can't forget how they treated her – treated us both, I suppose – when we got married.'

'But her own parents wouldn't have anything to do with her, either.'

'True, but then they left her all their money.'

'I don't think that money could ever compensate me for having been hurt and rejected.'

'No, but it's still nice to have, and it made a lot of difference to your mother. She'd had a very rough time, you know, before the war.'

Catherine felt that her father was letting her mother off too lightly. Personally, she could find nothing at all to be said, in a lonely world, for stubbornly resisting offers of friendship, even if they did come from those who had once inflicted pain. But there was no point pursuing the subject: Tom's generosity and her own delicacy put further criticism of Joyce out of the question. 'And have you told your brother that you're bringing me?' she asked.

'Yes, I phoned yesterday when you were at the shops. I didn't go into any details, of course, but I dropped a hint that you were over here for a long visit because, well, because your marriage is going through a bit of a difficult patch.'

'"Going through" implies you think it will survive in the end.'

'And I hope it will. You've both been happy together for so many years now that I don't like to think of you splitting up.'

'Günter was very bitter about me.'

'Bitter about you? I thought the problem was another woman?'

'Yes it is, but he seemed dissatisfied with me over and above that.' Catherine found herself, for the first time, attempting to reflect disinterestedly on what had happened. 'I can't decide whether he needs to convince himself that I was the wrong wife for him just to make his conscience easier about Anna, or whether he really does believe it.'

'People make the mistake of expecting perfect happiness in their marriages. And if it's easy for them to get divorced, then they make the even bigger mistake of supposing that they are more likely to find perfect happiness in a second marriage than they did in the first.'

'Then you think people should stick it out till death, whatever happens?'

'Oh, I wouldn't care to say anything quite as sweeping as that, but yes, it's true I can't see what is so very wrong in regarding as binding the only really solemn promise most of us ever make.'

They were nearly there. Father Quinn's church stood in a road not unlike the one in which his brother lived, though his parish contained both more Catholics and, among them, a more substantially respectable, well-to-do element than was now to be found in Childwall. He had been moved there ten years previously from Liverpool 8, where he had, in truth, felt more at home. But it was not in his nature to pine and he had, through hard work and the sweetness of his disposition, quickly won the affection of his new congregation. He had been genuinely pleased when Tom showed that he was willing to forget the past, since he had long reproached himself for failing to make any conciliatory gesture to his brother and his family once he was grown up enough to act independently. He knew that only a cowardly fear of his mother's reaction had prevented him from behaving in the proper Christian spirit. For old Mrs Quinn, God rest her soul, had never wavered in her conviction that Tom would burn in hell for letting his children grow up outside the Faith and Gerard had been quite inadequate to arguing against such certainty. Of course, she had remembered Tom in her daily prayers, but nothing short of the conversion of his wife and children would have induced her to speak to him again. After her death Gerard had continued to put off making the first move – he was always so busy and he feared a rebuff – until their common relation by marriage did it for them. Now they saw each other regularly and enjoyed the meetings for their own sake: there was more of real sympathy between them than between Gerard and the other members of the family.

Tom drove his car on to the drive in front of the presbytery, a double-fronted red-brick house, and before they had reached the door, his brother was on the step to meet them.

'Tom, it's good to see you. And you've brought Catherine. Well, I think that's splendid. Lovely to see you, my dear.' He shook hands warmly and led them into a large room at the back of the house which served the priests as both dining-room and parlour. There were only two armchairs, so they sat down at the great table in the centre, on high-backed leather-covered chairs. 'I'm afraid we're going to have to make our own tea,' he explained. 'Poor Miss Whelan was rushed off to hospital last week with acute appendicitis. The operation seems to have gone all right but of course it'll be a while before she's back.' He turned to Catherine. 'And how are you liking Liverpool? Is it good to be back?'

'Oh, yes, it always is.'

'You must find it a bit shabby and impoverished after Germany. There's no "economic miracle" here, though God knows we need one.'

'Do you know Germany at all?'

'I went there once – in 1960 to see the Passion Play in Oberammagau. I took a party from the parish – not this parish, you understand, I was in Liverpool 8 at the time. We had a grand holiday. Have you ever had a chance to go?'

'To the Passion Play? No, I'm afraid I haven't.' To please the priest, a note of regret, which she didn't feel, crept into her voice.

'You should try to go. It's an unforgettable experience. I brought a lot of slides back with me and gave talks about it for years. But of course we didn't just see the play, we had a jolly good holiday as well. The scenery was fantastic.' Father Quinn began to tell them, with mounting enthusiasm, about the trip: about the skill of the untrained actors and the reverential mood in the theatre; about the baroque churches and the hot rolls at breakfast-time; about the mountains and the women in their peasant costumes at mass. Catherine marvelled at his capacity to find so much to enjoy, even in the recollection of something which had happened more than twenty years ago.

'Goodness, it's nearly half-past four!' He jumped up as he spoke. 'You must have your tea!' He moved towards the door, not the one through which they had entered but the one in the far corner of the room which led directly into the kitchen.

'Can I help you?' asked Catherine, as though they had known each other for years.

'How nice of you to offer. I got the tray ready before you came but you're very welcome to follow me out.' Catherine did so. Tom remained seated: he had found something to read. The kitchen was large with fittings that had once been considered ultra-modern. The sink was full of dirty dishes, a pan on the stove contained the remains of a tin of vegetable soup. 'I think I've remembered everything. Perhaps you'd like to put out some biscuits from that tin over there, and I've bought a cake as well.' He opened a paper bag and took from it a bright pink and yellow chequered 'Battenberg'. 'Oh, good, the kettle's boiling.' Catherine noticed that he made the tea with great care, investing the business of warming the pot and measuring the spoonfuls with an almost sacramental importance. He appeared to read her thoughts and said, 'It's not at all nice to be without Miss Whelan but I confess I do enjoy making a good cup of tea. The good woman is inclined to make it rather weak. Everyone to his own taste, of course.'

Back in the dining-room the conversation passed to family matters. Catherine knew none of the people involved but listened all the same. Gerard spoke with affection about them all, including one great-nephew who was thought to be taking drugs. 'But you must find all this very boring,' he said at last. 'They're only names to you. Tell me about yourself.'

The suddenness of this request should have unnerved her but she found herself saying quite naturally, 'It's not a good time for me to do that, I'm afraid. I don't quite know where I am.'

'No, no, Tom put me in the picture about all *that*. But I didn't mean your personal affairs. Just tell me what you like doing.'

'I like cooking.' As she spoke, she realized what she must now do with a clarity that had been missing from her actions over the past ten days. 'I thought, actually, that you might like me to come and cook for you. Until your Miss Whelan has recovered.' Both men were completely taken aback, so she went on, 'You could surely do with someone to feed you properly and I am very much at a loose end just now. You would really be doing *me* a favour.'

'She does cook very well, Gerard,' said Tom, as though Catherine's qualifications were in question.

'I've no doubt she does, and I'm bowled over by such kindness. My sister Teresa said that she might consider making our Sunday dinner for us, but under no circumstances should I expect her to do any more. It's a funny life, you know, cooking for priests.'

'I don't see why it should be any different from cooking for anyone else. I think I'll enjoy it. My own thoughts are beginning to bore me to tears and it'll do me good to have something useful to do. Shall I come out tomorrow morning? I'll shop on the way.'

Catherine allowed no more argument and the matter was decided. Soon afterwards, it was time for them to go: Joyce would not appreciate their being later than usual. In the car, they were at first silent, and then Tom said, 'Have you thought what your mother's going to say to this?'

'I suppose she won't like it, but it'll be better for me than twiddling my thumbs all day.'

'She'll think you're lowering yourself.'

'What? How can it be lowering to do a good turn?'

'She'll think it lowering for *you* to stand in as a housekeeper.'

'Well, I can't help what she thinks. I'm surely old enough to make my own decision.'

'Oh, yes, there's no doubt about that. I'm just concerned that you'll be hurting her feelings. You'll have to break it to her very gently.'

'Of course, she expects that, at the very least, doesn't she?' Catherine was surprised by the degree of bitterness in her own voice. 'Why should we have to break it gently? You break the news of a sudden death or a car crash gently; all this amounts to is that I am choosing, for a couple of weeks, to do something which she – for reasons that do her no credit – would probably rather I didn't do.' While her words expressed exactly what she thought, she was conscious of their callousness. It was unreasonable of her mother to assume the right to order her life for her but by going her own way, even in something as trivial as helping out in the presbytery, she knew that she would, as her father said, be hurting Joyce's feelings. Her mother regarded all dissent as betrayal.

The front door opened as they drove up. Joyce was maintaining her good behaviour and welcomed them with a cordiality that Catherine found almost disarming. Tom disappeared upstairs to his racing results and Joyce poured her daughter's sherry. 'Now tell me all about your Uncle Gerard,' she said. 'I never get any gossip from your father.'

'I don't know that he's the sort of man who generates gossip, exactly. He looks quite young for his age – Daddy says he's sixty-five – and he talks a lot, but not at all scandalously. He told us about going to Oberammagau for the Passion Play in 1960.'

'How interesting for you.' With something like relief, Catherine heard the old sarcasm returning. 'And did you have a proper tea?'

'There was a cake and biscuits.'

'Home-made?'

'No, the housekeeper is in hospital with appendicitis.'

'Oh, dear, the poor man won't be used to fending for himself. I hate to think what your father would do if anything happened to me. I doubt he'd even be able to light the stove on his own.'

Catherine, reminded of Günter's resentment at her 'nannying' of him, said, 'Perhaps he's not as helpless as you like to think.'

'Like to think, indeed! I'm sure I'd have no objection to him being rather less helpless. I shouldn't at all mind a bit of help with the dishes or an occasional cup of tea in bed of a morning.'

'And does he know that?'

'What are you getting at?'

'Oh, I just thought that perhaps you give such a strong impression of independence yourself that it has never occurred to him that you'd actually like to be spoiled a bit from time to time.'

'Well! That really is the limit! I wish I knew what I had to do to get the same consideration from you that your father gets without even trying. You really think he can do no wrong, don't you?'

'Not necessarily. I just don't understand why you should think he can do no right.'

'So that's it – you think I'm to blame for ever finding fault with him.'

'Of course I don't think you're to blame – for anything. It's only that I never hear you giving him credit for being, well, for being what he is: a kind and very tolerant man. Do you realize that he never says – never even hints – a bad word about you?'

'Oh, that's very big of him, I must say. And apparently, from the way you talk, you think there are any number of nasty things he could say. Personally, though, I should have thought it was just a bit too easy being a saint if all that's required is to refrain from criticizing anyone. It's what people actually do that counts with me. And as far as your father is concerned, it's not the fact that he refuses to see any wrong in people, but the utter, deep-down selfishness of his own behaviour. Do you know that in all the years we've been married I've never once known him to put me – or even one of you children – before his own pleasure? He's taken the money for his books and his gambling and left me to find the money for the bills as best I could. And before the war, when there wasn't enough money coming in to pay even the most essential bills, he let me go out cleaning just to make ends meet. But he never went short of the things that mattered to him, and if by any chance he was able to sell more papers than usual or a winner came up at 50-1, he didn't let me have the extra money to pay off the grocer but used it to buy some bloody stupid present for Peter and Jennifer. And then of course they thought he was marvellous, whereas I was only the mean old crow who couldn't even find coppers for them to buy chocolate. He makes me sick with his moral superiority, but it makes me even sicker that you should fall for it.'

Joyce was by now very worked up indeed. Catherine, fearing that to remain silent would imply hostility, spoke thoughtlessly, responding to the substance of what her mother had said instead of to the passion behind it. 'But all that was nearly fifty years ago. Even if he was as feckless and selfish then as you say he was, might he not have changed for the better by now?'

'"Even if..." – you don't believe me, do you? You think I'm inventing horror stories of bad times long ago because I'm jealous of the way you idolize him. I sometimes wonder why I ever bothered to put myself out for any of you. I'd like to know whether he'd still strike you as so angelic if he'd had sole charge of you. You wouldn't have lived here, then, you know, and there certainly wouldn't have been any grammar school or university education. He'd have sent you all out to work at fifteen and while, of course, never letting a bad word about you pass his lips, he'd have relied on you to finance his betting.' Joyce started to cry. Catherine was horrified. Only once before had she seen her mother in tears: the day she announced finally that she wanted to marry Günter, there had been a hysterical outburst, dreadful while it lasted, but quickly over. At the wedding itself, Joyce had remained stoically dry-eyed. It crossed Catherine's mind that on both occasions she had been the cause, not only of the distress, but of the rare inability to control it. It was up to her, then, to offer comfort. She wanted to go to her mother, to put her arms round her, to tell her that she was mistaken, that what she had said in no way meant that she slighted what her mother had done for her, for all of them. But she was unable to get up from her chair. The assurances of her love which her mother so needed to hear would not come spontaneously and by forcing them out she would, she believed, deprive them of all conviction.

'Please don't cry,' she said at last, lamely, but Joyce continued to sob. 'Please. You know really how much we all care for you.'

Her mother stood up and Catherine saw the old will asserting itself again. 'I'm supposed to know that, am I? Well, I think you've got a bloody funny way of showing it.' She went out, leaving Catherine miserably aware of her own inadequacy.

It was not long before Tom came down. 'Goodness, are we indulging in pre-prandial drinks again?' He spoke with mock formality, putting 'pre-prandial', as it were, in inverted commas. 'It's going to be very hard having to go back to the real world when you leave us. I could get used to this.' He sat down with his whisky and began to recount the day's bad-luck story: this time he had narrowed the field to two potential winners, put his shirt on one and the other had romped home. Catherine endeavoured to look interested but her thoughts were with Joyce who, she imagined, would be busy in the kitchen, stifling the outward signs of her anger while inwardly raging more bitterly than ever at the injustices she was made to suffer, had always been made to suffer. She was sorry for her mother but aware that her sympathy was somehow hollow. She saw her father too clearly as a harmless, easy-going creature to accept that he could ever have inflicted lasting pain on so tough and self-confident a woman.

'If you two boozers have finished, the dinner is now ready.' Joyce appeared at the door, her eyes still red but otherwise apparently recovered. Tom, who never looked closely at his wife's face, noticed nothing but drained his glass and got up. As soon as they were seated at the table and she had served them with their braised steak and onion, Joyce said, with a brightness which Catherine felt must be forced, 'Peter rang up just before you got back. He was quite bursting with news. I thought at first that he must have been promoted to principal at least, but it turned out that it was something about Anthea that had got him so excited.' She paused, letting her words sink in.

'Is she having a baby?' Catherine guessed wildly.

'Don't be ridiculous. She's forty-seven.'

'Then what is it?'

'She has been accepted – and I hope you both appreciate what a very great distinction this is – as a marriage-guidance counsellor. To my shame I must confess that the honour of it all was initially lost upon me. I said all the wrong things, in fact, and even asked if she would get paid on a commission basis for the marriages she saved. Peter was very shocked. It is a purely honorary function – honorary and honourable.'

'And what sort of people will she be dealing with?' asked Tom.

'God alone knows. I shudder to think of the despair people would have to be driven to before they'd seek help from the likes of Anthea. But for their sake it's to be hoped she restores the marriages more successfully than she restored the old furniture.'

'I think I've read that they don't actually always even try to patch up the marriage – if they think both parties would be better free of it,' said Catherine.

'And how are they to know what's best for anyone? But, of course, if people are stupid enough to go to strangers for advice in the first place, then they deserve all they get.'

'Well, they don't force anyone to go to them and I've never heard of them doing any harm,' said Tom. 'A lot of people just need someone who'll listen to them.'

'I can't imagine Anthea listening in silence to anyone for very long and whatever she says is sure to be silly. But Peter impressed upon me that the interviews she had to go through were very rigorous indeed and only the best are taken. It was because the competition is so strong that they hadn't told us she was going in for it – they wanted to keep a possible failure to themselves. He even had the nerve to suggest that Catherine might *now* find it more useful than ever to go round for an intimate chat with her sister-in-law.'

'Oh dear,' said Catherine, 'I don't think I'd care for that at all.'

'Of course you wouldn't, and I wasted no time telling him so, but there's really no limit to his admiration for Anthea. It beats me what he sees in her, but then I never have understood what intelligent men see in stupid women.'

'Perhaps they feel more comfortable if they're not being challenged all the time.'

'And will Günter find his new girl less challenging?'

Catherine laughed. 'I very much doubt it. She'll be too busy working hard at her own self-fulfilment for him to get much peace. The irony is that although Günter belongs to perhaps the last generation of men who didn't see anything wrong with their wives giving up their careers in order to marry them – on the contrary, I think at the beginning he might even have felt guilty if he had not been *able* to support me – he is probably going to find it much harder to cope with Anna's emancipation than a boy of her own age would. Günter instinctively defers to women and when men defer to women who have been talked into believing that all they're after is making a slave of you, they're inclined to get their heads bitten off.'

'And you have never believed in the slavery to begin with?'

'I just don't think you can generalize. No two marriages are the same – it's certainly not at all like real slavery where you can say that the slave-owner, by definition, invariably owns the slave. Even apparent economic dependence doesn't necessarily mean that the woman is the inferior partner: there have always been plenty of women who look upon what their husbands earn as theirs to spend by right.'

Mrs Quinn look sceptical. 'I suppose being able to think so well of men does have its compensations and of course until Günter left you I would have said that one of them was your husband's gratitude.'

'Joyce, really!' Tom, who had had no interest in a theoretical discussion of marriage, now came to his daughter's support.

'It's all right, Daddy. Mum's point is a fair one. I'm beginning to realize, however, that gratitude is bad for you, both for the giver and the receiver.'

'Now there I don't agree. Of course giving has always been considered especially blessed, but I don't think myself that to be able to show gratitude properly is any less of a virtue.'

'All this abstract talk is a bit above my head.' Joyce made to clear the plates. 'I don't suppose, Tom, that you'd like to show your gratitude for another good meal by carrying some dishes into the kitchen?'

'Well, if that's what you want, dear, of course I'll carry them out.' Tom, looking bewildered, did not move, while Joyce, with a contemptuous little smile, piled all the plates on a tray and left the room. Tom turned to Catherine, 'Should I have taken the tray?' he asked. 'She's never said anything like that before.'

'She was proving a point,' said Catherine. 'And I don't think you really disappointed her.'

'Well naturally I hope I would never disappoint her. Do you think we're getting any afters?'

'Of course you're getting afters,' Joyce, returning to the room with an apple crumble, heard his question as she came in. 'Don't you always?'

'Yes, I suppose I do. You're very good to me, very good indeed.'

They ate in silence for a while and then Catherine decided to plunge for a quick announcement of her plan. She could hardly annoy her mother more than she had already. For a moment she considered what to call her father's brother. To start referring to another adult, at her age, as 'Uncle' seemed incongruous, but she felt that a bald 'Gerard' was also not yet quite appropriate. She rephrased what she wanted to say and avoided the problem. 'You know I mentioned the housekeeper had appendicitis?'

'Housekeeper?'

'In the presbytery. I told you when you asked what the tea was like.'

'Oh, her. Yes, I remember. What about her?'

'I've decided to go and help out a bit while she's in hospital.'

'You've what?'

'I'm going to go and cook for the two priests.'

'Now I know you've taken leave of your senses.' In spite of her words, Mrs Quinn was less shocked than Catherine had expected. Perhaps her distress before supper had been so exhausting that she had no more energy to argue.

'I think I need a breathing-space before I make up my mind what to do next and this'll give me something to do at the same time. I enjoy cooking.'

'Oh, yes, we know that well enough. It's what we sent you to Oxford for.'

In the kitchen afterwards, as they were starting the dishes, Catherine tentatively put a hand on her mother's shoulders. She wanted to say she was sorry if she had upset her and that her mother had no cause to feel bitter. But Joyce turned sharply away, shaking her off. 'Now, don't be going all sloppy on me,' she said. 'It won't wash. You've not been in the house a week yet and you've already had to find a way – and what a way! – of escaping from me.'

'Oh, mother, I'm not escaping from you. Don't be so touchy.'

'Oh, so I'm touchy now, am I? Well maybe I am a bit hurt that you've got to go and seek consolation for your broken heart peeling potatoes for a couple of strange men. You're hardly an advertisement for giving women higher education, are you? But, never mind, there's no point arguing about it.' And before Catherine had had time to work out her reply, Joyce had revived their old discussion on the usefulness of dishwashing-machines.

Eleven

Any hopes that Günter had that Anna would change her mind about going to Frankfurt were disappointed: she was still asleep when he left for work on Friday morning and when, later in the day, he tried repeatedly to phone her, there was no reply. He toyed with the idea of driving south after work on the off-chance of being able to find her but rejected it; not so much because he had no real clue where to begin his search as from fear that she would not be glad to see him. The possibility of a rebuff in front of those too-youthful friends, whose conversation had been so little to his taste, appalled him. By the time he was ready to leave the office, he was feeling extremely sorry for himself, for he could see nothing in his own behaviour to justify Anna's desertion of him for the whole weekend, the one time in the week when he could put himself entirely at her disposal.

On entering the flat he was struck by its utter cheerlessness. Perhaps he should have gone back to his own house but he feared Catherine's invisible presence; sitting among the elegant furnishings she had chosen he imagined he would soon be hearing her voice reminding him how she had judged the affair straight away to be 'an aberration'. But Anna's rooms were just as full of ghosts, and if the good taste and comfort of his old home epitomized everything he had given up, then the disorderly grubbiness of the flat most certainly underlined what he had taken on. Unable to concentrate properly even on the newspaper, he tried to find some release from fruitless introspection by cleaning the lavatory. It was high time someone tackled it and he had had experience of this particular chore during his national service. But doing it now only increased his resentment, though it was not, he insisted to himself, that he felt the task itself to be beneath him, but merely the fact that Anna had, apparently, never thought to do it at all. After working with petulant vigour for about a quarter of an hour he had little to show for his labours; there was a limit to what he could accomplish with a balding brush and a tiny remnant of scouring-powder. Anna, of course, rejected most patent cleaning products on account of the chemicals they contained, but tomorrow he would stock up with bleach and deodorizing rinses and to hell with the effect on the water table!

He fetched a beer and sat down to drink it, letting his eyes wander from the drab second-hand sofa and scattered newspapers to the posters adorning the walls. Absent-mindedly reading what was written upon them, he soon found in the crudeness of their messages a new source of irritation. Slogans which had, with Anna beside him, seemed to speak only of a laudable youthful longing to put the world to rights – stop the arms race! ban nuclear weapons! say NO to atomic power! save the forest! – began, the longer he looked at them, to infuriate him with their over-simplification, by what he saw as a wilful refusal to think through the consequences, in the unlikely event of such imperatives ever being obeyed. Would the world really be a better place if those countries where he felt most at home, the ones whose civilization he found most attractive, gave up their arms and left the bomb for the future in possession of the Libyans or Argentinians? And if saving the forest meant dismantling certain industries, then at what point did saving trees become less important than saving people's jobs? He was aware of the irony of such arguments going through his head at all since he had never had much active interest in contemporary politics: he and Catherine had shared a common-sense, undogmatic liberalism, an assumption – slightly arrogant and probably wrong – that there was a prevailing wisdom among thinking and influential people which ensured that society would continue to become ever more tolerant and humane. Only rarely had they commented on the news, for they were secure in the unanimous rightness of their reactions to it. They gave generously to famine and disaster appeals but turned off the television pictures of starving children; they shuddered when the United States started executing criminals again but found any actual discussion of the death penalty redundant; they favoured *détente* but fully understood why it couldn't, for the time being, quite work. Anna had shaken him out of such complacency and even infected him with a little of her own contempt for wishy-washy liberals, but she had not fully converted him to the green gospel, with the result that he was now, with neither wife nor mistress for company, thinking through in jejune terms issues which he had long regarded as too remote and implacable to be worth a busy man's consideration.

Ruefully he wondered if the upshot of his reflections would be a realization that he could not share Anna's views on anything. Certainly, as soon as they began to discuss specific issues, they tended to disagree; the charm of Anna's convictions lay more in the way she presented them than in their actual content. But charm there had been and it would not do to underestimate it. Sentimentally he recalled that first evening when, he was sure, her idealism and sympathy for his professional frustrations had beguiled him before he had the smallest inkling that she would invite him to bed. Should he not give her credit for the passion of her beliefs and stop quibbling about the *naïveté* of her solutions? After all, he had not fallen in love with her because she had all the right answers to the world's problems, but because her heart was so emphatically in the right place.

Fallen in love? He remembered with what sour disbelief Catherine had reacted to his assertion that it was love which bound him to Anna. But the affair, by showing him what exciting possibilities lay beyond suffocating common sense and decent restraint, *had* brought a new purpose to his life. Nevertheless, it was important to him that he should be able to see his love for Anna as something deep and enduring; above all he could not bear to think that he was merely putting a conventional romantic gloss on physical pleasure. For there was an element of puritanism in Günter which inclined him, deep down, to condemn infidelity on principle while finding his own – Catherine, he knew, would have been very scathing of such self-serving morality – less culpable if there were more than just sex to it. At the same time, another part of him felt slightly cheated to have missed out so completely on the more easy-going atmosphere of the last twenty years. His relations with Catherine had from the outset reflected this contradiction: having hoped initially that, as a native of the country which had invented the Swinging Sixties, she would liberate him from the hang-ups implicit in a conservative Bavarian upbringing, his disappointment, on finding that she was sexually even less experienced than himself, was mixed with relief that he was, after all, getting involved with a totally irreproachable girl. The sixties' revolution, however, had not altogether passed him by: he was almost ashamed of his residual straitlaced attitudes and his pre-marital chastity had remained a more closely guarded secret than the identity of many a public figure's mistress.

Significantly, it was Anna who had initiated their affair; the ambiguity of his perception of what was right inhibited him both from making the first move and from resisting when she did. For Günter, the intensity of Anna's love-making had been revelationary and he wondered if it was the very ferocity of the pleasure it gave him which made him now so eager to assert the non-physical side to their relationship. Perhaps he was wrong even to try and separate physical from non-physical. At least towards sex, Anna's attitude was a good deal more straightforward than his own: the pleasure she found in bed was unmarred by the pessimism and anxiety which clouded her view of life in general. Thinking such thoughts led him to want her with an urgency that caused him nearly to cry out in anger and frustration. What would he do if she left him? What could he do to keep her? He remembered her tears the previous week when he had been late coming home. Surely they had shown that she needed his love, that she was frightened of losing it? But for every occasion when she had sought reassurance that he cared for her, there had been several when she had striven to prove her independence. Günter was by no means insensitive to the Zeitgeist and even if it would never have occurred to him spontaneously that women were getting a raw deal from society, he was soon convinced when other people put the case for greater equality. Catherine had made it easy for him to escape charges of male chauvinism by being both so self-confident – it would take a brave man to look down upon *her* – and by insisting that she wanted to stay at home and look after him. Anna was so much younger, so much less sure of herself, that it was only natural she should worry he was going to take her over. Probably her going down to Hesse had been no more than a way of proving to herself that she was still her own woman. Somewhat comforted, he got another beer and switched on the television.

    Since the news came on at almost hourly intervals throughout the evening, it was not long before he was hearing the pundits' predictions of the election. They were all agreed that the Greens would poll more than five per cent and would therefore be sending representatives to the next Landtag. There followed an interview with a party spokesman, an untidy man of about thirty-eight, who appeared to have spent his life ever since the student unrest of the late sixties in a state of continual agitation. He spoke fluently and shirked none of the interviewer's questions, but still he made Günter uncomfortable, with his open shirt and tennis shoes, his five o'clock shadow and unkempt hair. Why couldn't he dress like everyone else? He wasn't even that young any more. And in all that he said Günter was aware of the same dogmatic refusal to concede any ground to his opponents which had upset him in Holger. Of course, the big parties did not agree with each other much either, but you knew all the same that they had a certain respect for consensus, whereas these wild new men wanted to push their programme through at any price, even through they did only have the support of a small fraction of the electorate.

Günter crossly switched channels and caught the opening credits of an old Ingmar Bergman film, by an odd chance one which he had seen with Catherine in Munich during the first summer of their acquaintance. He recalled how, when he had first suggested they go to see it, she had replied that she thought Bergman overrated, personally she found his films tedious and pretentious. Her outspokenness in those days had startled him, since it seemed out of character in the demure young girl whose perfect manners precluded open disagreement with the company she was in. He had argued with her about Bergman's merits and, her German not then being quite up to putting her own case adequately, it had ended with her giving way gracefully and going to the cinema. Afterwards (having had time to work out the vocabulary) she had commented devastatingly on what they had seen and forced Günter to agree with her, thus setting the pattern for years of deferring to her superior taste. To see the film again now would, he feared, almost certainly be to see it through her eyes, and was the last thing he wanted to do. The third channel was in the middle of a cheerful documentary about Crohn's disease, one of a highly successful series about conditions for which doctors as yet have found no cure, and Günter, despairing of ever being entertained by television, switched off and decided to go for a walk.

The nearby streets, full of turn-of-the-century terraces, were too near the motorway to be fashionable and were mostly sublet to Turkish 'guest-workers' and students, whose ancient cars – rainbow-coloured Beetles and little Citroëns adorned with Donald Duck stickers – were densely parked on the once elegantly broad pavements. During the week commuter traffic was so heavy that the residents were campaigning for restrictions upon it and many had festooned their windows with huge black flags bearing a white death's head, to draw attention to the poisoned, lead-filled air. The roads were quiet now and a light breeze was blowing, but the flags accorded well with Günter's spirits. Solitary introspection was new to him and he wished he could break free from the tyranny of his own thoughts, the recurring self-pity, the dull sense of futility which hung about his marriage, and the growing fear that his affair with Anna was moving out of his control. But stronger than anything else was the desire simply to have Anna there, near to him, to be able to touch her and hold her and prevent her ever going away again.

Anna, meanwhile, was sitting in a Frankfurt Weinstube, one of a noisy group at a large round table. She had not, in the course of the day, given much thought to Günter. Their journey – five of them packed tightly into Holger's Ford Taunus – had begun inauspiciously when they were stopped by the motorway police. The officers were hardly older than themselves but for all the informality of their dress – they were bare-headed and wore light-brown slacks with matching shirt and the most discreet of green shoulder flashes, nothing to polish anywhere – Anna regarded them with all the hostility she felt men in uniform deserved. When Holger's papers proved to be quite in order, she sensed their disappointment, though all they said was that even if the twenty-year-old car had been considered roadworthy at its last compulsory inspection, it was still unwise to overload it with so many hefty young men on a two-hundred-kilometre drive. With more than a touch of condescension in his voice, Holger thanked them for their solicitude and drove off. After arriving in Frankfurt they had spent the afternoon distributing broadsheets until it was time to go to a CDU rally. There they had waved their banners and heckled, much to their own satisfaction if not to the significant discomposure of the main speaker, a tough, sharp-tongued man who was not easily put off from his standard speech, as long as his loudspeakers were in good working order. And now they were relaxing, together with some local activists whom Holger had got to know on his previous visit. The conversation had turned to the sort of people who were likely to be voting for them.

'There was an old man in the shopping precinct this afternoon who promised to vote Green,' said Anna, 'and I thought he was so creepy, I nearly told him we'd rather not have his vote.'

'Don't you know yet it's quantity, not quality, that counts at an election?' snapped Holger.

'But you didn't hear him talk. I'm sure he was an old Nazi. He went on and on almost mystically about the forests and the German oak tree and how as a young man – that would have been in the thirties – he'd gone on nudist holidays to the North Sea coast. And then he looked at me in this slimy way and asked me what *I* thought about nudism.'

'So what did you answer?'

'I said I'd never given it a thought and that he was mistaken if he supposed the Greens wanted to sentimentalize nature; our aims are much too serious and our policies too radical for that.'

'Hear, hear!' A woman in her late thirties with a solemn, unmade-up face, who had been introduced as Iris Schmitz, the local secretary, suddenly smiled her approval at Anna.

'Of course, he didn't like the word "radical" at all and complained there were quite enough radicals in Frankfurt already – and a fine mess they'd made of the city, too. I felt I had to agree with him about some of the new building development, but then he started on about it all being the fault of *Jewish* speculators.' Anna gave a little shudder of distaste at the recollection.

'Well, as Heine said, Jews are like the people they live among, only more so.'

'And what's that supposed to mean?'

'Simple. Your old man has seen his home town growing more and more hideous and inhuman and he also knows that some people – a few actually *are* Jews, though of course we're too nice to say so – have made millions out of it all. So he decides something must be done. He can't help blaming "radicals and Jews", because they were the bogeymen of his formative years. But what he is actually condemning is unfettered free-enterprise capitalism and it's the dissatisfaction of people like him that we have to exploit – if, that is, we really want to win power – because they're the ones who are really representative of German society. We might not care to admit it, but there aren't actually all that many voters who share our own brand of academic post-radicalism. Unless we widen our appeal we'll end up as a mere bolt-hole for cranks and potty minorities – very therapeutic for the cranks, of course, but not what I'd call adult politics.'

'I still don't like to think of us harvesting an anti-Semitic vote. Surely the whole point about forming a new party is that it should be different. We don't just do what is politically opportune, we do what is right.'

'And how are you ever going to be able to do what is right if you turn away all the voters who don't conform to your own high ideals of moral purity? The opinion polls say that we'll clear the five-per-cent hurdle on Sunday and that'll give us a few seats, but if we're ever going to *do* anything, we'll need a majority.'

'It strikes me,' said Iris, whose expression had become increasingly hostile as Holger had got into his stride, 'that your pragmatism is both premature and misplaced. Three years ago, we didn't even exist as a party and "clearing the five-per-cent hurdle" as you put it is a very respectable achievement for the time being. But what worries me more is that if your rush to sell out every principle we stand for in order to win a few more votes from petit-bourgeois malcontents were to catch on, then we would forfeit once and for all our chance to bring about genuine, useful change. All the big parties have made the mistake of ignoring completely how society itself has altered and there's a huge gulf already on an awful lot of issues between what is said in manifestos and what ordinary people think. We don't want to "exploit" – to use your nasty capitalist word again – purely negative dissatisfaction for our own ends; we want to articulate instead what so many voters really feel on subjects like atomic power, the environment, disarmament and sexual equality.'

Holger, never inclined to give way in an argument and particularly unwilling to be routed by this plain, schoolmarmy woman, hesitated for a moment before picking up her last point. 'Sexual equality? Surely you're not suggesting that *that's* a burning issue with your ordinary people? It's not just old-fashioned men who run a mile from putting too many women in power – most women don't like to be represented by their own sex, either.'

'Really? Well, there's a stag-bar assertion, if ever I heard one. I believe that the very reason why so many people are disillusioned with politics lies in its predominantly masculine nature. The very basis of party politics is competition, the need to win rules out solidarity with anyone not clearly on your side and real co-operation – I don't mean the sort of coalition-building that goes on because parties want to cling to power – doesn't exist. Politicians pride themselves on being objective, on understanding the facts and eliminating all emotion – in other words on deliberately excluding the feminine virtues which society so desperately needs.'

'I don't give a hoot for the feminine virtues when they're invoked by childless spinsters with a good job. Can't you see that they wither away as soon as you free your sisters from their traditional feminine role? It's easy to be sweet and gentle and emotional when all you have to cope with is a loving family, but put a woman out into the big bad world and she'll soon be as tough as any man. Or has it escaped your attention that all the women prime ministers we've had so far – Golda Meir, Indira Ghandi, Margaret Thatcher – have not only been as hard as nails personally, but have actually dragged their countries into bloody wars as well?'

'Now *you* are becoming emotional. And even though what you said was very silly, it's still a welcome sign in itself. It would be a good thing if more men took to expressing their views in a less inhibited way. But now it's time for me to be going, as I want to make an early start in the morning. There's a spare bed in my flat, if anyone wants to make use of it.'

Most of the party were still far from ready to turn in, however early the start next day, but Anna jumped at the chance to improve her acquaintance with this intriguing woman. She collected her overnight bag and they set off together.

'I hope your bag's not too heavy. It'll take us about a quarter of an hour to walk. I try to use the car as little as possible these days.'

'Great. It's a lovely evening and I always travel light.'

Iris walked briskly and hardly spoke but when they had reached her apartment, she suggested they have some tea before going to bed. While she was occupied in the kitchen, Anna looked around the neat little living-room. With its white walls and black leather armchairs, it had a rather severe look and even the abundant bookshelves were tidily arranged. Only a collection of African masks and sculptures saved it from thorough-going old-maidishness.

'Is Holger a close friend?' Iris poured the tea and offered Anna a wafer-thin almond biscuit.

'Not really. He's the one with the car who drove us down this morning.'

'I don't know what boys like him are doing with us. You were quite right when you said that the point of forming a new party in the first place was to be *different*.'

'He's a very good debater.'

'Oh, yes, I can see that he's good at winning arguments – but it's hearts that we should be out trying to win. People may be momentarily impressed by forensic skills but they don't necessarily vote for the cleverest debaters. They tend to think that smooth talking and insincerity go hand in hand. And they're probably right. There's a terrible cynicism in politics today and I don't just mean the obvious cynicism of ambitious men out to win power, but the cynicism of voters who increasingly think that all the parties are the same anyway and all politicians equally untrustworthy – that they're all out for what they can get. If too many people like Holger are allowed to put our case for us, then I'm afraid we'll just be lumped together with all the rest.'

'But isn't it in the nature of politics for good speakers to attract more attention that the idealists who are not so good at scoring debating points?'

'At the moment, yes, it is. And that is precisely what we have to change.'

'How?'

'By insisting that on every candidates' list there are at least equal numbers of women and men. Personally, I should like to see men removed altogether from the top places – they've had it their own way for far too long. When will people see that these dreary, dreary men with their identical dark suits and unobtrusive ties will be the ruin of us all? They like to pretend that they judge each issue on its merits, that they know the facts and won't be swayed by emotion, but where has it got us? What is the *fact* of atomic power, the *fact* of the neutron bomb, the *fact* of genetic engineering? The fact is that human life is being destroyed by their damned facts.'

'I'm with you all the way. But how do you get enough women interested in taking a really active role? I should say that nearly three-quarters of our membership in Bonn is male.'

'Oh, it'll take time, but we mustn't leave it too late to start or the Holger-types will have bagged all the important positions. But if there are a few of us willing to speak out, then I think there's a good chance – even against a male majority – of forcing through statutes laying down parity for all our committees and so on. One good thing about our membership is that most of the men are at least benignly disposed towards us and they'd feel uneasy voting against anything which laid them open to a charge of prejudice.'

'I'm not myself awfully good at making speeches in public.'

'Then you must practise till you are. You were able to hold your own this evening – the size of the audience shouldn't make such a difference to you. But for goodness' sake make the most of your opportunity *now*. Women are at last starting to gain a little confidence in their own abilities and to see that they're cut out for more than just ironing shirts and changing nappies. When I was your age the pull of convention was still very strong: a girl was made to feel that she shouldn't ever be quite as clever as a boy and, moreover, that there was something shameful about being left on the shelf. And what was the result? We all rushed into marriages – I did myself – that were destined to end, more often than not, in misery. But that won't happen to you. You know that it is absurd to spend your whole life in the shadow of some man. Don't you know in your heart that women are actually more capable than men; and, what is more important still, that we can do without men a lot more easily than they can do without us?'

'Gosh, do you really think that's true?' Anna, impressed from the outset by the woman's calm assurance, was elated at the opportunity of escape from her personal difficulties which these last words seemed to hold.

'Of course I do. I'm only surprised that the notion should surprise you.'

'Oh, I suppose I just don't feel I've been all that successful so far at going it alone.' Anna knew that she would soon have said so much that telling Iris everything would become inevitable. Before plunging into full disclosure she reflected, fleetingly, on how Iris might react. Would her indecision and dependence appear merely contemptible? It was a risk she felt she had to take, for even in the couple of hours since their first meeting, she had found too much to admire in Iris for her to continue the conversation on the dishonest assumption that she was indeed the sort of super-emancipated girl Iris took her for. 'Actually, I'm pretty heavily involved with a man right now.' She paused, waiting to see the effect of her words.

'I hope,' said Iris, pleasantly, 'that you don't think I disapprove of all contact with men on principle. Of course, it's possible to have an equal, mutually satisfying relationship.' A slight emphasis on the word 'possible' betrayed her scepticism.

'You'd be sure to disapprove of this relationship, though.'

'The question is whether you would think me wrong to disapprove. If you are so certain that *I* will disapprove, then I rather fear it means you disapprove of it yourself.'

'So I do, in a way. When I try to be objective about us, then I think, yes, he does just want to impose his attitudes upon me, and on pretty well everything, from politics to food and the way I dress. But the problem is that at the same time I get a very strong impression that it isn't his *intention* to dominate me at all, and I'm also sure that he really does love me.'

'Tell me more about him.' So Anna did. Her sense of Iris's sympathy was so strong that she took a lot of time describing the beginning of her affair with Günter before even mentioning that she was pregnant. In doing so, she felt that she was doing greater justice to the complexity of Günter's emotions, as well as her own, than had been possible in her confidence to Steffi, where the arguments for and against an abortion had impeded proper discussion of what had led to her becoming pregnant. She was harsh, though not, in her own view, unjust, in her comments about Catherine, whom she depicted as a superficial materialistic parasite, a woman who readily accepted the role of housekeeper to her husband in order to enjoy a higher standard of living than she was prepared to earn for herself. Had Catherine not ignored Günter's emotional needs; had she not been, both in and out of bed, such a chilly creature; then, Anna was convinced, he would not have been attracted to herself. In describing Catherine she half-consciously attributed to her many of the characteristics she associated with her own mother: in all externals the perfect wife while at the core a hollow egoist.

'And was it Günter who told you all about his wife's shortcomings?' Iris's feminism, more deeply rooted than Anna's, instinctively sought to mitigate such severe criticism of another woman.

'Oh, no, hardly at all. He's terribly loyal. But I got to know her for myself when I visited with Wolfgang and then I can guess a lot, just from the way he behaves, especially, you know, about sex.'

'I am beginning to think you are in love with him, after all.'

'No,' said Anna, surprised at the certainly in her own voice. 'No, I'm not in love. I was in love with Wolfgang, in the abominable, degrading way that girls in cheap novelettes are in love, and I would have let him walk over me, too – anything to stop him ditching me. But Günter's too ... too good a man for me to let you assume that he's just some stereotype male chauvinist who, after taking up with a young girl because at his age it flatters the ego, only wants to turn her into a submissive little wife and mother.'

'Your anxiety to make me think well of him does you credit, but I'm afraid it obscures the main issue, which is whether you want to be his submissive wife.'

'No, no, of course I don't, even if I thought it was possible for me to be the way he wants me to be. But I'm still terrified of finishing with him, and even more terrified of telling him that I intend to get rid of his baby.'

'Are you physically afraid of his anger?'

'Perhaps, just a tiny bit, though he's really a very gentle man – as far as I can tell. I've only seen him cross once and that was with Holger – actually you and he probably have much the same opinion about poor Holger.' Anna smiled.

'Well, then, leaving aside the rather odd inference that the child conceived inside *you* is *his* before it is *yours*, why are you terrified? If he is as decent as you say he is, then surely you can put it to him that you are just unable to commit yourself to him in the way you believe he wishes and perhaps deserves. You might even suggest that you continue to be, as the film stars used to say, "just good friends".'

Anna shook her head. 'You don't understand,' she said, sadly aware that she was about to cry. 'He's the first person who's ever told me he loves me and it just seems terrible to me to reject his love.' As the tears began to roll down Anna's cheeks Iris moved over to her and put her arm round her. Anna found the gesture inexpressibly comforting and, relaxing, cried even more. When at last her sobs had subsided Iris fetched a bottle of wine and poured them each a glass before saying, 'You're right to grieve. It is terrible to reject love but it's even more terrible to deceive someone who really loves you. And you would be doing precisely that if you let him go on thinking that you love him the way he loves you. It would be a false and foolish foundation for a marriage and I know, I really *know*, that you would regret it – and he would too.'

Anna's relief at hearing at last what she wanted to hear was overpowering. It did her good to hear Iris emphasize that, though everyone should be allowed to make mistakes, nobody should have to live for ever with the consequences. Anna had a vital role to play in changing society: for the first time this century there really was a chance of breaking the hold of the military-industrial complex and of creating a world which was fit to bring babies into. 'For far too long,' Iris insisted, 'women have accepted what men have told them about their function in life: that the best they could do for coming generations was to stay at home and take care of their children. Their feminine strengths – their compassion, their refusal to see the wood for the trees, to insist on looking at how grand policies affect individuals – all these things, they were told, would find their best outlet within the home. Poppycock! By restricting a woman's influence to the domestic hearth, men actually showed how little importance they attached to the qualities to be found there. Kindness and unselfishness, they implied, could usefully contribute to family harmony but they weren't much good to you if you wanted to make your way in the world. And the proof that these female virtues, to which everyone paid lip service, were held in contempt is the way all the little boys, who had been so carefully nurtured by their utterly devoted mothers, grew up. For of course they didn't grow into kind and generous men, but into soldiers and policemen, into ruthless politicians and greedy businessmen, who, while carrying a sentimental image of a perfect mama in their breast, lived their adult lives according to the law of the jungle. If they are ever to be of any use, the feminine virtues have to be asserted *outside* the home; and when we put society to rights, life inside the home can be left to take care of itself.'

They talked well into the night, leaving Anna's own little cares far behind as they expanded upon a brave new world in which women would break out of the prison of their fitted kitchens and challenge the deadly arrogance of male power. Unlike men, women had the imagination to believe that utopian yearnings properly belonged to politics; indeed that they *must* belong to politics if catastrophe were to be averted. Anna spoke quite as much as Iris and was aware that, the longer they talked, the more confident she became. At last she had found someone who listened to what she had to say with interest and respect but without the ultimately insulting – because patronizing – admiration of Günter.

When she went to bed she felt more in control of her life than she had ever felt before; Iris had given her the courage not just to make up her own mind on big issues – she had been doing that already – but the courage to sort out smaller, personal issues in a way that was consistent with her general philosophy. Tomorrow she would phone Günter and tell him gently that she would be staying away a few days longer but that if he was very anxious to see her, he might come down on Sunday. She would make it clear, however, that she would not have a lot of time to spare him; he must take her as he found her.

Twelve

Catherine and her mother kept up their inconsequential chatter at breakfast on Friday and it was not until Catherine asked for advice on where to do her shopping that Mrs Quinn showed any sign of the irritation she felt.

'I've no idea where you should go,' she said. 'We have a couple of nice little shops right here and the meat at Tesco in Allerton Road is also very good. But I'm sure that wouldn't do you with your high-falutin ideas. And, any way, you'll surely want to find somewhere local to depend on in Crosby.'

'Yes, that's true. I just thought that if you knew of anywhere particularly good, I might take everything with me for day one. What about the fish shop?'

'Oh, yes, that's all right – with all the Jews round here it'd have to be.'

'And would you like me to bring anything back for you?'

'No, I wouldn't. If you insist on going, I'd rather you went as quickly as possible.'

Catherine decided to say no more. She packed her case and was ready to leave before her mother had finished washing up the breakfast dishes. 'I'll phone you this evening to let you know how I've got on.' Catherine kissed her mother's cheek.

'There's no need,' said Joyce. 'You won't have anything much to say – unless, of course, you want to bore me with the menus you've presented. I hope they appreciate *"haute cuisine"* – Catholic priests are a rough lot, you know.'

Catherine went into the sitting-room to say goodbye to Tom, who was already engrossed in the day's racing-card. 'It's good of you to go and help them out,' he said, squeezing her hand. 'Give Gerard my regards and tell him I'll come over one day next week. You can bake me one of your Dundee cakes.'

Catherine drove away and did not stop at the local shops, having decided that it would be disagreeable to have to exchange small talk with any neighbour who remembered her. In Crosby, she parked at a promising row of shops and looked critically into each window before going inside. The fish seemed good, though the selection was limited; she bought hake and, from a cooling-cabinet in the corner the sort of very thick cream which, to her chagrin, was unobtainable in Germany. The vegetable shop also proved satisfactory; the weekend supplies were just being unpacked and by opening her purchases with two expensive pineapples and giving a sympathetic ear to the assistant's complaints about the deliveryman's thoughtlessness, she managed to ensure that she was served only the freshest produce. It was now past ten o'clock and time to go to the presbytery. It would be sensible anyway to check the store cupboard there before buying anything else. As she drove off with her car full of good things to eat and smelling agreeably of fresh fruit, she felt her spirits rise. Years ago she had read a remark by a prolific writer of the sort of romantic fiction which was beneath her contempt, to the effect that buying groceries gives many women a *frisson* akin to sexual pleasure. Of course it was nonsense but such memorable nonsense that she rarely did a big shop without its occurring to her. Poor Günter, she thought, it was no wonder he'd gone off in search of some real sex!

Father Quinn was delighted to see her and insisted on making her a cup of tea before she did anything else. 'It really is marvellous of you to come – I thought you might have had second thoughts. But you must promise that you won't stay a moment longer than you really want to. I see you've done some shopping already, and I haven't even given you any money. No, don't be silly – here's fifty pounds to be going on with and I think Miss Whelan keeps petty cash in the bottom drawer of the sideboard in her own little parlour – I'll show you round later. Are you going back to your mother's each day?'

'Not if there's a bed here for me – it's a long drive and I might as well watch television here as there.'

'Oh, d'you like the telly? I would have thought you were too intellectual to bother with it.'

'Not at all. Actually, the more mindless the entertainment it offers, the more I like it. German TV is awful because it's always trying to inform and educate.'

'All serious people over there, are they? A bit like some of my parishioners round here – nothing but BBC2 and the Third Programme. But they're good souls, very good.'

'Do you like your main meal at midday or in the evening?' Catherine felt that it was time to be getting down to work.

'At midday – that is, at about one o'clock if you can manage it. And then we have a light supper, or high tea or whatever you call it at 6.30, so that we're free for evening meetings.'

'And is there anything that either of you can't stand?'

'Oh, no, we can't afford to be faddy. It'll be a treat to have anything hot, especially if it hasn't come out of a tin.'

'I've bought fish for one meal today – is that all right?'

'Oh, yes, fish on a Friday – old habits die hard, don't they? And they say it all started because the Spanish fishermen were going out of business. Personally I could never see the difference between a *nice* bit of fish and a piece of meat. On the other hand, if you want to know the real meaning of mortifying the flesh, then you should have tasted my mother's salt fish on Good Friday. That *was* diabolical!'

Father Quinn seemed about to pour himself another

cup of tea and settle down to more reminiscences but the phone rang. 'I'm afraid I'll have to go out,' he apologized, after he had answered it. 'And I haven't shown you where anything is yet. I hope you'll manage all right. Take a message if anyone phones – I'll be back before one and Father Michael should be in any time now, he only went over to the school.'

It did not take Catherine long to find the essentials in the kitchen, which had been left in immaculate order by Miss Whelan and only superficially disarranged by the two men, who appeared to have been living on tinned soup (economically heated in the same pan) and bread and cheese. The vegetables were simmering for a leek-and-tomato soup and she was already rolling out the pastry for an apple pie when the door opened and a young, slightly-built man with an abundant beard poked his head round it.

'Hullo,' he said, 'you must be Catherine. I'm Michael.'

'The curate? How do you do?' It struck Catherine as absurd that the cure of souls should be in such extremely youthful hands.

'And are you really going to cook for us? We won't know ourselves.' The young man spoke with assurance in the flat tones of native Merseyside.

'You sound as though you've been starved.'

'Nyer, not really. Just a joke. It's about time we got used to looking after ourselves, anyhow. It's not easy to find housekeepers these days and Monica won't last for ever.'

'Monica?'

'The boss calls her "Miss Whelan", but it seems daft to me not to be on first-name terms with the people you live with.'

'And does the lady herself have a preference?'

'Ooooh! "The lady herself" – aren't you posh? Yeah, well, I suppose she's all for being formal too. I can't get her to drop the "Father" with me, even. To be honest, I don't call her Monica to her face very often, either – she reminds me of my grandmother.'

He smiled suddenly in an engagingly open way and she laughed. 'I hope I don't run that risk, at least.'

'Ha! Funny grannie you'd make. Have you even got any children?'

'No.'

'But you are married?'

'Oh, yes, we just never had any children.'

'And did I hear your husband was a German? I read somewhere that the Germans don't have babies any more. It's always a struggle deciding between the second car and the kid, and the car usually wins.'

'I've read that sort of thing too, though I've never actually met anyone myself who remained childless for purely financial reasons. It certainly wasn't that in our case. I just couldn't have children.'

'Ah, I am sorry, honest. I didn't mean to put my foot in it.'

'It's quite all right. I got over any regrets I may have had long ago.' Catherine remembered how bitterly Günter had reproached her for not seeming more upset about her infertility. She wondered if he would have had his affair with Anna just the same if they had had children. She believed that probably he would; indeed she doubted whether anything could have prevented the whole stupid business from happening, once Anna had wanted it. Her instinct told her that the first impulse had not come from Günter.

'We haven't had a real apple pie for ages. Just between ourselves, I think Monica's getting a bit past it. She's still a dab hand with the tin-opener, though, and we get through a fair bit of Marks and Sparks meat pie. What are you making now?' Catherine was creaming butter and sugar.

'Almond tarts – I found some ground almonds in the cupboard and as their death date is next week, I thought I should use them at once. And you'll be wanting something to eat with your tea.'

'Smashing. I can hardly wait. I'll take any telephone calls that come now and leave you in peace. And thanks a lot for coming.'

Catherine found herself reflecting, in a matronly sort of way, that he seemed a 'nice boy' and, following on from this, that he had chosen 'a funny sort of life'. But then she checked herself: surely she should be one of the last people to share the fashionable distrust of celibacy. Moreover, most of his life must be spent in a highly satisfying way: close to a large circle of people who knew and respected him; particularly admired, no doubt, for becoming a priest at all at a time of falling vocations; and with ample opportunity to help others through the ordinary crises of life. During an earnest phase in her teens, Catherine had started to keep a commonplace book and in it she had given special prominence to a sentence from *Our Mutual Friend:* 'Nobody is useless in this world who lightens the burden of it for anybody else.' The words still rang true to her, even if she had become too outwardly cautious and sceptical to be caught saying anything which implied she gave much thought to such profound matters as the purpose of life. Sadly, she could not tell herself with any conviction that she had succeeded personally in 'lightening anybody's burden'. There had been a time, perhaps, when she had made Günter's life very comfortable, but it could hardly be said that he had ever had any significant burdens to bear. He had never been ill, never been without money or a job, never been without a certain recognition that his work was worthwhile and that he did it well. Nor was she convinced that, had she refused to marry him, he would – even briefly – have been inconsolable. She had entered his life just when he had begun to think it was time to get married and, finding her generally acceptable, he had asked her to be his wife. She would not flatter herself that there had been any more to it than that.

So what of Anna? How had she managed to sweep him off his feet? How much credence should she give to his assertions that he was in love, that the feeling which bound him to Anna transcended anything he had ever felt before? Catherine was very tempted to put it all down to 'sex', though she hated herself for thinking in what she regarded as vulgar clichés. Her mother might say, 'Men are all the same – vain and only interested in one thing,' but she prided herself on never reducing her fellow human beings to such crude simplicities. Günter, she was starting to realize, might have changed over the years and have been looking for something which she could not give and which Anna could. But for the sake of his – and her – self-respect, she hoped it was more than mere sensuality.

Catherine's first meal was received with rapturous praise and it pleased her particularly for seeming utterly genuine. There was nothing in what the two men said that smacked of formal compliments or resembled the sort of pretty speeches made by the affected wives of Günter's more senior colleagues, which Catherine had often said would probably have been the same had she served them beans on toast. So, she thought, as long as she remained in the presbytery she could be sure she was doing something useful. With renewed energy she set about her weekend baking, finished the shopping, and prepared pancakes stuffed with spinach and cream cheese for supper. The afternoon flew by and it was eight o'clock before she had time to sit down in the little housekeeper's room with her own meal and the newspaper she had bought that morning. She had also bought wine, though not without some misgiving. There was no sign in the kitchen of any alcohol (the house did not possess a cellar), and of the sparkling Waterford crystal decanters on the sideboard, one was empty and the other less than a quarter full of sweet sherry. Should she not adopt the same abstemiousness herself? In the end she decided that she deserved her customary glass or two of wine and that it would be hypocritical to forgo it. After all, she was only helping out as a friend, not seeking a job for life.

She had cleared away her dishes and was looking at the television programme when, towards half-past nine, there was a tap on the door and Gerard came in. 'Hello,' he said, 'mind if I join you? The disco's started at the youth club and I think I'm more than a little superfluous.'

'I'm delighted to see you. It's not every day one acquires a new uncle. What can I offer you? Some wine?'

'Oooh, are we celebrating then?'

'Well, I suppose we could say meeting after all these years is worth a toast, but actually I just usually do drink wine in the evening. I hope you don't think it very sinful.'

'Sinful? Of course not. Why, St Paul himself told Timothy that he should take a little wine on account of his stomach.'

Catherine fetched a glass for him. 'Would you like anything to eat? Some cheese?'

'Oh, dear me, no. I've eaten more than enough for one day, thank you. And very delicious it was, too. Every bite of it.'

There was a moment's silence. Catherine felt suddenly awkward, for the first time inhibited by the dog-collar Gerard was wearing. She feared a *tête à tête* which might touch on her own religious beliefs – or lack of them. And yet at the same time she was aware of an urge to say something to please him, rather as she had wanted long ago to please her father by appearing to enjoy their irregular attendance at mass. And once, when she was about fourteen and they were studying the Reformation at school, their history mistress had set an unusual piece of homework: to write a transcript of what might have been said had Luther met Pope Leo X in a television debate. Catherine had written fluently from a precociously early age but what surprised her teacher this time was the force with which she put the Pope's case; proof, it seemed, of an extraordinary imaginative leap since their lessons had dealt largely with the validity of Luther's criticism. Catherine showed her father her exercise book after she had duly received her A+, but although he congratulated her on the mark, he shook his head at the sophistries which she had attributed to Leo and muttered something about what a good Jesuit she would have made. Much later, when she was already at Oxford and they had strayed on to the subject of religion, she told him she had sometimes thought of converting to Catholicism.

Her father answered that he had suspected as much, but he was glad it hadn't happened – doing 'the right thing for the wrong reason', he added, should always be strenuously avoided. Catherine understood his meaning and even agreed with him, but still she had puzzled, from her father's point of view, at such a lack of proselytizing zeal.

'Did you phone home? To your mother, I mean?' Gerard's question broke in upon Catherine's thoughts and she found, stupidly, that she was surprised it had nothing to do with them.

'No, not yet. Why do you ask?'

'Why not? I'm sure they'll want to know how you're getting on.'

'They'll hardly be in suspense – if there's one thing they both have complete confidence in, then it's my ability to cook.' Catherine was sorry to hear a sour note in her own voice.

'Well, now, I didn't mean that I really thought they'd be waiting by the phone, all agog to hear whether you'd burnt the spuds! It's none of my business, of course, but your dad did say enough for me to understand that you're having a bit of a rough time just now and so it occurred to me that he and your mother would probably be more than usually anxious to know how you're bearing up.'

The temptation to talk was very great. For all the affection which her family had shown her, there had been powerful constraints upon confiding in them. She had come nearest, on their way out to Crosby the previous day, to discussing with her father what had really gone wrong with her marriage, but Tom was both too bland and too uninterested in detail for her to feel their talk would lead anywhere. As for her mother, the obstacles to candour there were greater still, since everything Catherine said was reinterpreted by Joyce against the background of her long-felt hostility to Günter and her hopelessly idealized image of her favourite daughter. Catherine had no idea whether the man sitting on the other side of the tiled fireplace would turn out to be the confidant she needed but she knew that she required very little encouragement to find out.

'I'm bearing up very well,' she said, refilling their glasses. 'It's done me good to come here and be busy. I don't know about the devil making work for idle hands, but he certainly fills idle heads with very tedious thoughts. My mother meant well, I know, but by insisting that I took things easy all the time, she made sure that I dwelt solely on my own miserable self.'

'And is that such a bad thing?'

'Of course. It's not even as though I find myself very interesting any more. Before all this happened, you see, I had settled into a very comfortable rut and believed that I'd put soul-searching and solipsism behind me – that I'd grown out of such silliness. And then Günter decides to leave me and I find that I'm devastated, but not quite in the way you'd expect. The awful thing is that I'm not so much upset at losing him as worried that the fact of his going makes a complete nonsense of my life. This seems a terribly self-centred view and I would like to be able to shake myself out of it. I don't want to be the most important thing in my own life, but just now I find it very difficult to focus on anything else.'

'What a very stern moralist you are! Not at all how I'd have expected Tom's daughter to turn out. He was always a very happy-go-lucky sort of chap.'

'But he has come back to the Church.'

'Yes, and thank God for that. But it's not got much to do with morality, you know – more the fear of death. Our generation and type of Catholic, even if we don't talk about it any more, still believe, deep-down, in hell – and naturally we don't want to go there.'

'But will he want to escape hell if that's where all his family – his wife and children – are?'

'Oh, how literal-minded you Protestants are! He doesn't suppose for one moment that nice people like you will be damned.'

'Why do you call me a Protestant?'

'It's what I thought you were. Aren't you?'

'No, I'm not anything. That's hardly unusual but I sometimes think that it is unusual never to have been anything. We grew up in an extraordinary religious vacuum, without even token attendance at Sunday School or membership of the brownies. It's true Daddy took me to mass occasionally, but he never encouraged me to enquire about the Catholic faith, and my mother is bitterly anti-Catholic without having any more time for a religion of her own. And as I'm a very rational person, there could be no question of me seeing the light on my own. Indeed I don't particularly want to, though I sometimes feel a certain spiritual loneliness. I take George Eliot's view that there is no God but we must be good, while envying the insouciance of what Myers is supposed to have replied – that there is a God, but we don't have to be good.'

'I should be the last person to talk anyone out of trying to be "good", but I do think that the effort increases enormously in value if it springs from faith in God. Without Him, man becomes so small and insignificant.'

'Perhaps that's the point: man is small and insignificant. And instead of creating a God to give ourselves some reflected importance, we should strive to obtain the fortitude necessary to face up to our own irrelevance.'

'And is it fortitude that you think you need to cope with your husband's behaviour?'

'Mainly, yes. You see, I'm not short of sympathy and in fact I'd probably get a lot more if I gave people the chance. But I'm really too proud to want it – I find it distasteful to be regarded as a mere victim, as the weak creature who was ditched because something better came along. I don't even believe this wretched girl is "something better".'

'Do you know her well?'

'Quite well. She came to our house fairly often at one time – she was Günter's cousin's girlfriend. I'm afraid I thought her a bit pathetic: she seemed to find life a terrible burden and she was potty about the cousin, who treated her like dirt.'

'Then Günter may have felt sorry for her? Not, of course, that anything can excuse him.'

'Can't it? That's something else that bothers me. I find it very difficult not to blame him – not so much for falling for her but for failing to check the affair before it went too far. And yet at the same time I hate myself for being so censorious. What right have I, when I don't even believe that marriages are made in heaven, to begrudge him the happiness he claims to have found?'

'Goodness me, you really are amazingly fair to the man. Too fair, I should say. I wouldn't treat him so gently if I had the opportunity to tell him a thing or two.'

'Ah, but you're wrong. I haven't been at all fair to him. For while the outside world has been congratulating him on his super wife, he has really been longing for someone with qualities I not only don't possess, but resolutely refuse to acquire. It may seem admirable in me to try to see his point of view, but my impartiality is only possible because I am such a cold person, and for some time now Günter has desperately needed a wife whose emotions aren't so magnificently under control.'

'You're much too hard on yourself. Even if it's true that he needed a wife whose emotional make-up is so different from yours, then it must be said that no man has the right to expect his wife to be made to measure, and especially not like some made-to-measure suits from expensive tailors who will do all the necessary alterations if the customer's waistline changes.'

'In principle I agree with you, but as far as sorting out my own problem goes, I don't think I should let it concern me unduly whether Günter has behaved wrongly or not. It's for me to decide only whether my own actions have been right or wrong.'

'The need to decide between right and wrong throughout life makes good theology.'

'Theology without God?'

'If you don't mind me saying so, I think you sophisticated people – oddly enough – are rather prone to foisting upon God the sort of nursery image which we simpler souls have successfully outgrown. And that is what makes it so hard for you to believe in Him.'

Catherine smiled and nodded but thought it better not to say anything. Her preoccupation with right and wrong had probably made this kind man think her nearer to God than she was. After they had sat in silence for a few moments she asked only if he would like more wine.

'No, thank you, dear. I must be off. I still have a couple of letters to write. But I hope there'll be time for lots more chats while you're here. I don't meet people like you – let alone ones I'm related to – very often.' At the door he squeezed her shoulders and kissed her lightly on the forehead. 'Good night,' he said, 'and God bless.'

Thirteen

Anna woke on Saturday with an extraordinary sense of wellbeing. The austere cleanliness of Iris's flat pleased her; in surroundings such as these she could feel at home in a way that had eluded her, not only amid the relative luxury of her parents' house, but even in the consciously protesting squalor of her own lodgings. The home-made müsli which Iris offered her for breakfast was delicious and she ate with gusto. There was a novelty for her in enjoying food and a bonus in the knowledge that this müsli was also ideologically sound. Before they left to set up their information table in a suburban shopping-centre, she asked Iris if she might phone Günter. As she dialled she felt her heart beating faster. Her friendly little speech was all prepared but she was not quite sure that she would be able to remain firm if he persisted in pleading with her to change her plans. But there was no reply; after a restless night Günter was washing his hair under the shower and did not hear the ringing. She put the receiver down relieved that there had been no unpleasantness, but also disappointed at being thwarted in this first attempt to bring greater tidiness into her affairs. At midday she tried again but he was out and when her third attempt in the late afternoon also failed, she began to think that he could not be really interested in hearing from her at all, and decided that she was under no further obligation to get in touch that day. The evening, in any case, promised to be more than interesting enough to put Günter out of her mind: she was to join what Iris called her 'female caucus' at a vegetarian restaurant.

Günter, however, was far from having lost interest in hearing from her, though the fierce longing for her physical presence was increasingly mixed with anger at the thoughtless manner of her absence. He had gone to bed bitterly disappointed that there had been no word from her; it had always been *his* practice, when away from home on business, to telephone Catherine last thing each night. He remembered with a growing sense of injustice how ready Anna was to reproach him for any lack of consideration which she perceived in his behaviour; why, she had not even fully accepted that it was sometimes necessary for him to work late. On the other hand, his harmless desire to see her in a pretty frock was taken as a sinister attack upon her right to self-determination! How differently he would have reacted had she made him a present, say, of a sweater; however hideous, he would have worn it happily as a token of their love. But there was no equality in sexual relationships, he thought, and, as far as he was concerned, the inferior partner seemed always to be himself. Catherine, once she'd got over her initial homesickness or whatever it was – perhaps the little flat in Frankfurt just depressed her – had taken control of everything. She knew, and expected him to agree, what was best and would brook no dissent on the way they furnished their home, entertained their friends, or spent their leisure. Sitting now over his crispbread and Nescafé, he would not deny that such efficient management had its compensations but equality, let alone male domination, it was not.

With the weekend stretching before him, Günter realized, with something close to panic, that he had no idea how he was going to spend it. He had hardly experienced anything like it before. Whenever Catherine had popped over to Liverpool for a few days, she had left him with a plentiful supply of food in a comfortable, tidy house and there had been, in addition, the pleasure that goes with solitude when it is exceptional: however harmonious a marriage may be, it is refreshing occasionally to have only oneself to please. But he was still at the stage of wanting Anna all the time; they had barely begun to get to know each other and, had she chosen to walk through the door that moment, he would willingly have shaken off his sense of pique in the joy of seeing her. Sadly he conceded that she must be less in need of his company then he of hers, or how could she have gone off like this, merely to offer her paltry bit of help to a derisory party in a state election of limited significance? Perhaps he really should have accompanied her and risked feeling out of place among her friends. After all, if they were to spend the rest of their lives together, he would eventually have to find a way of coming to terms with them. Alas, the likelihood of their ever settling down permanently seemed just now very remote indeed. But he must continue to believe in it, if only because the alternative was too terrible to contemplate.

Looking around the dingy little kitchen, he wondered to what extent his surroundings were increasing his gloom. Things might not seem quite so bad if he got out and surely, in any case, it was absurd to allow one spoilt weekend to sour his whole attitude to Anna. But where should he go? Solitary walks would hardly divert him from his own troubles: he needed company. Unfortunately, Catherine and he had always held their friends at a slight distance and there was nobody to whom he felt sufficiently close to call on uninvited. Yet even if there had been someone, he would be received still as Catherine's husband, with all the embarrassment which that involved, for not only had he kept his affair with Anna completely secret, but also his marriage had generally been regarded as secure as the Rock of Gibraltar. How different it was for Catherine! At the first sign of trouble she had scurried off home to Liverpool, back into the arms of those adoring relations who had always regarded him with such reserve, implicitly denying that he was good enough for their darling. Doubtless they would see in his present behaviour the vindication of all their antagonism: for them, Catherine could do no wrong and by deserting her for the sake of a shabby affair, he would have proved his unworthiness once and for all.

It really was essential that he do something; at least, as it was nearly lunchtime, he could go out and look for something to eat. He went down to the car and drove away. The centre of Bonn would be very crowded and there would be long queues for the multi-storey car parks. Much better to get to the Autobahn and just drive. Günter was not a reckless driver and he did not love speed for its own sake. Nevertheless he was used to getting the best out of a car and, as the speedometer touched 160 kilometres per hour, he at last began to relax. In no time at all he was approaching Coblenz, where he decided to stop and find a restaurant. Eating would fill in the time and he was free to choose a place – perhaps one run by a Munich brewery that specialized in rustic fare – in which Catherine would have disapproved of the quality and Anna of the quantity of the food. Later, replete with Leberknödelsuppe and Sauerbraten, he would buy a mildly pornographic bestseller at the station bookstall and go back to the flat to read it while he waited for Anna's telephone call.

Iris's friends were very like her: independent, professional women in their thirties who, while welcoming Anna in the warmest possible way, conveyed to her without words an impression that life must be shorn of all trivial and extraneous matters – love affairs, for example – if anything useful were to be accomplished. Conversation flowed without pause but it remained on a high plane; the election was in the bag and they were now more concerned with planning their tactics for the meeting of the party executive on Monday. Anna did not contribute much to this discussion, partly because she was not very good at mastering detail and constitutional procedures were beyond her; partly because she was feeling unwell. It was nothing, as yet, very definite and she could not even properly identify her symptoms, but it was enough to interfere with both appetite and concentration. When they got home, Iris remarked that she had been very quiet and looked rather washed out. 'I'll make us some tea,' she said, pleasantly, 'and then you must get to bed. It was very late last night and you were on your feet and running round all day.'

'I'm not usually so feeble,' said Anna, 'I'm the thin, tough sort.'

While Iris was in the kitchen, Anna went to the lavatory and found that she was bleeding, though so slightly that she was more puzzled than alarmed. When she returned to the sitting-room, however, Iris saw that something was wrong. 'Are you sure you're all right?' she asked. 'You're deathly pale.'

Anna, who had enjoyed perfect good health all her life, was indeed beginning to feel frightened, not so much by the symptoms she was experiencing – they were not severe enough for that – as by the fact that her body was behaving inexplicably. She was immeasurably glad that she was not alone with her fear and quickly told Iris what was happening.

'I suppose,' said Iris when she had finished, 'that you really are pregnant? That it's not just a late period?'

'If it is, then it's a *very* late one. It's weeks since I had the test done.'

'The labs can make mistakes. We'll have to get you a doctor – as it happens I have a friend who is very good and probably willing to make a house-call. I'll phone her.'

'I'm glad it's a woman.'

'I don't think gynaecologists should ever be anything else. How would men like it if nine out of ten urologists were women?' She went away to telephone. When she came back, she said, 'Christa says you should go to bed and she'll come round in the morning. There's not a lot she could do for you, now, but rest is essential. Bleeding does not automatically mean that you will lose the pregnancy.'

'How very comforting,' Anna began to cry. Iris was at her side in an instant. 'It's all so stupid, utterly absurd,' she sobbed. 'I've been worried sick for weeks about how to break it to Günter that I want an abortion and now it's just happening to me without me having had to make any decision at all. I should be laughing, not crying.'

'Now, now. Take it easy. It's perfectly natural to cry. Part of you always wants the baby, however irrational that may be.'

'I rather thought you disapproved of irrational behaviour.'

'Oh dear, did you really? No, what I believe is that we should try to see more clearly what it is that makes us tick. You won't ever be able completely to root out what is irrational, but you can make a bigger effort to recognize it for what it is. Don't be misled into thinking, for example, just because you're a bit weepy at the moment that all you ever really wanted was to have a baby.'

Although Anna did not speak she showed no sign of wanting to get up but Iris insisted she go to bed. Reluctantly she said goodnight. Alone in the little room which only that morning had seemed the perfect setting for her new start, Anna felt as miserable and lonely as she ever had as a child when her mother, gorgeously arrayed, had bestowed a brief peck on her cheek – she was discouraged from returning the kiss lest she spoil the immaculate make-up – before hurrying away to her evening engagements. Her thoughts turned to Günter. She did not doubt that if she phoned him now and told him she was ill he would rush to her aid immediately. He would comfort and sustain her and, if she were really having a miscarriage, then the tricky question of an abortion would also be shelved and they could go on for a little longer without her feeling forced into the sort of permanent commitment she was so unready to make. She began to entertain a picture of unalloyed happiness: did he not love her more than enough, provided there were no baby pressing its claims upon her, to allow her to find her own role in life, without expecting her to assume passively the one he had chosen? Would it not be nice if she could enjoy her independence without forfeiting the security his love gave her? It was not yet midnight, she would phone him at once; unless she had misjudged him completely, he would be with her in the morning.

She got out of bed and crossed the room noiselessly on bare feet. But as she opened the door, Iris came along the passage, on her way to the bathroom. 'Is something the matter?' she asked, concerned.

'No, no, nothing's the matter. I just though I'd try to phone Günter again. I think he should know.'

'Oh, Anna! What do you think he should know?'

'Well, that I'm not quite all right. He'll want to be with me.'

'And of course you want him to be with you.'

Anna bit her lip. Whereas the previous evening Iris had, with her sober common sense, seemed able to inspire her with the confidence she needed to act alone, she sounded now more like a hostile inquisitor. Aware of a terrible weakness in herself, Anna turned away to go back into the room. Iris followed her and straightened the bed as she got into it. 'Of course you must phone him – or I'll do it for you – if that's really how you want it to be. But don't drag the poor man all the way here and fill him with hope that you're ready to marry him and cherish him for ever, if all you actually want is someone to hold your hand while you have a miscarriage. If it's only a vague feeling of loneliness that you're trying to stave off, then I am more than willing to hold your hand – in every sense.' Iris sat down on the edge of the bed.

'I feel awful,' said Anna, allowing her hand to remain in Iris's. 'I'm so helpless all of a sudden.'

'This is hardly the time for being dynamic, you know. Even if your attitude to the baby has been equivocal all along, your body has been adapting to its presence and, if you are about to lose it, then your body has to adapt to that, too.'

'And you don't think I should even let Günter know?'

'Only if you're clear about what effect that will have on

your relationship. It would be very easy to have him come down and console you for the loss of the baby and, as you wallow in his sympathy, to lose sight of the fact that you were about to get rid of that baby against his wishes. And what will you do, if you don't miscarry after all? If you let him come now, when you are so particularly susceptible to all that is nice and tender in him, you will make it infinitely harder for yourself to break free later of the other side of him which wants to control you.'

'Maybe I was wrong about him wanting to control me.'

'Well, naturally, I can't be a proper judge of that, one way or the other. But you did give me the distinct impression last night that you were *very* worried about the future, if you did end up giving yourself to him heart and soul.'

'The way he's given himself to me.'

'But has he, Anna, has he really? Oh, I dare say he makes very fine speeches, but do you think he would ever give up anything of significance for your sake?'

'He gave up his wife.'

'Oh, that! Men are giving up their wives all the time, especially when they think something better has come along. But would he change his way of life? Would he give up his job? Would he take a cut in salary in order to stay at home and take his share of minding the baby? And I'm not talking about the occasional magnanimous gesture like putting it to bed once in a while so that you can go to a hen-party, but actually involving himself in every aspect of its upbringing while you finish your education and develop a career of your own?'

'He said we might get someone in to mind it until I get my degree.'

'Exactly! Use his money to employ someone as your substitute. And how long would it be before he was reproaching you for leaving his child to the tender mercies of a paid help?'

Anna was about to stick up for Günter but something – perhaps Iris's mention of his money – made her recall the pleasure in his face when she had appeared from the cubicle in the elegant dress shop wearing the clothes he was buying for her. Oh, yes, he loved her in her jeans all right, but he loved her even more when she conformed to his tastes. Iris, anxious to make the most of Anna's hesitation, went on, 'I'm not urging you to have nothing more to do with him, you know, just to wait a little – perhaps only a day – before you get in touch. After all, you've tried several times already to reach him since you came down here and *he* wasn't there, so your conscience can afford to be clear. But wait till Christa has seen you, at least, before you rush into something you may regret. After all, twenty-four hours ago you thought you had made your final decision. Now you're not so sure but in another twenty-four hours you may have changed again.'

Anna had to concede the sense in what Iris said. 'Will you stay with me for a bit?'

'Of course, with pleasure.' So Iris continued to sit at Anna's side until she fell into a fitful sleep. Early the next morning she woke with a much clearer sensation of pain than she had had before and struggled to the bathroom. She was no longer in any doubt that the pregnancy which had caused her such distress and confusion was at an end. Recollecting that the technical term was spontaneous abortion, she thought grimly to herself that spontaneity – as one might expect – was very messy. But at least the fruit of her womb bore scant resemblance to the half-grotesque, half-appealing little figure so familiar to her from the banners and publicity of the Pro-Life campaign. And for that she was profoundly grateful.

Fourteen

As Catherine cut julienne strips of vegetables for consommé on Sunday morning she sang odd snatches of song. Her repertoire was limited and strongly influenced by what Jennifer's taste had been thirty years ago, since she had never been much inclined to take an interest in music on her own account. Moreover, if she thought about it at all, she believed that the old songs were superior: Cole Porter and Johnny Mercer knew how to use words as well as how to compose agreeable tunes. Having started on several songs without being able to get beyond a line or two, she decided to sing something from *Kiss Me Kate,* which Jennifer had had on a record and which she had once learned off by heart. She was in the middle of 'I Hate Men' when Father Michael appeared.

'Oooh,' he said, 'I hope you don't mean it.'

'No, not at all. But now I think of it, my mother stopped me singing it years ago, on the grounds that it would hurt my father's and brother's feelings. At least, that was the reason she gave me at the time, but I decided afterwards that what she was really worried about was the impropriety of the lyrics:

>   Than ever marry one of them,
>   I'd rest a virgin rather ...
>   Of course, I'm awfully glad that mother
>   Had to marry father...

Pretty tame stuff nowadays, but I was only about ten years old.'

'What else do you sing?'

'Not much. As there's not a lot of tune in my voice, I like to know the words and that restricts me to a few old musicals, Christmas carols and the first verse of innumerable hymns. It's funny how it's only ever the first verse I remember, even though we always sang several at school.'

'We could do with you in church here. The singing's pathetic.'

'You flatter me, though I do rather enjoy belting out a hymn, whatever the pain it may cause music lovers. The only problem is that it has to be one I've known for at least twenty years, as I'm quite incapable of learning new tunes.'

'Right, then I'll leave you to choose the hymns next Sunday – OK?'

'Certainly, if I'm still here.'

'Ah, d'you have to be leaving us already?'

'Not necessarily, but I assume Miss Whelan will be coming out of hospital quite soon.'

'Oh, she'll not be back just yet, I'm sure. The boss said he was getting her fixed up in a convalescent home somewhere in Wales. The operation must have taken a lot out of her – well, it took an appendix out, anyway!'

They were both laughing rather in excess of this little witticism's worth when the door opened and a tight-lipped woman of about sixty walked in. 'Oh, Father Lee,' she said, unctuously, 'I'm very sorry if I intrude. I didn't think there'd be anyone here. I only came to make the dinner.'

'Oh, crumbs, didn't anyone tell you?'

'Tell me what?'

'Well, that Catherine's taken over. She's been cooking the most fabulous meals for us since Friday.'

The woman looked coldly and uncomprehendingly at Catherine, who now stepped forward saying, 'Hello, I'm Catherine Hemmersbach, Father Quinn's niece.'

'His *niece*?'

'That's right, one of Tom's children.'

'Oh, one of *his* children. That, of course, explains it. I am your Aunt Teresa.'

The woman said this with such exaggerated formality, even a touch of grandeur, that Catherine could not help smiling. Worse, her eye caught Michael's and he gave her a wink. Regaining her composure, she said quickly, 'Well, I'm very pleased to meet you.' Michael, looking at his watch, excused himself, leaving them alone with their embarrassment.

'Michael's a very nice boy, isn't he?' Catherine was desperate to break the silence.

'I am not myself in the habit of referring to ordained priests as 'boys', *or* of calling them by their Christian names.'

'Oh dear, I'm sorry if I've offended you. But I really believe that *he* prefers to be on first-name terms.'

Teresa merely sniffed and Catherine, anxious not to be enveloped once more in her disapproving silence, forced herself to go on. 'I realize now that Gerard did say something about your offering to help with dinner today when I was here on Thursday. I came just on the spur of the moment with my father and, as I've got time on my hands, I took pity on the pair of them and came to save them from a diet of tinned soup.'

'That was very kind of you, I'm sure, particularly as you're a stranger. But I don't think they were doing so badly. I had been keeping an eye on them myself and would have come yesterday, only my back was bad. I could hardly move.'

'Oh, I'm so sorry. Wouldn't you like to sit down? Can I get you anything? A glass of sherry, perhaps?'

'Oh, no thank you. I never drink.'

'Well, what about a cup of tea?'

Teresa hesitated but then replied, 'No, nothing at all, thank you. I really couldn't have *you* waiting on me in my own brother's house.'

'Well, perhaps it won't be too long before Gerard's free. He's saying the eleven o'clock mass – I don't know how long that takes.'

'You don't know?' Then apparently recalling some unpleasant fact, she added, 'No, I suppose you wouldn't. Your parents' marriage was a great tragedy for the family – but at least our prayers for your father have been answered. God is very good.'

'I do wish I could get you some refreshment while you wait.' Catherine, who wanted to get on with her own preparations, spoke rather too forcefully. 'Have you seen this morning's paper yet?' She made to hand Teresa the *Observer*.

'No, I don't read that sort of thing, thank you very much. But I've got the *Catholic Pictorial* in my bag, if you're worried about me disturbing you with my chatter.'

'Oh, no, of course not. Please make yourself at home. I only thought you'd be more comfortable in the other room and I really must get on with one or two things in here.' She set about separating the eggs for a soufflé but all the while she was conscious of Teresa's hostility. She had never known anyone to convey so completely, without saying a word, such a sense of her own implacable injury.

'Did you serve your time as a cook?' Teresa's question, after five minutes' observation, implied accusation rather than curiosity.

'No, not a bit of it. I taught myself.'

'And what is your job then?'

'I don't have one. I'm just a housewife.' Catherine, as a rule, avoided describing herself in this humble way but she was dimly aware that the grumpy old woman's resentment might have something to do with her own superior manner and she therefore wanted to make herself sound as ordinary as possible. But it was no use: the inquisition continued.

'And did you never work?'

'I taught for a few years.'

'Oh, a teacher, like your dad. Go to training-college, did you?'

'No, actually I went to university.'

'Liverpool?'

'No, to Oxford.' Catherine felt as though she were confessing, under duress, to a guilty secret.

'Ah, that explains why you sound so posh.' Satisfied to have wormed it out of her Teresa asked, with somewhat less asperity, 'And what are you making for today's dinner?'

Catherine relaxed, foolishly assuming that food was a great leveller. 'A clear soup, roast duck with braised celery and chocolate soufflé. I'm a little worried that the soufflé will be a bit too rich after the duck but I asked them if there was anything they'd especially like and Gerard said he hadn't had duck for years and Michael said he'd never had a soufflé in his life but had heard so much about them that he'd like to try one. I couldn't resist doing a chocolate one because I'm sure they'll both love it – more, I think, than any other sort – and it'll be so much easier for me to time it with me being in the kitchen while they're eating. Hot puddings have a luxury all their own, but they are dreadfully difficult to get right if you have to sit at the table with your guests.'

'I shouldn't have thought being a skivvy would be so much in your line.'

'Well, of course, I wouldn't care to be somebody else's mere kitchen maid but I look upon the creation of a whole meal almost as a work of art.' The skittishness which Catherine had hoped to impart to these words failed to come off and she was immediately punished.

'Oooh, get you!' said Teresa contemptuously. 'Works of art in the kitchen! But it's no wonder my brother prefers your cooking to mine. I was only going to give him lamb chops and rice pudding.'

'But I'm very fond of rice pudding, especially yours, Teresa. There's nobody cooks a tin of Ambrosia better than you.' Gerard joined them and his sister stood up to greet him, offering him her cheek to kiss without allowing her face to relax into a smile.

'I know you're very busy, Gerard, but I do think you might have let me know you'd made other arrangements for your Sunday dinner.'

'Yes, love, I'm very sorry you've had a wasted journey. I hadn't realized that you thought we'd made a firm arrangement – I expected you to ring up before you came out.'

'I should have thought you'd know me well enough by now – I always keep my word. Even though my back is so bad at the moment.'

'Oh, that is a shame. Why don't you stay here for your dinner, then. And I'll run you home this afternoon?'

Teresa looked sceptically at Catherine and said, 'No, I'd rather not, thank you. Fancy food doesn't agree with me and I'd be sure to suffer if I ate duck. Much too greasy. But of course I'll stay if you'd like me to help with the washing-up.'

Catherine laughed. 'Certainly not! I don't need *any* help with that.'

'Well, then, I'll be getting along. I'll just go into the church to say hello to Our Lady before the twelve o'clock starts. I wouldn't want Her to think I'd forgotten Her when She's so good to me.'

'I'll walk across with you,' said Gerard, adding with a smile to Catherine, 'I don't think there's ever been such a good smell in this kitchen. It's like living in a luxury hotel.'

Catherine worked on, reflecting with some dissatisfaction on her part in this last encounter. Though not in any doubt that Teresa was a disagreeable woman, there was too much which was pitiable about her for Catherine to feel easy about indulging her dislike. There were in her appearance so many signs, if not of poverty, then of straitened circumstances: her shabby coat and imitation-leather handbag; cheap stockings that wrinkled round the ankle; a crimplene, home-made dress. She had never married, probably she had had to look after her mother, a lifetime of grudging self-sacrifice. Surely it was hardly fair to reproach a woman whose life had been spent within such constricting limits with narrow-mindedness. 'And how stupid to offer her sherry!' Catherine was disgusted at her own tactlessness. What she should have done, she realized too late, was make tea without asking whether Teresa wanted any, and then sit down with her to drink a cup, even if it had meant leaving the soufflé for a later meal.

The delight with which Gerard and Michael received their pudding, however, left little doubt that, as far as they were concerned, Catherine had got her priorities right. 'Your husband must be an awfully lucky man,' remarked Michael, when she came in to clear away.

Touched that Gerard had obviously breathed no word of what lay behind her being there, she smiled and said, 'Ah, but you know, husbands don't live by chocolate soufflé alone.'

'I bet there's a few who wouldn't mind trying,' he replied, genially, scraping the last mouthful out of the dish before getting up to help her carry the plates into the kitchen.

When Catherine at last sat down at nine o'clock that evening with the review section of the Sunday paper, she felt more pleasantly exhausted than she had for years. She remembered Günter's jibe, as indeed she remembered everything he had said that night, about their marriage being nothing but 'one long dinner party'. Perhaps, she thought with an ironic smile, this was how she wanted life to be: provided she had appreciative people to feed, cooking for them was arguably what she did best, while offering at the same time a certainty of satisfaction which had been missing from teaching and most of the other things she had dabbled in over the years. She started reading the review of some lengthy feminist tract by an Australian, but her attention kept wandering to what seemed for the moment to be the more important question of whether she could obtain flour in Crosby suitable for making successful ravioli.

'Am I disturbing you?' Gerard paused in the doorway.

'Not in the least. I was only reading a review of a book which seems to be too silly for words. Apparently it is now considered treachery to the feminist cause to accuse *any* woman of confused thinking or unclear writing: if women write badly and think in a muddled way then it is because that is the only valid way *for* them to write. Such nonsense would make my old headmistress weep.'

'You should write a book yourself.'

'I've thought that too, sometimes. But while I'm the perfect letter-writer, I don't think I've got the staying-power required to write a whole book.'

'But you do like writing letters?'

'Almost as much as I like cooking. The only trouble is that these days so few people are willing to be proper correspondents – you embarrass them with unsolicited letters, which they haven't the wit or the time to reply to, almost as much as the *Reader's Digest* irritates them with all those unsolicited special offers.'

'Do you think you could write to me? I promise to reply, though I don't know that there'll be much wit in what I write.'

'But I'm living here!'

'Yes, well, that's what I've come to talk about.' Gerard looked uncomfortable. 'I went to see Miss Whelan at visiting-time this evening.'

'And is she all right?'

'Yes, perfectly all right. That's the point. They're going to discharge her on Tuesday.'

'Michael said you wanted her to go and convalesce somewhere.'

'I did indeed. And I'd already been in touch with a nursing-home in Prestatyn – a nice place run by some nuns who would have been happy to take her for a fortnight, even longer if she'd wanted. But when I told her about it, she just wouldn't hear of it.'

'Why ever not?'

'I'm afraid that Teresa visited this afternoon – they're quite good friends, you know – and, well, it sounds silly, but I think she told some tall stories about what you're doing for us. Poor Miss Whelan feels her nose has been pushed out and, well, not to beat about the bush, she says she *insists* on returning to *her* kitchen the very moment the doctors say she can leave hospital. I tried to reason with her but she seemed to think I was only interested in enjoying your cooking a bit longer.'

Catherine was surprised at the force of her disappointment. Another two weeks or so, she was almost sure, would have provided just the period of calm which she needed, with enough useful activity to prevent her dwelling exclusively on her own concerns. She found her relations with both men undemanding and pleasurable; she had looked forward to getting to know them better. But a glance at Gerard's face told her that he was clearly very distressed on her behalf and she realized she must check her own feelings.

'I won't pretend I'm not a bit disappointed,' she started, cheerfully, 'I really do like it here, and you're the best guinea-pigs I've ever had. But of course I understand how Miss Whelan feels as well. Cooks are terribly vain and hate to have anybody else's achievements praised – they seem to think it implies denigration of their own efforts. I'm just the same myself.'

'I'm quite sure you're not, my dear, but it's very good of you to put it like that. I must confess that I feel I have let you down – of course, it was smashing to have you cook for us – but, without wanting to deny how much we liked the food, I was beginning to think we were offering you a sort of refuge as well.'

'A refuge? What a lovely word that is! And, yes, you've got a point. It *was* refreshing for me to come here – it was so different from sitting about at home all day, and you both made me feel so welcome. And it also gave me a good excuse to postpone actually deciding what I should do next.'

'I sincerely wish we could have given you the excuse for a bit longer.'

'Oh, it can't be helped. I'm only sorry that Miss Whelan looks upon me as a usurper. I hope she doesn't overdo things when she gets back, but if she should need her convalescence after all, then I'm sure I'll be in Liverpool for a little while longer, and you can always ring me up.'

'You're very kind, really very kind.'

Catherine fetched a bottle of wine and encouraged Gerard to talk, but on very general topics. In restraining her own dismay at being prematurely ejected from the presbytery, she had had to harden her heart and the urge to confide, so strong two nights ago, had altogether left her. Gerard was a kind and worthy man whom she genuinely liked but it seemed increasingly unlikely that she would find counsel and solace in anybody; personal problems were for sorting out on your own and she only hoped that, if she persevered, she would soon be able to face life again with all the composure Günter so deplored.

Fifteen

Günter got up on Monday morning relieved that the weekend was over and he could go to work again. Sunday had seemed interminable but he had forced himself to stay in the flat all day since it had occurred to him, once his rage on Saturday night that Anna still had not rung subsided, that he might have missed her through spending so long in Coblenz. As the day dragged on and there was still no word, he tried hard to make excuses for her: long-distance telephone lines were notoriously busy on a Sunday and if, as was probable, she had to use a public call box, then it would not be easy to keep dialling with an impatient queue forming outside. Ostensibly plausible as such reasoning might be, however, it could not quite dispel his fear that her silence proved she just did not care enough. By evening this fear was turning into a dull conviction that she wanted to be rid of him altogether.

He watched the election results come in, learned that the Greens were in the Landtag with nine out of 110 seats and saw the jubilant scenes at the party gathering in Wiesbaden. His eyes scanned the crowds for a glimpse of Anna and a couple of times he thought he had found her, but he could not be sure: considering their contempt for the uniform dark suits of the male establishment, it was extraordinary how alike all these green women looked. Even the natural differences in their figures, he thought, were largely obscured by several layers of loose, shapeless overgarments. The commentators were agreed that the success in Hesse meant almost certain entry to the Bundestag in the forthcoming federal election. Someone mentioned that the party, being so young, was short of experienced candidates: there would be some very new, probably youthful, faces in the new parliament. It crossed Günter's mind to wonder if one of them might be Anna's. On balance, he rather doubted it; for all her conviction, she had struck him, on the night he argued with Holger, as being too hesitant, even too shy, to pursue a public career. Ruefully, he reflected that, along with her party, she too was young enough to learn how to overcome her shortcomings.

On arrival at the office he was told that a colleague, who was to have gone to a meeting in Brussels that day, had been taken ill and that he was required to go in his place. He would have to hurry home for his overnight bag and then be driven to the airport at once. He really had no choice in the matter and perhaps, under the circumstances, a night in the sanitized comfort of the American hotel where the company would put him up was just what he needed: at least the bathroom would be spotless. The driver was to follow him home, so that he could leave his own car there, and then take him to the airport. It meant going to his own house, for not only had he left his small cases there, he was also reluctant to let the driver see Anna's scruffy dwelling, even from the outside.

As he put the key in the front door, he felt it was an age since he had last done so and, familiar though everything was, that he was entering a stranger's house. Almost like a burglar, he hurried upstairs, anxious to make no noise and to disturb as little as possible. He had no difficulty in selecting a couple of shirts and other essentials but with horror he realized that he had no idea where his overnight bag was. When had he had it last? On a trip to Geneva; on the way back his plane was delayed and he had not arrived home until the early hours of the morning. Of course he had not unpacked at that hour and next day, by the time he returned from the office, Catherine had tidied it all away. What had he said to her, here in this very room? 'Don't think I ever wanted you to nanny me.' He sat down on the bed and put his head in his hands, suddenly wondering if he could have meant it.

But he must pull himself together or he would miss the plane. He looked once more round the room and then ran down to the cellar, where their large suitcases were stored. There he found a rather shabby hold-all which he had had as a student and although aware that it might raise an eyebrow at the Hilton, he decided it would have to do. He gave it a cursory wipe with his handkerchief, packed hastily and went out to the car.

The driver was passing the time reading a popular tabloid newspaper, which had chosen for its main headline not the results in Hesse but the news that a famous television personality was dying of cancer ('sixty cigarettes per day!') and had only a few days left to put his affairs in order. Would he be reconciled to the children of his first marriage? Would there be a deathbed marriage to the 'live-in girlfriend' (thirty years his junior), who had already been seen at nightclubs with another man? It was hardly a suitable topic for conversation on the drive and they talked about the traffic instead.

Late that night, before settling to sleep, Günter phoned Anna's flat. He was nearly certain that there would be no reply, but at least he wanted to be able to tell her that *he* had been assiduous in trying to get in touch. But hadn't she said something about a party conference being held today? He should have listened to the German news on the radio, but he couldn't be bothered now. Tomorrow he would be home again and since she could hardly intend to stay in Frankfurt or Wiesbaden or wherever she was for ever, it could not be very much longer before he saw her.

The driver brought Günter back to his house at about half-past five the next afternoon. He went straight to the telephone and dialled Anna's number. There was still no reply. He was now distinctly uneasy; if she had been motivated to go away for a day or two primarily in order to show him that she must sometimes lead her own life, then surely she had more than proved her point. But was her continuing absence still to be interpreted as a message to himself – a cowardly way of breaking off their relationship altogether – or had something happened beyond her control to prevent her coming back? He thought of Holger's ancient car and the reckless way that young men drive. Might she have had an accident? He shuddered and felt a pang of guilt that his thoughts up to now had been wholly selfish: wounded by her apparent neglect, he had not paused to consider that her silence might be involuntary. Oh God, if she were in hospital and unable to speak for herself, how long would it be before he was informed? Her parents did not know of his existence and those few friends of hers whom he had met would scarcely have taken in his name. At the same time, he could not very well initiate inquiries for himself, since it was still possible that nothing had happened, that she did only want to be free of him.

The longer she stayed away, the less he felt he really knew her. It was as though he could only aspire to understanding her when she was near enough to touch and then, by contrast, how utterly transparent she became! And yet, for all the secrets which her personality kept hidden from him, she was expecting his child, the first he had fathered. Perhaps because it had come to him so late in life, the very idea of parenthood filled him with awe. He vividly remembered every detail of the day she first told him she was pregnant. It was a wet Sunday and he had been desperate to see her, although jogging – the cover for their secret meetings – seemed out of the question. Nevertheless, he had decided to brazen it out with Catherine, certain that she would attempt to talk him out of going. In fact, she had only remarked caustically that since he was mad enough to go jogging in the first place, he was presumably more than mad enough not to mind getting wet. On the way home there had been such a downpour that, to corroborate his alibi, he had parked his car in a lay-by and stood out in the open until he was thoroughly soaked. It had not dampened his spirits: he was immensely, uncontrollably happy that Anna should be carrying his child. It gave a new, altogether more serious, dimension to the affair which a part of him at least suspected of being rather unworthy. Of course it would mean that he must soon tell Catherine but he was in any case ashamed that he had deceived her for so long.

For some time afterwards he had assumed that Anna's tears that morning, when he took her in his arms and kissed her, incoherently expressing his delight about the baby, their baby, were tears of relief that at last he was talking seriously to her about the future, that he was committing himself to her frankly and wholeheartedly. Only gradually had it dawned on him that Anna did not quite regard her pregnancy as an unmixed blessing. Now, thinking back to the manner of her announcement and putting together, in the context of her prolonged absence, odd little remarks she had made, the ugly fear presented itself to him that she had gone away to have the abortion which, he suddenly realized, had probably been in the back of her mind all along.

No sooner did the idea present itself than it became the only possible explanation for her behaviour. Angry with himself for not having thought it all out before and angry with Anna for daring to take matters into her own hands without consulting him, he stood up, impatient to do something. He would go once more to the flat, collect all his things and leave her a letter which he would compose as he was driving and write when he arrived. In it he would describe the anguish he had suffered and challenge her to justify her treatment of him, although he was not yet sure whether it was prudent to put his worst suspicions in writing. In any case he would make it clear that he was not prepared to continue living in her wretched rooms on his own but would await her answer in his own house.

As he mounted the stairs to the apartment which had witnessed within a few months far greater extremes of emotion in him than he had experienced in all the rest of his adult life put together, his heart leapt as he heard sounds from within, clearly indicating that she was back.

He felt that he was waking from a nightmare: his fears were still upon him but they were already fading and soon they would disappear. Anna had not had an abortion and there would be a perfectly mundane explanation for everything. He let himself in, calling her name as he did so. There was no reply and he walked on into her living-room, where he found a woman, whom he had never seen before, with some of Anna's books in her hand. She turned and came towards him, her other hand outstretched to greet him.

'My name is Schmitz,' she said. 'You must be Herr Dr Hemmersbach. Anna has told me a lot about you.'

'She has told me nothing about you.' Günther, completely taken aback by the unexpectedness of the encounter, stumbled over his words, unable to match the woman's composure.

'No, nor could she have done. We only met for the first time last Friday, but a lot has happened since then and so I feel I have really known her for much longer.'

'Where is Anna now? What are you doing here? Why hasn't she been in touch with me herself?'

'There's so much to tell; wouldn't you like to sit down? We tried to phone you yesterday but your secretary explained that you were in Brussels. Anna was naturally surprised that you had not mentioned to her that you would be leaving the country.'

'I didn't know myself until I got to work yesterday morning.' Günter replied without thinking and then regretted the apparent defensiveness of his words. 'Leaving the country', indeed! She made it sound as though he had tried to emigrate. And what right had she, anyway, to imply that he was in the wrong? What business was it of hers? He spoke again, with exaggerated formality. 'I really have very little time. Would you just be so good as to tell me where I can get in touch with Anna?' He was on the point of saying that he too had been ignorant of Anna's whereabouts for the last few days, but checked himself.

'I'm afraid she's in hospital – but there's no need to be

alarmed. She has –'

'She's having an abortion!' he broke in. 'You're the one who's arranged it for her.'

Iris frowned at his outburst but went on calmly, 'I do not know why you should suppose any such thing, but I assure you that you are quite mistaken. Anna happened to be staying with me over the election and she had a miscarriage in my flat early on Sunday morning. The doctor thought it advisable for her to be kept under observation for a couple of days – merely as a precaution – but she's leaving the clinic tomorrow. I've come to get her some more clothes and the books she needs, since she's agreed to stay with me until she's fully recovered.'

Günter was inclined not to believe a word the woman had said, beyond the fact that she had apparently taken over the running of Anna's life. She was so sure of herself, he thought, so typical of the new confident female making her way in a man's world: capable, certainly, but also humourless, unfeminine, even vaguely inhuman. He would of course no more have owned to an instinctive antagonism towards such women than he would have confessed, had he been taken ill in Africa, to wanting a white, rather than a black doctor to treat him; but his prejudice was no less real for being suppressed. Still, he could not call her a liar to her face. 'But Anna was perfectly fit,' he protested, 'she didn't even appear to suffer much from the usual symptoms – morning sickness and so on.'

'Unfortunately these things often just happen, though that hardly makes them any less upsetting when they do.'

'I suppose she overdid things on Saturday; she probably didn't eat properly and didn't get enough sleep.'

Iris smiled, but not unsympathetically. 'The doctor says there's actually nothing you can do to prevent a miscarriage of this sort – just as all the horseriding and hot baths in the world won't dislodge a good pregnancy.'

'I find that very hard to believe.' Günter could dispute a medical opinion without needing to impugn Iris's own honesty. 'The real point, I'm afraid, is that Anna didn't properly want the baby. You claim to have got to know her very well – did she give *you* the impression she wanted it?'

'I won't deny she had some doubts, yes. She's very young and she felt – I think quite rightly – that a baby at this juncture would sadly inhibit her chances of developing her own potential.'

'Potential to do what? Isn't becoming a mother a worthy enough end in itself?'

'Perhaps it isn't quite the only one which interests her. She was naturally frightened of being sucked into the role of housewife and mother at the very moment when her life was opening out in other, very exciting directions.'

'So you talked her into getting rid of the baby and then kindly made all the arrangements for her?'

'I have told you she had a miscarriage. If you wish, you can see the doctor's report.'

'Whether it was an abortion or not, it wouldn't have happened, I'm sure, if she'd taken proper care of herself; if she'd let me look after her instead of gallivanting off to Frankfurt.'

'I see that you'll have to read the diagnosis for yourself. Then you will know that this particular pregnancy was incapable of producing a baby, under any circumstances.'

'What on earth are you talking about?'

'The technical term is blighted ovum. It happens quite often. What it means is that although everything starts normally, the cells don't divide the way they should and a viable foetus simply doesn't develop.' Iris paused and, seeing the look of hostile disbelief on Günter's face, added spitefully: 'They say the probable cause is some deficiency in the sperm.'

Günter stood up. 'Thank you for enlightening me. You must forgive my gynaecological ignorance. And now if you would just let me have the address of the clinic, I'll be on my way.'

'I'm afraid I can't do that.'

'What the devil do you mean?'

'Anna does not wish me to.'

'You mean that you've decided seeing me might be bad for her feminist principles and are therefore deliberately withholding her address.'

'Rubbish! Anna has a mind of her own and is more than able to reach a decision about seeing you independently of me or anyone else.'

'Then why isn't she able to communicate her decision to me personally?'

'As I said before, she tried to phone you yesterday.'

'And what prevented her ringing on Sunday? I spent the entire day sitting by the phone.'

'She was in no state to speak to you.'

'Do you mean she lost her voice? Or was she unconscious?'

'I don't find your sarcasm very helpful. If you had any real feeling for her, you would surely understand that she was in no condition to do anything on Sunday.'

'My feelings for Anna are no concern of yours, but there is nothing callous in my assertion that she must have had the strength, if not to speak to me directly, then to arrange for someone else to do so.'

'Anna needs time to sort herself out.'

'How dare you presume to know what Anna needs? But I suppose you are so consumed with hatred of men yourself that you can't even begin to imagine that a girl just might need a man's love more than all your self-fulfilment and consciousness-raising nonsense.'

'I will not deny that Anna is very fond of you ...'

'Thank you, but I really do not need you to tell me that.'

'Of course you don't. I just want to say that you must be patient. When Anna has got over the strain and shock of the miscarriage, then she will come back to Bonn and you will be able to discuss the future more soberly than was possible while the pregnancy was complicating everything.'

Günter exploded. 'You mean-spirited bitch! You really can only see pregnancy as a complication, can't you? As something that awkwardly stands in the way of women taking over the world? I expect you'll not be satisfied until there aren't any women left foolish enough to have babies at all.'

'If you only want to abuse me, then there is no point in continuing the discussion. I had hoped that you would be less self-centred and rather more willing to see what should be done in the light of what is best for Anna.'

'And naturally you're the only one who knows what's best for her.'

'We could both, I think, help her to find out for herself. She has been very neglected by her parents.'

'Frau Schmitz, while I grant that Anna may well be seeking a mother figure in yourself, I can assure you that I am not prepared to cast myself in the role of father to her.'

'No, your vanity wouldn't permit it. But it's a pity that the love you talk about so grandly isn't magnanimous enough to support her while she considers how she really wants her life to be, even if that turns out to be very different from what you had in mind for her.'

'This is becoming altogether too absurd. You say you have only known Anna for a few days and yet you talk about her in a manner that I should find presumptuous in a parent. She is, after all, turned twenty-one and more than old enough to order her personal affairs without the help of an intermediary. I must ask you again to give me her address.'

'And I must repeat that I promised Anna I would not give it to you.'

'I see. Then I'll have to leave without it. I won't ask you to give Anna any message from me, since I doubt that anything I might wish to say to her would pass your censorship.'

The anger and sense of hurt which had been building up in Günter over the last few days were now concentrated upon Iris to such an extent that he almost feared he might hit her if he stayed any longer. He moved towards the door but she, observing the emotion in his face but mistaking its violence, spoke again in what she intended to be a conciliatory voice. 'Herr Hemmersbach, please don't go away with the impression that I am exercising some sort of evil influence upon Anna. Sometimes a girl has to have a woman, older and wiser than herself, to confide in, however much she may know she is loved by a man. And, just like you, I only want Anna to be happy. I too have grown very fond of her.'

'Really? Did she seduce you as well?'

Iris, her face suddenly very red, for the first time came near to losing her self-control. 'As it happens,' she said, forcing the words out with some difficulty, 'I do not personally see anything shameful about love between women, but as you so obviously do, I shall take the question for the insult you intended. I have nothing more to say to you.'

Günter shrugged and left, almost running out of the house and not stopping until he was back in his car. The Autobahn was barely a kilometre away but before he reached it three cars had hooted at him on account of his aggressive driving. Even when he was out on the motorway and doing nearly 200 kilometres per hour, he had no real sensation of speed. Hardly aware how he got there, he arrived home, put the car in the garage and went inside to find himself a drink. He had just poured himself a large brandy when the phone rang. The sound he had been waiting for since Friday took him completely by surprise and for a few seconds he could not move: the ringing seemed to become more insistent. He crossed the room to the hall and lifted the receiver. So certain was he that it could only be Anna at the other end that he answered not, as usual, with his name, but with a barely audible 'Yes?'

'Günter, Günter, is that you at last?' It was his mother's voice, excited and anxious, but he was still too disorientated to speak. 'Where have you been? You haven't phoned us for over two weeks. And we tried all day Sunday to reach you. There is terrible news.'

'Oh, really? What's happened, then?'

'Günter, you sound so strange. Are you ill? Where is

Catherine?'

'In England.'

'What is she there for? When will she be returning?'

'I don't know. Probably never.'

Günter had answered honestly enough but his mother, understandably, deduced from his reply that Catherine was to blame for his distraught state. 'Oh, dear God,' she said, 'I was always afraid something like this would happen. How could she do it to you? Oh, my poor boy!'

'Mother, I'm afraid you don't really understand.' With an effort Günter attempted to correct the misunderstanding, but his heart was not in it. He could not face explaining anything, least of all to his mother; all he wanted was to be left alone to get drunk.

'Günter, I am so sorry for you, so very sorry. But I'm afraid there is even worse news.' Her voice trembled and she sighed before going on. 'Your father is in hospital. He hasn't seemed quite well for a few weeks but he wouldn't see a doctor – you know how stubborn he is – and then on Sunday he collapsed, in terrible agony. They say he has something ... has a ... has a lump in the bowel. They have to operate, tomorrow. We must pray that's it's benign, and that they have caught it in time.'

'Yes, yes, of course. What do you want me to do? I can come down at the weekend.'

'Not before? It would be good to have you with me.'

'But you have Monika and Klaus, almost next door.'

'That's not the same. You could stay with me; I'd have you here in the house.'

'I have to go to work. I'll see about getting away early on Friday.' Günter knew that his mother would think herself ill-used and her querulous tone would continue to reproach him, but she would not argue: she never did argue with a man, husband or son.

'I promised your father that if I managed to get in touch tonight I'd ask you to phone him – he has a phone by the bed and he would appreciate speaking to you before the operation. He wanted to speak to Catherine, too, he can't understand why she's not rung up as usual. He always was so fond of her.' Frau Hemmersbach sighed audibly at her husband's folly. 'And he believed she was just as fond of him. Ah, well, that's how things are. But don't tell him she's left you – spare him that till the operation is over and he's feeling stronger. God help him, the news could kill him.'

'Mother, I'm afraid ...' Günter's voice trailed away. What could he say? That Catherine had not left him, that it was he who had left her because his mistress was having a baby? That this baby was now dead and that its mother was probably having an affair with a vile, middle-aged feminist? It was impossible. He could not do it. Later, of course, when the shock had subsided, he would have to exonerate poor Catherine, but for the moment it was all he could do to speak the platitudes of comfort about his father which his mother expected to hear. And then he would have to say it over again to his father before, at long last, drinking himself into oblivion.

Sixteen

Catherine spared no effort to make the last meals she prepared for her priests memorable and she stayed up into the early hours of Tuesday morning in order to leave a full larder for Miss Whelan. She kept her departure as businesslike as possible, giving Michael detailed instructions about where she had left the cakes and pies and how long the soup and pâté would keep. As she drove away, she felt the same mood of helpless pity for the world coming over her which had afflicted her the week before in Lewis's. Stopped at a zebra crossing, she saw a small child stumble and start to cry, only to have his ears boxed by his mother for undisciplined behaviour in the middle of the road. Catherine, finding that she was close to tears herself, was angry at her own weakness. What had happened to the famous equanimity which Günter hated? Why had her rational approach to life deserted her now, when she was more in need of it than ever? The child would get over the injustice of his mother's treatment; and indeed he might ultimately find it a useful preparation for all the subsequent injustices he would have to suffer. But she still felt desperately sorry for him.

Mrs Quinn accepted her daughter's return with a coolness that indicated she was still smarting from the circumstances of her going away in the first place. 'Oh, well,' she said, 'we'll try to make the most of you while we've got you. No doubt you'll be off again as soon as you can find another lame duck.'

She had not been in the house very long when Jennifer called, having snatched a few minutes from her lunch-hour to see if all was well. 'I'm so glad you're home,' she told Catherine. 'I was quite jealous of this new uncle getting to see so much more of you than we do. Peter and Anthea are coming over to supper tonight and I thought you might like to come too. Carolyn's just got home and Peter wants to ask her where they should go if they decide to drive to France next Easter. She has a friend with her and will be off to Leeds again before the end of the week. That's why it's all a bit rushed. Will you come?'

'Thank you, I'd like to very much.'

Jennifer, to her mother's unsurprised dismay, had no time for a cup of tea but had left them again without apparently pausing for breath. 'She's silly to try and cope with entertaining in the middle of the week,' said Joyce. 'She'll only end up doing two jobs badly.'

Catherine welcomed the opportunity to agree. 'Even though I never taught as many hours as Jennifer does, I must say I avoided having guests on the days I worked.'

'Yes, well, not everybody puts the effort into cooking that you do. You look quite worn out from your stint in Crosby.'

'I was up very late last night – I did a bit of baking and things. The housekeeper probably won't feel up to doing a lot the first few days she's home.'

'You needn't have overdone it. Bought cakes wouldn't have killed them.'

'I did enjoy it, though. And I've nothing to do this afternoon – I might take a nap after I've unpacked.'

'Goodness! Fancy sleeping in the middle of the day at your age!'

'Of course I don't have to sleep, if there's something you'd like me to do for you.'

'I don't want you to do anything *for* me. But it would be nice if we could have a comfortable natter again, the way we used to.'

'I'm sorry, mother. It never occurred to me. I thought

you'd be busy – you usually say you have too much to do to be able to sit around all day.' Pleased that Joyce was no longer cross with her for going away, Catherine settled herself to give an interesting account of her weekend. 'Did I mention Teresa's visit on the phone?'

'Only the fact that she'd been. What's she like?'

Catherine told her, describing in graphic detail the way Teresa had looked and what she had said, including her announcement on leaving that she would pop in to say 'hello' to Our Lady. Catherine felt a slight qualm at passing on something which would only serve to feed her mother's anti-Catholic prejudice, but it was so much easier to make an entertaining tale with such gems than it was to convey her own strong sense of Gerard's goodness. As they talked, it became clear that Joyce had an extraordinarily vivid recollection of all the Quinns and was far more curious about them than Catherine would have thought possible after fifty years' estrangement. They were still talking at four o'clock when Tom, who had been watching racing on television, came in to ask if there were any chance of a cup of tea. Catherine jumped up to make it, wondering if it might be possible to find some common ground with her mother other than malicious gossip. Over tea Tom told them his latest hard-luck story, with Catherine feigning interest and Joyce sunk in reverie.

Jennifer was a busy woman who had for years managed to fulfil her most pressing obligations while retaining both her good humour and a total lack of organization. Since housework came very low on her list of priorities, it was in her living-room that she appeared at her most disorganized. Most people took her as they found her but Joyce never visited without passing some critical comment about the place looking 'more like a disaster area than ever'. But Jennifer was not offended: 'I like a room to look lived-in,' she would reply and cheerfully remove a cardigan and a couple of books from the chair which Joyce should sit on. Catherine, at heart as censorious as her mother though superficially more polite, also experienced a shock of distaste on entering her sister's house. As she was this evening the last to arrive, the chairs had all been taken and she was offered a bean bag, borrowed from Sally's room, on to which she uneasily lowered herself. Anthea, sitting at the other side of the fireplace, caught her eye and winked conspiratorially, implying that they were both rather slumming it. Catherine ignored her.

'Have some of my latest,' said Bob, bringing her a glass of pink liquid. 'There's a prize for anyone who can tell me what it is.'

'We're all hopeless,' said Anthea. 'The girls aren't allowed to help either, because of course they know what it is. And Bob, dreadful man, won't even tell us how potent it is. It tastes absolutely delicious, though, and I'm already on my second.'

Even before Catherine had taken a first sip – it tasted like indifferent white wine – she had guessed what it was and said, as she put down her glass, 'Could it be kir?'

'Gosh,' said Bob, a mixture of disappointment and wonder evident in his voice, 'you *are* clever!'

'And what, pray, is kir?' asked Peter.

'White wine with a shot of crème de cassis.'

'Carolyn brought the liqueur home from the duty-free,' said Jennifer, giggling, 'but when it runs out we're going to try making it with Ribena. I'm sure most people won't be able to tell the difference.' Everyone laughed and Peter and Anthea exchanged pitying glances. Jennifer left them to see to the dinner and Bob, who was the headmaster of a primary school in the Dingle, embarked upon an involved and embarrassing anecdote from one of his sex-education classes. There was general relief when he got to the end and several people started to talk at once.

'You're looking awfully well, Catherine,' said Anthea, energetically. 'That really is a lovely dress you're wearing, exactly the right colour for you.'

'Thank you.' The compliment jarred on Catherine, who felt that she was far from looking her best, but she tried to credit Anthea with a well-meaning intention to boost her own confidence. 'Actually it was a bit of a rush getting ready,' she said. 'Mum and I got talking and didn't notice the time. I've been meeting some of the Quinns over the weekend and I had to tell her all about them.'

'And can there be that much to tell?' Peter joined in, a little disdainfully.

'Oh, there's always a lot to tell about people, and Mum's memory is phenomenal. I think she remembers more about Daddy's family than he remembers himself.'

'Knowing him, that wouldn't be hard. He's hardly renowned for his strong feelings.'

Catherine was surprised by the bitterness of Peter's words; her adult observation of his attitude to Tom had led her to think he held his father in mildly amused contempt and she would never have supposed that he was hankering after a warmer relationship. 'He's very affectionate, I think.' Her reply sounded rather lame.

'Well naturally, he's always had a soft spot for *you*.' Jennifer now appeared to announce supper and saved Catherine from further exploration of Peter's jealousy, which had astonished her even more than his apparent resentment of his father's lack of feeling.

Jennifer had had her kitchen extended soon after Sally was born and the family always ate there, at a large, battered pine table. It seemed to possess an elastic quality and room could always be found at it for the extra friends whom the children were constantly bringing home. Jennifer refused to allocate places to her guests and Catherine ended up sitting between Peter and Carolyn's friend, Harriet. Carolyn was on the other side of Peter and, when the spaghetti had been served, they were soon deep in discussion of the relative merits of *gîtes* and touring holidays. Catherine turned to her other neighbour, who had so far hardly opened her mouth.

'Do you know Carolyn from Leeds?'

'Yes, we're sharing digs next year.'

'Will it be finals for you, too, next year?'

'Yes.' The girl pushed a straggling lock of pale hair out of her eyes and took a large mouthful of noodles.

'Have you any plans for afterwards, or are you too busy concentrating on exams?' Catherine plodded on with her commonplace questions; she had not come out to dinner to sit in silence.

'I want to go to the States. I've got a provisional place in the Department of Women's Studies at a university in Iowa and hopefully I'll stay and do a doctorate there.'

'And on what aspect of women will you hopefully write your thesis?'

'Well, I've not worked it all out precisely yet, but I feel there's scope for reinterpreting the famous women novelists of the last century. When you think how much of women's writing has been largely ignored, you can't help being struck by the disproportionate amount of attention that has been paid to Austen, Eliot and the Brontës. Personally, I think their recognition comes from them being so utterly conformist – they fully accept the inferior place society allots to women and their heroines – even one as rebellious as Cathy in *Wuthering Heights* – don't stand a chance of finding happiness unless they're able to win the affections of some man, and invariably he's a man they look up to, in a pathetic, degrading way. People always complain that Dickens' heroines are wishy-washy and unrealistic – too good to be true – but at least they're not as craven as Gwendolen Harleth is towards Daniel Deronda or Emma towards that prick Knightley.'

The word took Catherine by surprise: the vocabulary of her small family circle in England had not moved with the times. 'I've always had a rather soft spot for Mr Knightley,' she said, 'and his proposal could hardly be more humble, but it's a matter of taste whether you like him or not. Still, I do think you're wrong to use a word like 'craven' in describing heroines as spirited as Jane Austen's. The fact that they regard marriage to the right man – and they are most assiduous in rejecting the wrong men – as offering them the greatest chance of happiness and personal fulfilment surely only reflects the preoccupations and aspirations of most women since time immemorial.'

'But don't you see that it's the form these marriages

take that is so sickening? Why should Knightley's disapproval be so upsetting to Emma? Why should Elizabeth Bennet's shame at having misjudged Darcy be so acute? Why does Fanny Price have to have her opinions formed by Edmund and why does he never question his right to form them? Why does Anne Elliot let herself be bullied by her father only to mope for years after Wentworth? Why can't they be their own women?'

Catherine smiled in a way Harriet found patronizing. 'No doubt because Jane Austen was not interested in writing a feminist manifesto. Had that been her aim, then of course her books would not have been so good, nor would they have received the wide recognition which you find so remarkable.'

'"Feminist manifesto" — at least the way you say it — sounds very pejorative. I suppose you would dismiss any work by a woman who was struggling to break free of the bounds men have imposed upon literature.'

'I'm really not aware of literature having bounds imposed upon it by men or anybody else. Women have had as much freedom as men to experiment in their writing.'

'Huh! Most women weren't even taught to read.'

'Nor were most men until comparatively recently. Naturally we're talking about a small group of literate people ...'

'And don't you see anything wrong with literature being left exclusively in the hands of a small élite?'

'Right and wrong don't have anything to do with it. The study of literature is the study of what has been written and it's just plain silly for the student of literature to concern himself with what might have been written if more people had learned to write.'

'I notice you assume all students are male.'

'Nonsense! Whatever gave you such an idea?'

'You said "concern *him*self".'

Catherine made no effort to hide her exasperation. 'That is merely a civilized usage and no more rules out the possibility of girls being students than a phrase like the "birth of mankind" excludes women from the creation.'

228

'That's not the way most women see it nowadays. All these civilized usages, as you call them, are nothing but forceful reminders of our subordinate position. We may have the vote and certain rights that we used not to have but we still live in a world that was formed by men who will, if they can, resist all our attempts to reshape it. The trouble with women like you is that you don't even realize what a huge confidence trick has been played on you. You were probably so proud of yourself at getting to a university where women were hugely outnumbered that it didn't occur to you that your chance of success was undermined from the outset by the fact that the criteria for doing well had all been established by men and for men.'

Catherine thought it would be cheap to mention just how successful she personally had been within this very system but said instead, 'I have always supposed that academic disciplines possess internal standards to which the sex of the scholar is irrelevant.'

'Of course, that's what I'd expect you to say, and by saying it you only prove your subservience to the male view of the world.'

'Not at all. There must be an objectivity – '

'Objectivity! The word stinks of men. There's no such thing as objectivity – there's just male subjectivity – which they've conned us into thinking is the same thing – and female subjectivity, which is now at last beginning to come into its own.'

The girl had become very worked up and Catherine mistakenly thought she might take the heat out of the argument by laughing. 'That really is awful nonsense,' she said, pleasantly, in a manner intended to convey that she believed Harriet must know herself what nonsense it was and be doing it for a joke.

'Don't you dare call it nonsense!' Harriet almost shouted. The other conversations which were going on at the table fizzled out and everyone looked at her. 'It's bad enough having to fight men on basic principles but it's a fucking sight worse having to defend yourself against women who ought to know better.' She stood up angrily and ran from the room.

'Oh, dear,' said Jennifer, in the awkward silence that followed. 'D'you think you should go and see if there's anything you can do, Carolyn?'

'Not just yet, she's best left on her own when she has one of her fits. It's nothing personal, Catherine, she's trying to get over an unhappy love affair.'

Catherine, who had been momentarily shaken by Harriet's outburst, now began to laugh, to the questioning looks of her companions. 'That really is awfully funny,' she said. 'A real case of *plus ça change, plus c'est la même chose*. There was I imagining we were to have a rather jolly argument about the feminist view of literature and all the time her opinions were nothing but a front for being jilted. All the same, it does make one rather "ashamed that women are so simple".'

'I'm glad that you at least are still able to laugh,' said Anthea. 'We all think you're being awfully brave.'

'Brave?'

'Well, yes – after the way Günter's treated you. But I know that deep down you must regret having let him turn you into a domestic drudge with no life of your own. Even if it's sometimes easy to laugh at "loony feminist nonsense", I do think the work women's groups do in restoring the confidence of deserted wives and girls like Harriet is most tremendously useful – I support it all the way.'

Anthea obviously thought she had spoken rather well and Peter looked across at her admiringly. Catherine was stunned. Harriet's generalized attack upon her as the sort of woman who gave the sex a bad name had not affected her in the slightest – on the contrary, if Harriet had had the courage to remain she would have enjoyed the discussion and looked forward to winning the argument – but Anthea's expression of pity for her as an ill-used wife was altogether different and offended her deeply. Before she had time to collect her thoughts sufficiently to speak, Anthea was continuing: 'You know, if you decide to stay in Liverpool a while, I could take you along to a very interesting group that meets near us. I think women of our generation who were brought up to look on marriage as the be-all and end-all of existence have got to make a positive effort to shake themselves out of their submissive attitudes. You could learn so much from the way some of the younger ones look at the world.'

'Thank you,' said Catherine, taking great care to keep her voice low and steady, 'but I take pride in having long ago worked out my own way of looking at the world.'

'Oh, but that's where you're wrong,' began Anthea, confident that she was at last in a position to help this sister-in-law who had for so long had the advantage of her in youth, brains and money. But Catherine interrupted, no longer even trying to disguise her anger.

'How dare you tell me I'm wrong? I have nothing but contempt for the sort of feminism which refuses to see women except as helpless victims of their sex. Of course, soft-option courses in Women's Studies and consciousness-raising sessions for inadequate suburban housewives are useful for reassuring the feeble-minded that they're not total failures after all, but any sensible women will cope with her life without having to take refuge in the daft notion that as history has been against women for thousands of years, all her personal shortcomings today can be blamed upon a historical male conspiracy.'

'Oh, come off it, Catherine,' said Peter, aware that his wife would not be up to fighting her corner. 'You're not going to deny that women have been grossly disadvantaged.'

'*People* have been disadvantaged,' retorted Catherine. 'The common man *and* the common woman have led utterly miserable lives until very recently – and of course they still do in most parts of the world. Good heavens, your own father was denied a university education because his family was too poor, and his great-grandparents came to Liverpool to escape actual starvation! Compared to the Irish Famine, the trials and tribulations of a Caroline Norton pale into insignificance. But the injustices and hardships which the Quinns suffered over a century ago haven't caused you to go through life with a chip on your shoulder, so why should I get worked up about the way women used to be treated?'

'Well, obviously because those wrongs haven't yet been fully eradicated. You only have to look at yourself – because true equality still doesn't exist, you threw away a splendid career just to go and keep house for a man who hasn't even had the decency to be grateful.'

'Rubbish! Wilful, stupid rubbish! I married Günter because at the time I wanted to marry him more than I wanted to do anything else in the world. It was my own decision, freely made, and for most of the past sixteen years I have been extremely happy. If that happiness is now at an end then it is because something went wrong in the very personal relationship between Günter and me and it has no more to do with the status of women in general than a pain in your belly has to do with the national debt.'

'Gosh,' said Jennifer, laughing a little nervously, 'I feel we all ought to applaud.'

'I can't help thinking that perhaps you protest too much,' said Peter, with a smirk.

'Naturally,' said Catherine, who was quite calm again, 'if you have nothing to say of substance yourself, you can claim I was saying the opposite of what I really think. Why can't you understand that I just don't have any hang-ups about not going to work? I love my leisure. I detest the prospect of having to find a job, now that Günter's left me, but not because I'm lacking any confidence in my own abilities. I'm simply upset that a way of life that I found perfectly satisfying has been destroyed. And it infuriates me to have people ignore me as an individual in a situation that for me at any rate is unique, in order to lump me together with a lot of awful, helpless women who aren't individuals at all but mere statistics in a sex war that has never interested me in the slightest. I refuse to be one of Anthea's marriage guidance cases: "deserted wife, rising forty, desperately in need of re-education prior to acquiring long-overdue economic independence".'

'I marvel at your self-assurance but I'm afraid you may be in for a rude awakening – it won't be all that easy for you to find a job in the present economic climate and you really may find you need retraining of some sort.'

'Oh, Peter,' said Jennifer, anxiously, 'don't be so pessimistic. Catherine isn't going to be penniless and I've no doubt that there are all sorts of things she can do – and you know she'd be an asset anywhere she worked.'

'I hope so,' Peter sniffed. 'But of course you won't be able to start at the top – and at your age and after the standard of living you've been used to in Germany, you may find life a bit hard.' Catherine shrugged; she was still reluctant to talk about specific plans for her future. Peter went on: 'Anthea and I have thought for some time that you were rather too complacent about your "*Hausfrau-existence*". There aren't many women these days who would feel able to justify doing nothing more useful than cooking a superb meal once a day.'

'Oh Peter, don't be tiresome. All you mean is that you were both jealous that I could live in comfort without having to work for it.' Catherine's words were spoken lightly enough, but her tone betrayed a certain fatigue.

'Jealous? Certainly not. If anything, we were very concerned about you living in a fool's paradise. When one in three marriages ends in divorce, it seems to me positively foolhardy to make no effort at all to secure the means of supporting yourself.'

'Oh, I have the means to do that, all right.'

'I shouldn't think even Günter will be able to allow you enough to set up house on.'

'Then I shall get a job. I shall ask Uncle Gerard if he knows any priests who are looking for a housekeeper.'

'Catherine, you can't be serious!' Anthea squeaked in horror.

'Why shouldn't I be? Peter's just warned me that I'll have to start at the bottom, but not as a housekeeper, I wouldn't. I flatter myself that I am, in that profession, without compare.'

'You must be mad!'

'Maybe. We all go mad in different ways. And then I could always write in my spare time.' Catherine tossed in this possibility as a mischievous afterthought, amused that Peter and Anthea should be so much in earnest.

'Oh,' said Peter, 'now I understand. You think you'll be able to dash off a masterpiece as effortlessly as you write those letters everybody raves about – though personally I've always thought your style dreadfully artificial. And you'll probably find that it's not nearly as easy to get your work published as it is to write it.'

Maliciously sensing that she would annoy Peter most by appearing serenely confident, Catherine replied, 'We'll see about that. I gather there's a boom in poetry at the moment and I might start with some modest verses. If only I pretend to speak from the depths of my poor broken female heart, then I'll surely be able to get some feminist publisher to take me on.'

'How arrogant you are! I suppose, though, that it's inevitable that you should have a high opinion of yourself when nobody has ever crossed you and everything has always come so easily to you since the moment you were born.'

'Quite. Everyone should have my luck.' Catherine saw with spiteful satisfaction that she had at last silenced her brother. 'Jennifer,' she went on sweetly, 'do you think I could have a tiny drop more wine?'

'Of course, certainly.' Jennifer jumped up. 'Bob, get another bottle will you? There's some cheese here as well. With all the talking, I'd quite forgotten about it.'

While Jennifer bustled about, Catherine pointedly engaged Carolyn in conversation about her stay in France. Peter and Anthea said little and when Bob suggested they all move back to the sitting-room with their coffee, they excused themselves, saying that they would have to leave as they both had to be out early next morning. Conversation continued in a desultory manner among those who remained until Catherine also said she must be going. 'I'm awfully sorry about all those things Peter said,' muttered Jennifer as she saw her to the door. 'I can't think what came over him.'

'Oh, don't give it another thought,' replied Catherine. 'I don't like him much, either.'

'Oh, it's not that!' Jennifer was shocked. 'I'm sure he doesn't *dislike* you. It's just he has a funny way of showing that he wants to help.'

'Ah, well, you don't believe anyone ever does really dislike anyone else do you? It's a wonderfully endearing trait in your character, but you're dead wrong, all the same. Most of us find more to dislike than to love in our fellow men.'

'Oh, Catherine.' Jennifer squeezed her sister tightly. 'Don't let all this rotten business make you cynical, please.'

'Cynical? Is that what I am? Günter said the same thing, so perhaps it may be true. Never mind, cynicism's healthier than despair.' Catherine returned her sister's embrace and went quickly to her car.

Seventeen

Joyce and Tom were having their milky drink and discussing the television news when Catherine got home: that is, Joyce was pouring out invective against the prime minister, to whom she only ever referred as 'that woman'. But she insisted on getting up to make Catherine coffee, assuring her that her own drink could be reheated without its taking any harm. By the time they sat down, Tom had finished his and was off to bed with Evelyn Waugh's letters. Joyce saw his departure with satisfaction: his presence interfered with her desire for a *tête à tête* and his half-baked remarks on subjects on which she possessed clear and unambiguous views irritated her.

'Now tell me all about it,' she said, sincerely eager to receive a full account. 'What was the meal like?'

'Filling – spaghetti and meat sauce.'

'Funny thing to give people you've invited specially. Was it at least nicely cooked?'

'There was rather a lot of tinned tomato in the sauce, but it was otherwise OK.'

'Any befores or afters?'

'No starter, no. There was some cheese at the end, when Jennifer remembered it.'

'And did you get wine?'

'Yes, from Marks and Spencer's. I didn't even know they did wine.'

'Oh, yes, they're into everything nowadays. You should

see the queues at the food counters on a Saturday. It's all these working women with no time to shop or cook properly and more money than they know what to do with – their food's not cheap. Now tell me what Anthea had on.'

Catherine described Anthea's dress and, on the basis of her description, Joyce was able to declare with confidence that it was home-made. Then she wanted to know how the children had looked and finally what they had talked about. Catherine hesitated. The evening had left her very low-spirited, saddened by Peter's hostility but also dissatisfied with the figure she herself had cut. By contrast, her mother's persistent interest, in spite of everything, in all that concerned her, was very soothing. More than that, she seemed to feel some of the old certainty that her mother's love was the surest source of her own strength – a certainty that had underpinned everything she did until Günter came between them – returning to her. At the same time she saw Joyce herself as changed: the woman sitting opposite her was no longer the indestructible and pugnacious character who had dominated her children's lives but rather an old woman made terribly vulnerable by the very strength of her love for those children and the completeness of her identification with their affairs. What, Catherine asked herself, did she hope to prove by holding out against such love? The more unloved she felt herself to be, the more absurd it was, surely, to spurn the affection that had never wavered, however much her own behaviour had led to its expression being thwarted. She decided not to fob her mother off, then, with a superficial account of mere table talk, but to open her heart.

Without dwelling on the substance of her conversation with Harriet – it was enough to tell Joyce that she was a silly girl whose head was filled with feminist clichés – she launched into an examination of what she had found so troubling. 'I hated having Anthea patronize me with her new-found knowledge of group therapy but I still shouldn't have let it get under my skin so. I think that if I hadn't lost my temper, then Peter wouldn't have said all the spiteful things he did.'

'What spiteful things?' Joyce's voice was sharp.

'Well, it wasn't just that he wanted, like Anthea, to make me out to be some feeble little woman who had cringingly allowed herself to become her husband's creature and was now being quite properly punished for it – although that was bad enough. It was more that he seemed intensely jealous of me and the more he said how sorry he was for me, the more I felt that he was gloating over the fact that I'd got my come-uppance at last.'

'But you're not surprised, are you, that Peter should be jealous of you?'

'Well, yes, frankly, I am. He can't still be jealous that I made it to Oxford and he didn't.'

'Oh, I think he very well may be, but that's not as important as his general feeling of inferiority.'

'But, mother, don't be silly!'

'I'm not being silly. It's not so much that you're brighter than he is or that your standard of living is higher – though he did come home very peeved after his visit to your lovely new house. No, it's more that you're so sure of yourself whereas he's full of doubts about almost everything he does. Poor Peter had to work so hard to get even as far as he has and although Anthea being so stupid must have helped him to feel mentally superior for the first time in his life, she's such a snob that she's made him worry about his social standing. Nobody really cares two hoots about what sort of job his father had when he was small or that his mother went out charring, but it bothers *him,* and every time we get invited to his house and he can't avoid having other people there to meet us, he's terrified that we're going to let him down. Now you're different, and so is Jennifer – you couldn't care less who knows your parents came from Scotland Road, and of course that's how it should be.' Joyce paused and shook her head, then added, almost to herself: 'I'm afraid I failed altogether on Peter.'

Catherine, who had not expected the conversation to

turn away from herself, asked almost mechanically, 'What makes you think that you've failed?'

'Well, isn't everything the mother's fault in the end? I probably should have done more to build up his confidence when he was little. Instead I was inclined to nag him for not being cleverer – even Jennifer did better at school. You know my parents never wanted a daughter and for as long as I can remember they made me feel that they would rather I'd been a boy. I thought that was dreadful and I absolutely refused, when I was expecting my own babies, to say what sex I was hoping for. But when I had Peter and the doctor and the nurses congratulated me on a fine *son* and went on about how *proud* I must be, I snapped their heads off and bent over backwards to prove that I didn't see anything special in boys at all. I suppose he must have noticed eventually that I preferred girls – just as I knew with my parents.'

Catherine was so astonished that her mother should even be subject to self-recrimination, let alone admit to it, that she could make no comment. Joyce went on, 'But I wasn't much good to my daughters, either, although Jennifer's managed all right because she doesn't dwell on things. She keeps busy and doesn't want more from life than she gets – she's a lucky woman. But I expected too much for you and for myself. I wanted you to be brilliant and independent *and* to go on needing me. Ridiculous, of course. You had to get away and even if I'll never quite forgive you for marrying a foreigner, I understand why you did it: it was to escape from me. It was the only way you could be sure of getting to live your own life. I'm just sorry that it hasn't worked out more happily for you.'

'Oh, mother, you've got it all wrong, really you have.'

'Have I? I doubt it. I'm not such an old fool as you think. I know that I've come to be a bit much for my children and I also know that they're good enough to put up with me because they believe I meant well. But I know really that it's wrong to set such store by your kids, even if you don't have anything else in your life that offers even a fraction of the satisfaction that they do. I would have been quite happy living my life through you, if only you'd gone the way I'd wanted you to go, the way I might have gone myself if only I'd been born thirty or forty years later than I was. But you know what they say about "if only"? That they're the saddest words in the English language.'

Catherine got up and moved over to where her mother was sitting. She put her arms round her and kissed her and knew not only that comforting her mother was of greater importance, just then, than anything else, but also that for once she possessed the power to comfort. 'Please, please, don't be so sad. Don't run yourself down in this way. You're marvellous, we all think you are, I *know* you are. And it's just not true that I ever wanted to escape from you – I've often wished actually that I had you living round the corner.' Joyce raised her eyebrows and Catherine realized that simple assertions that her mother was mistaken were not enough. She thought for a moment and then said, 'It's funny you should have said you could forgive anything but my marrying a *foreigner*, because I actually think I married Günter because he was foreign – I wanted to get away not from you but from England.'

'Surely you don't mean to say that you prefer Germany to England.'

'Well, yes, in a way I think I do, even if I've never really bothered to think it out. Of course, I'll never feel as strongly about anything German as I do about things English. There's no German politician that I really either loathe or wholeheartedly admire, for instance. But this is part of the charm. England is always forcing you to belong to some group or other – when I talk to Sarah's in-laws then I feel I'm a Liverpudlian first and foremost and I detest their rich southern vulgarity; when I argue with Carolyn's friend then I know I went to the better university and have the automatic advantage; when I talk to poor Teresa then I find I'm almost struck dumb by all the privileges I've had and I don't dare to regard her as I'd regard someone who I felt was more nearly my equal.'

'You're surely not trying to tell me that Germany has a perfectly classless society?'

'No, of course it's not perfect either. But the inequalities and the snobbishness don't confront you everywhere you turn. Maybe, with not fully belonging myself, I am less sensitive anyway to the nicer points of social position. But the fact remains that ordinary encounters over there are not riddled with the nuances of class and education the way they are in England.'

'The Germans wouldn't be human if they never looked down on anyone.'

'That's not the point. What matters is that there's no sense of being superior or inferior built in to people's dealings with each other. I talk exactly the same language as my hairdresser and the plumber; here I can't even exchange a few words with my own father's sister without her reproaching me for sounding so posh.'

'There's nothing wrong with speaking nicely. Some people these days actually seem to want to sound more common than they are. Jennifer's boys are getting to sound more scouse every time I see them. Let's hope it's only a phase they're going through. But to go back to what you were saying about why you married – I'm not at all sure that I wouldn't rather you *had* done it to get away from me, as I don't at all like the idea of you disliking your native country so much.'

'Now, mother! It's my turn to take your words with a pinch of salt. You wouldn't surely be happy if I loved England more than I loved you.'

'Oh, love! You can't help love – it's like being stupid.'

'You sound, though, as if you'd like to do something about it if you could. Isn't it what makes the world go round?'

'Huh! The world goes round anyway, and love is as likely to bring pain as happiness. I've loved you more than I ever loved the other two and look where it's got us.'

'It's got me here tonight. I really do think I'm extraordinarily lucky to have you to come back to.'

'You're only saying that to cheer me up, but I won't pretend I don't like to hear it all the same.'

'Then I'll have to say it more often. I'm afraid it's a long time since I did much to make you happy.'

'You make me happy just by being here.'

Catherine was struck by the sincerity in Joyce's voice and suddenly it seemed clear to her what she should do next. 'Then I'll have to stay a long time,' she said.

'Oh, Catherine, would you?'

'Why not? I just don't know why it's taken me so long to get round to asking if you'll have me.' For the moment the glum certainty that they would remain estranged for ever was dispelled and the barriers between them were down. They talked long into the night, touching with asperity on most of their circle, from the guests at Sarah's party to Günter and Anna. Catherine found that she could, after all, talk freely about the affair and no longer felt any compunction in declaring that it must have been sex and sex alone which attracted Günter to a girl whose other qualities it would be hard to underestimate. Her mother, long hungry for a fuller picture of the young woman capable of displacing Catherine in Günter's affections, listened eagerly. By the time they went to bed they were both light-headed from the illusion of having somehow put the clock back twenty years and of being able once more to face the world in the confidence of a shared outlook.

Nothing happened on Wednesday or Thursday to spoil the new harmony between mother and daughter. For Joyce, a long period of mourning had come to an end and the daughter whom she had given up for lost had been restored to her; she could hardly believe her good fortune. Catherine, having given more thought than Joyce to the nature of the obstacles which time and circumstance had put in the way of their intimacy, was the more surprised of the two at their apparent elimination. She remained aware of the changes in herself and of her mother's limitations, but these no longer constituted any impediment to the strong affection which bound them.

On Thursday evening she forced herself to try to get in

touch with Günter, telephoning first Anna's flat and then the house. There was no reply at either number. She was relieved, in the fatuous way that someone with toothache is relieved when his appointment with the dentist is postponed. And then on Friday the phone rang. Joyce answered it and although the person at the other end was speaking passable English, she called to Catherine with near panic in her voice: 'Come quickly, it's someone from Germany, I can't make out what they're saying.' Catherine came at once, her heart beating, and took the receiver. Her mother, who had never cared to hear her 'jabbering away in German', went into the sitting-room, shutting the door behind her.

'Catherine, hallo, this is Monika.' Catherine was taken completely by surprise; Günter's family had played no part in her reflections over the past weeks. 'I am so glad I was able to get you at home and I hope you will not be angry with me for getting in touch like this. But I felt you must know about Günter.'

'Has something happened to him?' Catherine's stomach was churning but her words had a hard, raw edge.

'He looks so ill, so miserable – Catherine, can't you come back to him, please?'

Catherine, imagining Günter to have had an accident, was rendered speechless by the unexpected inference that it was she who had left him.

'Catherine, Catherine, are you still there? Please don't hang up.'

'I'm sorry. I'm still here all right – just a bit puzzled. Do you mean Günter's down in Munich with you?'

'Well, yes, naturally. The funeral's on Monday.'

'Monika, I don't know about any funeral.'

'You mean Günter didn't tell you his father died?'

'Father is dead? But that's terrible. How did it happen?'

Monika, who had assumed that Günter must have informed his wife, even if they were living apart, of so momentous an event, explained that Herr Hemmersbach had died in the operating-theatre. The cancer had been very advanced and his heart was weak. It had been a terrible shock for them all but for Monika herself the shock that Catherine and Günter's marriage had broken up was, if anything, even greater.

'Does Günter know you're phoning me?' asked Catherine when Monika at last reached the end of her story, much prolonged by expressions of regret and incomprehension.

'Oh, no, of course not. He probably wouldn't want you to know how much he's suffering. You might call it stupid male pride but I think it's more likely that he wants to spare *you*.'

'He should still have told me about his father.' Catherine's voice was cold. 'Of course I must come to the funeral. What time is it to take place?'

'Eleven o'clock on Monday morning.'

'Then I'll have to come down the day before. If you don't hear from me again, I'll be on the Inter-City that gets into the Hauptbahnhof soon after six o'clock. Will someone be able to meet me, do you think?'

'Of course. I'm sure Günter himself will want to come. Oh Catherine, I'm so glad you're coming back.'

'I'm coming back to my father-in-law's funeral.'

'Yes, yes, I understand. But when you see Günter, I know your heart will go out to him. Till Sunday then. Goodbye.'

Catherine put the phone down and sat for a few moments on the little seat next to it. The tranquillity of the last couple of days had been destroyed and she felt old, too old almost to have a mother, let alone young enough to rely on her. With piercing clarity she saw that the direction her life had taken since her marriage could not, after all, be revised at will. The problems she was facing were not entirely of her own making but she had to face them, and if possible solve them, alone.

She went into the room where her mother and father were sitting. 'What was all that about?' asked Joyce. 'It was a very long call – it must have cost a fortune.'

'It's Günter's father. He died on Wednesday.'

'And who was it on the phone?'

'Monika – didn't she tell you her name?'

'I didn't catch it. The line wasn't very good.' Joyce, seeing the look of misery on Catherine's face, added, 'I'm sorry about the old man. You were quite fond of him, weren't you?'

'Yes, he was always very nice to me. We used to talk books – we shared a rather bleak view of modern literature.'

'Well, don't be too downcast by it, love. He was getting on and we all have to go some time. It's not as though you would have been seeing him again, anyway, with things as they are.'

'I didn't get in touch with them at all after Günter told me about Anna.'

'No, and that's understandable – you had other things on your mind.'

'But it was always me who saw to it that we rang them on a Sunday morning and let them know if we were going away. They must have wondered why I suddenly started to neglect them.'

'Günter will have explained it all – it's not your fault.'

'Certainly, if I had given the matter any thought then I would have assumed Günter would tell them, but apparently he hasn't and his father died probably believing that I didn't care.'

'Whatever makes you think that?'

'Monika – she didn't ring to tell me about the death but to beg me to come back to Günter. He must have given them the impression that *I* left *him*.'

'But that's preposterous!'

'It's what he's done, though.'

'What's got into the man? How dare he make up stories about you like this?'

'I don't know how it came about but I suppose it means the thing with Anna is off. Monika says he looks awful.'

'And well he might with so much on his conscience. I hope that now you'll appreciate once and for all that you're well rid of him.'

'But am I?'

'Of course you are, after the way he's treated you. As though it wasn't enough to run off with another woman, he has to go spreading lies about you as well.'

'I realize that's how it must look .. but I still think I'll have to go to the funeral.'

Joyce flushed with anger. 'What on earth can have put that idea into your head?'

'Well, one has an obligation, surely, to attend the funeral of someone so close.'

'Not under these circumstances. Travelling half across Europe, indeed, just to be given the cold shoulder by all those relatives who believe Günter's stories!'

'But I'm not going for their sake but as a last mark of respect to Günter's father, whom I liked very much.'

'And what will you say to Günter? The whole situation is ridiculous – and embarrassing.'

'It depends, I suppose, on what he has to say to me.'

Joyce, no longer in doubt about the seriousness of Catherine's intentions, sensed that their reconciliation had after all been too good to be true. 'Don't, for goodness' sake, tell me that you'd ever take him back.' Though the words she chose were forceful enough, her voice betrayed her hopelessness.

'I don't know whether I have any choice, if that's what he wants. We should all be allowed to make one mistake, I think.'

Joyce stood up and Catherine saw that her hands were trembling. 'I don't understand you at all,' she said. 'I was a fool ever to think I did. But I'm not going to shed any more tears over it. I've shed more than enough tears over you already. But not any more, not any more I won't.' Resolutely dry-eyed, she left the room.

Tom, who had kept his eyes on his paper for most of this exchange, now spoke. 'This'll be very hard for your mother. You'd led her into believing you were going to make your home with us here again.'

'I thought I was – how could I have known things would take this turn?'

'And do you really mean it – about taking Günter back?'

'Probably. But you of all people must understand why. What was it you said about regarding as binding the one really solemn promise most of us ever make? You know, the afternoon we went out to Crosby.'

Tom looked sheepish. 'Yes, well, I was talking generally. And I don't suppose I thought it would happen quite like this. After all, if Günter is sorry for what he has done, then he should be the one ringing you up. I wouldn't go running back to him just on Monika's say-so, if I were you – you have to have a little pride.'

'Do I? I thought it was a deadly sin.'

'Now, Catherine, don't try to pretend you believe any of that stuff.'

'How can you be so sure I don't?'

'Oh, I just can. I know my old sweetheart, she's too intelligent.'

'But, Daddy, you wouldn't say intelligence was a bar to religious belief, would you?'

'In your case I would.'

'But with you it's different?'

'Oh, yes, with me there's a great weight of atavistic superstition that stops me taking any chances in my old age.'

'Funnily enough, Gerard said something rather similar. But I still won't accept that doing the right thing is only a matter of superstition. Would you really want me to ignore my conscience?'

'That depends on what your conscience is telling you. I think it's altogether admirable that you want to go to the funeral – and brave as well, if Günter really has made them think badly of you. But I don't think you're under any obligation whatsoever to return to Günter as his wife. Unless, of course, you're so much in love with him that you'd pay any price to have him back. But I must say that's not the impression you've given since you came home.'

'No,' said Catherine, sadly. 'I could have resigned

myself to losing him, all other things being equal. But if he knows now that he made ghastly mistake and desperately wishes it hadn't happened, don't you think I must give him a chance to start again?'

'Oh, of course, if you put it like that, I have to agree with you. But I wish I could believe that doing the right thing was going to make you happy.'

'Maybe it will, in a quiet sort of way. Don't forget that I'm not the euphoric type. And needless to say I won't put any pressure on Günter to have another go at marriage to me if *he* would still rather make a clean break of things, with or without this girl's love.'

'So there is some hope that you may come back to us after the funeral, then?'

'I suppose so, but I wouldn't bank on it. My vanity tells me that he'll probably not have to struggle very long with *his* conscience before welcoming me back with open arms. Marriage has a lot of convenience to recommend it to a man.'

'Then why did he leave you in the first place?'

'Oh, he wanted a little adventure – or rather he didn't realize what he was letting himself in for until it had all gone too far. We're often so busy retrospectively imposing a pattern on our pathetic little lives that we overlook how much happens initially more or less by accident.'

'I wish you didn't sound so pessimistic. It's been lovely seeing you laugh again these last couple of days. I'd be a lot happier letting you go if you looked as though it was what you really wanted to do.'

'I'm sorry, I promise to be more cheerful the next time you see me. The problem is that I wouldn't be happy here either, now that I know about Günter. It's better for me to go.'

'Well, you're a grown woman and you must know what's best for you. I suppose you'll be off very soon?'

'Yes, just as soon as I've packed. I'm too late to catch the Hull ferry today, so I'll head for Dover and stay in a hotel overnight, then get a crossing tomorrow. I told Monika that I'd take the train from Bonn on Sunday –

I'll have had enough driving.'

'And your mother? Have you no time left for her at all?'

'We wouldn't know what to do with it, even if I had. But you can tell her when she's more herself that I *did* enjoy the last couple of days and that I would have liked to prolong them, if only ... Well, she knows all about "if only".' Catherine hurried off without giving Tom the chance to reply. She felt surprisingly calm again and packed with speed and efficiency, reflecting that she should have known all along that the attempt to recapture the spirit of her old, close relationship with her mother was doomed. The sooner she could be on her way the better.

Eighteen

The news of his father's death had reached Günter when he was still prostrate from the loss of Anna and he drove down to Munich in a dazed state, his mind unable to assimilate so much misfortune all at once. His mother's grief, on the other hand, was for the time being subsumed in the largely pleasurable activity of arranging a worthy funeral. Günter's parents had always been conscientious in their attendance, not just at funerals, but at the graves of their late relatives and friends, which they visited each year on All Saints' Day, Christmas Eve and whenever a new death brought them to the cemetery. Herr Hemmersbach was, therefore, not going to be laid beneath an unwelcoming, anonymous piece of earth: his last journey would take him to a familiar plot, hallowed by a lifetime's sentimental attention, where his grandparents and parents already lay. Long before he had had any reason to think that his own demise was imminent, he had specified what form his obsequies were to take and what should be inscribed on the family tombstone. Naturally his wishes were sacred to his widow and she derived a double satisfaction from knowing that she was not only doing what would please him but doing it in full view of a large circle of mourners, of whom she was the principal.

In face of what seemed to him unnatural serenity, Günter found it impossible to speak properly to his mother. Widowhood had altered her and she received him with a dignity, almost a grandeur, that was altogether new. Indeed, she gave him the impression that his primary function was to support *her* and implied that his own need to mourn was negligible. His sense of affront that she should belittle his loss was complicated, though not diminished, by a nagging suspicion that he really was not quite inconsolable. For the more he tried to pin down the memory of his father, the more elusive it became.

His earliest recollections were patchy: brief glimpses of a man home on leave, wearing a uniform that scratched his face; the forced cheerfulness of wartime reunions; the strain of railway-station goodbyes. The man who returned after the capitulation, lucky to have escaped captivity in a Russian prison camp but indelibly scarred by the privations of the long trek home, was moody and remote. Gradually, as bourgeois normality reasserted itself, his father relaxed a little but the respect with which Frau Hemmersbach treated her husband and which she sought to inculcate in her sons, was reinforced by the continuing need to spare one who had suffered so much from all trivial irritation. As a child of nine or ten Günter was not allowed to ask questions about the war because his father was trying to forget the terrible things war had done to him; later, as a teenager, when it had begun to dawn on him that Germany was not quite the nation of helpless victims which his parents' attitude suggested, he preferred not to ask any questions at all. The impossibility of reconciling his increasing knowledge of the horrors of the Nazi period with the character his father presented – stern, conservative but basically decent and honourable – led to his giving up all hope of achieving any sort of intimacy with him.

In the end it was Catherine's arrival in the family which brought them closer. Unencumbered by any personal guilt, either on her own or her parents' behalf, she had taken the older generation of Günter's relatives as she found them. While they were predisposed in her favour by her wholesome appearance and good manners, she was struck by the absence of animosity towards the British in their reminiscences, so different from the casual hostility of people at home to the Germans. In passing she learned that they had never been active Nazis: they had never turned out on the streets to cheer Hitler or hung his picture in their living-rooms. Catherine readily believed them, even though she knew well enough that the masses who had backed the Führer in the thirties had long since melted into thin air and many of those who now strenuously denied their allegiance to him must be lying.

Herr Hemmersbach had been particularly delighted with his new daughter-in-law who, on top of her social graces, had actually read *Die Wahlverwandtschaften* and could converse with him about *Faust* at a level which put to shame his sons' more superficial knowledge of Goethe's masterpiece. Günter discerned a special warmth in his father's congratulations to him on choosing such a wife and the deepening affection between Herr Hemmersbach and Catherine gradually helped to open his own eyes to qualities in both of them which he might otherwise have overlooked.

Lying in bed the morning after his arrival in Munich and trying to re-create an image of his father consistent with filial piety he came to the conclusion that all his best memories were those in which Catherine played a part. His conscience troubled him as he reflected on his failure, not only to inform Catherine of his father's death but, even more culpably, to correct his mother's inference that he was the injured party in their separation. True, he had demurred at her wilder assertions but this was taken as proof of his continuing loyalty to an undeserving wife and went little way towards rebutting the charges made against her.

Günter was shocked by the ferocity of his mother's dislike. Of course he knew that there had been little warmth between the two women but there had always been such propriety in their behaviour that deep-rooted antipathy seemed out of the question. He doubted there was any comparable illwill on Catherine's side: he could not recall her ever having spoken unkindly about her mother-in-law. Nor had she seemed to mind Frau Hemmersbach's frequent lectures on the importance of thrift as a virtue in its own right, unconnected with any economic necessity, in spite of the implied criticism of her own extravagant housekeeping which such lectures contained. Probably the worst that could be said of her conduct was that she had not taken the older woman seriously enough but treated her rather with a sort of benign condescension that ruled out all possibility of her having anything useful to say. Perhaps, thought Günter, the seeds of his mother's present fury lay in years of resentment that her advice on such matters as darning socks and using up left-over vegetables had invariably been ignored, a resentment made the more bitter by Catherine's having seemed at first only too willing to defer to guidance. But then Günter had also had to learn that his wife's scrupulous courtesy concealed an unshakeable confidence in the rightness of her own opinions.

Nevertheless, disappointment that your son has married a girl possessing qualities different from those you prize yourself and jealousy that your husband has also fallen for her should not amount to hatred. In vain could Günter try to remember anything which Catherine had done to make his mother believe she would betray him. On the contrary, he was forced to concede that she must generally be regarded as an exceptionally loyal wife. If in his heart he had come to miss the spark of passion in her, then that was a private shortcoming, apparent to no one but himself. Anna, he supposed, had given him his fill of passion but now that she was gone from his life for good and he had only a bleak bachelor existence to look forward to, he was inclined to think passion overrated. All in all, his awareness of the injustice of his mother's assertions, combined with the sympathetic images awakened by recollections of his father, had already begun to produce a softening of his own feelings when Monika called to tell him that she had been on the phone to Liverpool and that Catherine would be coming to the funeral.

'Why didn't you say you hadn't even told her Father was dead?' Monika sounded aggrieved.

'It didn't seem important that you should know.' Günter hated his sister-in-law to interfere in his affairs.

'She was terribly shocked. I wish you'd tell me why she went off like that. It's not a bit like her. I suppose there must be another man – though it's funny, in that case, that she should be staying with her parents.'

'There is no other man.' Monika's persistence led him into speaking more energetically than he had intended.

'How can you be so sure? She's attractive and very cultivated ...'

'I know because Catherine would have told me herself if there had been anyone else. She is quite the most honest person I have ever met.'

'Gosh, I don't think I've ever heard you speak with so much feeling! How long has she been gone?'

'Over two weeks, and I wish you wouldn't go on about it. I don't want to discuss it and I'd be extremely grateful if you could get Mother to stop telling her ridiculous lies to everyone.'

'But how was I to know they were lies? I assumed she was passing on what you had told her.'

'Well she wasn't. All I told her was that Catherine had gone to England and that I didn't know when she was coming back.' Monika nodded her head meekly, convinced by Günter's irritable defence of his wife that he was anxious to have her back and that she herself had done the right thing in contacting Catherine.

Frau Hemmersbach, on joining them, received Monika's news with angry astonishment, incensed that Catherine should have the nerve to show her face at the funeral of a man whom she had inexplicably neglected in the last weeks of his life. Günter cut her short angrily but still could not bring himself to explain what had really driven his wife to leave so suddenly for England. There was an awkward silence, broken by Monika who, feeling that no time should be lost in rehabilitating Catherine, said, 'She was quite stunned when I told her Father was dead –

there had always been such a very special bond between them and I'm sure she would never deliberately have done anything to hurt him.' Frau Hemmersbach only sniffed sceptically and Monika went on, with a glance at Günter for approval that she was complying with his request: 'There seems to have been an awful mix-up all round but talking to Catherine I got the impression – '

'I'm not interested in your impressions, Monika,' Frau Hemmersbach interrupted. 'Of course if she insists on coming to the funeral I can't stop her, but she'll not be able to stay in this house – I've already offered the spare room to Josef and Magdalena.'

Frau Hemmersbach's spiteful satisfaction was so evident as she said this that Günter felt he must get out of the house at once if he wished to avoid a scene. 'I need some fresh air,' he announced. 'Don't wait supper for me.'

He walked for hours, his thoughts struggling to sort out the full implications of Catherine's return. On the whole he regretted Monika's intervention since it deprived him of a pretext for getting in touch with Catherine himself, while furnishing yet another example of his wife's unfailing self-assurance. How characteristic of her to decide there and then, on the phone to a mere sister-in-law, that she would attend the funeral! Most people, he suspected, would have hesitated to discharge an obligation to the dead which involved such awkwardness among the living. With a shudder at what he took to be his own moral inferiority he reflected that, had their positions been reversed, Catherine would never have permitted *her* mother to think so badly of *him*. He recalled her remark at their last breakfast together, that she would never have left him 'on a mere selfish whim', her choice of words underlining both her contempt for his behaviour and an awareness of her own superior self-control. Not for the first time he wondered if beyond her stony rectitude she really did care for him a little. Her cool reaction to his leaving her would seem to prove that she did not; perhaps even her readiness to come to Munich indicated how little her emotions, as far as he was concerned, were involved.

It still did not occur to him that she might have been more upset by his behaviour than she had appeared to be or that she was returning in the hope that he wanted her back. He foresaw a difficult reunion and, for all his dismay at his mother's hostility and his shame at having given it substance by his cowardly equivocation, the self-pity in him remained stronger than the guilt.

Günter arrived at the station on Sunday evening with half an hour to spare before the train was due and he spent it wandering idly up and down, out of place among the crowds of people purposefully hurrying to or from their trains. He considered putting money in the 'twenty-four-hour flower shop' and buying, from one of its refrigerated glass drawers, a posy of welcome. But he decided against it: under the circumstances such a gesture was all too likely to provoke Catherine's sarcasm. A few minutes before the train was announced, he positioned himself at the end of the platform where he had a clear view of the passengers as they approached the barrier. He spotted her at once. She was not yet in mourning, but even wearing dark green, with a cream silk scarf at her throat, he thought she looked pale, even a little haggard, in spite of her carefully applied, unobtrusive make-up. On seeing him she smiled, but automatically and without warmth.

'Hello, I'm glad you're here,' she said, holding out her hand and offering her cheek to be kissed. 'I suppose I should have rung again from home yesterday to confirm my train time. I'm afraid I just didn't feel like it.'

'Did you have a good drive?'

'Yes, very smooth – Brussels is quiet on Saturday afternoon and I managed not to get lost on the Ring.' He took her case and led her out of the station, away from the parking-area. 'Where are we going?' she asked.

'I've booked us into the "Vier Jahreszeiten",' he said, trying unsuccessfully to sound matter-of-fact. 'Home is like a madhouse, completely overrun with ancient relatives.'

'But I like your ancient relatives.'

'Yes, well, before we knew you were coming, Mother offered to put up Onkel Josef and Tante Magdalena – they're not so good in the mornings these days and it would have meant a very early start for them tomorrow if they'd had to catch the train from Augsburg. But it's meant there isn't a room left for both of us.'

'And is there any significance in the fact that you've chosen the most expensive hotel in the city?'

'I thought you'd like it.'

'Mmm, then I'm sure I shall.'

When they had checked in and the porter had left them Catherine said, 'For a moment I was afraid you might have taken the bridal suite for good measure, but you know I really wouldn't have minded a put-you-up in your mother's sewing-room.'

'It's all been a bit difficult but I do want you to know how very glad *I* am that you decided to come.'

'Really?'

'Why should you doubt me?'

'Oh, just something Monika said which made me think you might find it a bit hard explaining my presence satisfactorily.'

'It's true mother has managed to get the wrong end of the stick but I swear I never wanted her to think badly of you.'

'No, she did that anyway.'

'You've never said anything like that before. What makes you say it now?'

'There was never any reason to mention it as long as she did the proper thing and made me welcome in her house.'

'I'm sure she would make you welcome now, too, only she couldn't very well put Onkel Josef off.'

Catherine looked hard at Günter and for a moment it seemed she could not be bothered to reply. But she changed her mind and said, brightly, 'Right, so now we've dumped my bags we can go home and I'll offer my condolences to your mother and say hello to them all – OK?'

Günter smiled weakly and picked up the room keys. 'There's a fridge here with drinks in it. Won't you have something?' He unlocked the discreetly panelled cabinet and went on, 'There's even champagne – quite a good one. Would you like a glass?'

'No, I don't think that would be very appropriate, do you? I'll have sherry, if you insist, though as I shall want at least two of those absurd little bottles it might be more sensible to give me fruit juice.'

'Hang the expense!' Günter poured out two miniatures and took a beer for himself. They raised their glasses and said 'zum Wohl', as Germans do, before drinking. Catherine waited for Günter to speak first. 'How are your parents?' he asked at last.

'Very well. I'm afraid I couldn't avoid telling *them* the whole truth, so they are rather surprised at my wanting to come back like this.'

'I understand. Dare I ask why you did come?'

'To attend Father's funeral.'

'Did you really care that much about him?'

'Yes, I did, and I'm very angry with myself for not having contacted him before I left for Liverpool.'

'I must take the blame for that.'

'No, you must not take the blame for *that*. My affection for your father went far beyond my relationship as a daughter-in-law. You had nothing to do with it.'

There was a hardness, a rigid scrupulousness in Catherine's words which Günter found very disheartening. 'I've had a lousy time since you went away,' he blurted out, hardly hoping for her sympathy.

'Have you really?' For a moment Catherine thought he would burst into tears. The possibility appalled her and, to stave it off, she added, more kindly, 'Do you want to tell me about it?'

Günter did.

As she listened Catherine was overcome by a colossal weariness, a dull conviction that his story would hold no surprises. True, she could hardly know the precise nature of Anna's perfidy, but as soon as he began to describe in detail how she had failed to return his love in the spirit it was offered and how she had aborted their baby without even wanting him near her, Catherine finally knew that there had only ever been one possible ending to the whole silly episode. She wondered why she had taken it all so seriously; instead of rushing, panic-stricken, back to England, should she not have acted with the very restraint Günter despised and waited calmly at home until he saw for himself the folly of trying to live out his romantic dream? Her irritation that he should presume to ask her to pity him gave way to kinder feelings: clearly he *had* suffered and it still came more easily to her to respond to his plea for sympathy than to seek any for herself. When he had finished she said, 'Do you intend to see Anna again?'

'How can I? She's made it plain she wants nothing more to do with me.'

'I'm not quite so sure that she has. She's impressionable and mixed-up and when she gets out of this formidable woman's clutches she may very well find that she misses you.'

'But *I* never want to see *her* again. Even if it was a genuine miscarriage she's shown that she didn't share *my* feelings for the child – why, she was hardly prepared to acknowledge it was mine as much as it was hers.'

Catherine shrugged. 'Yes, well, that's the fashionable view,' she said.

'Oh, Catherine, do you have to be so horribly detached about everything? You talk of the "fashionable view" as though you were an anthropologist commenting on the strange practices of a tribe of savages. Don't you understand that I'm trying to tell you what it was like for me personally to be rejected by the mother of my own child? And to have you tell me that Anna was acting in line with contemporary wisdom on the irrevelance of fathers is no consolation at all.'

Catherine was inclined to retort that he should be grateful she was listening so patiently and not press his luck by quarrelling with what she said. But she stopped herself; what was the point of a generous gesture if it was offered in a mean spirit? So she smiled and said, 'I can't change my spots overnight. If I'd been perfect in the first place, then you'd surely never have looked twice at poor Anna.'

Günter looked at her with sudden gratitude. 'Gosh,' he said, 'you are amazing! Not many women would be able to say "poor Anna" like that.' Catherine felt uncomfortable, as ruffled by his praise as by his criticism. A truly sensible man, she thought, would take his wife as he found her and keep a sense of proportion about both her shortcomings and her strengths. She bit her lip and said nothing. Günter, catching the uncertainty in her eyes and cheered by the unexpected hint of self-criticism in her last remark, drew his chair nearer to hers and said, earnestly, 'I'm almost afraid to put it into words, but would you perhaps be willing to have me back?'

'Of course, if that is what you want. Didn't I tell you straight away that I thought your great love affair was an aberration? It would be quite reprehensible of me to make you suffer any longer the consequences of having proved me right.'

She had found the familiar ironic tone again but this time Günter did not take exception to it: any reservations he may have had were far outweighed by the intensity of his relief that she would let him resume his old, orderly existence, the quiet life appropriate to a man of his age and station.

'I don't deserve you,' he said, with such emotion that Catherine again feared he might weep. She was aware of no similar emotion in herself. Sadly, it occurred to her that this was the moment when she should try to show the warmth he had made her realize she lacked. She should embrace him and with her kisses try to heal the wounds left by all the years when he had felt so unloved that even an Anna had been able to capture his heart. She should promise him that this time it would be different; this time she would try to love him as he wanted to be loved, she would do more than merely look after him. But all she could actually bring herself to do was to give his hand a little squeeze and then, standing up and looking at her watch, she said, 'Is it time, do you suppose, that we thought about getting some dinner?'